GOALKEEPER TRAINING PROGRAM

120 Drills to Produce Top Class Goalkeepers

WRITTEN BY
MAARTEN ARTS

PUBLISHED BY

GOALKEEPER TRAINING PROGRAM

120 Drills to Produce Top Class Goalkeepers

First Published March 2019 by SoccerTutor.com

info@soccertutor.com | www.SoccerTutor.com

UK: 0208 1234 007 | **US:** (305) 767 4443 | **ROTW:** +44 208 1234 007

ISBN: 978-1-910491-29-4

Copyright: SoccerTutor.com Limited © 2019. All Rights Reserved.

All rights reserved. No part of this publication may be reproduced, stored in a retrieval system, or transmitted in any form or by any means, electronic, mechanical, photocopy, recording or otherwise, without prior written permission of the copyright owner. Nor can it be circulated in any form of binding or cover other than that in which it is published and without similar condition including this condition being imposed on a subsequent purchaser.

Author
Maarten Arts © 2019

Diagrams by Tom McDermott - SoccerTutor.com

Edited by Alex Fitzgerald - SoccerTutor.com

Cover Design by Alex Macrides, Think Out Of The Box Ltd.
Email: design@thinkootb.com Tel: +44 (0) 208 144 3550

Cover Photo by Jason Dawson - jasonpix.co.uk

Diagrams
Diagram designs by SoccerTutor.com. All the diagrams in this book have been created using SoccerTutor.com Tactics Manager Software available from www.SoccerTutor.com

Note: While every effort has been made to ensure the technical accuracy of the content of this book, neither the author nor publishers can accept any responsibility for any injury or loss sustained as a result of the use of this material.

CONTENTS

Meet the Author: Maarten Arts 7
Peak Elite Advert 8
Goalkeeper Training Tips 9
Drill Format / Key 10

CHAPTER 1: CATCHING 11
Drill 1: Catching the Ball in Front of Goal 12
Drill 2: Side-steps and Catch 13
Drill 3: Catching After Quick Small Steps 14
Drill 4: Catching After Turning from the Near Post 15
Drill 5: Catching After Low Hurdle Jumps 16
Drill 6: Catching and Throwing with Slalom Through Poles 17
Drill 7: Catching with Quick Cone Touches 18
Drill 8: Catching and Awareness Drill 19
Drill 9: Throwing/Kicking and Catching in a Continuous Circuit 20
Drill 10: Throwing and Catching in a 4 v 4 Possession Game within the 6-Yard Box ...21

CHAPTER 2: FALLING 22
Drill 1: Falling Save at Close Distance 23
Drill 2: Falling Saves to Left and Right 24
Drill 3: Continuous Falling Saves from Opposite Sides 25
Drill 4: Jump Low Hurdle + Falling Save 26
Drill 5: Two Falling Saves in Quick Succession 27
Drill 6: Falling Saves and Awareness Drill 28
Drill 7: Changing Direction + Falling Save within a 4-GK Passing Combination ...29
Drill 8: Fast Reactions and Turning + Falling Save 30
Drill 9: Falling Save at the Near Post from a Cross 31
Drill 10: Falling Saves to Defend the Bottom Corners 32

CHAPTER 3: DIVING 33
Drill 1: Diving to Side from Kneeling Position 34
Drill 2: Falling with Ball in Hands and Maintaining Control 35
Drill 3: Moving to One Side and Quickly Changing Direction to Make a Diving Save ...36
Drill 4: Changing Direction + Diving Over Rope 37
Drill 5: Diving Out of Goal to Grab the Ball 38
Drill 6: Diving and Pushing the Ball Away from Danger 39
Drill 7: Side-steps and Dive to Save in the Top Corner 40
Drill 8: Back-steps and Dive to Tip Ball Over Crossbar 41
Drill 9: Diving to Save Free Kicks with Mannequin Wall 42
Drill 10: Jumping On and Off Bench + Over Rope to Make a Diving Save ...43

CHAPTER 4: PUNCHING 44

Drill 1: Training the Correct Angle and Position of Hands in a Basic Stationary Punching Drill 45
Drill 2: Punching from Sitting, Kneeling and Standing Positions 46
Drill 3: Throw, Punch and Catch in a 3-GK Juggling Group 47
Drill 4: Punching Over Mannequins from a Stationary Position 48
Drill 5: Punching Over Mannequins in a Continuous Throwing Circuit 49
Drill 6: Punching the Ball while Holding Another Ball in a 3-GK Juggling Group 50
Drill 7: Accurate Punching with Alternate Hands from a Sitting Position 51
Drill 8: Punching the Ball Away from Goal to Alternate Sides 52
Drill 9: Quick Footwork and Punching the Ball Over the Crossbar 53
Drill 10: Punch Ball Small Sided Game with Large Goals 54

CHAPTER 5: PARRYING 55

Drill 1: Parrying the Ball Away from Goal 56
Drill 2: Parrying the Ball to Alternate Sides from a Sitting Position 57
Drill 3: Dive and Parry + Get Up to Save Second Ball 58
Drill 4: Quick Side-steps, Dive Low and Parry Away 59
Drill 5: Quick Side-steps, Dive High and Parry Away in a Dynamic Goalkeeper Circuit 60
Drill 6: Parrying Shots Away from Goal with 2 Hands 61
Drill 7: Quick Sprint Forward, then Back + Parry Over the Crossbar 62
Drill 8: Quick Side-steps and Parry the Ball Over the Crossbar at an Angle 63
Drill 9: Diving and Parrying Shots to the Top or Bottom Corners 64
Drill 10: Continuous Quick Footwork and Parrying the Ball Over the Crossbar with 2 Goals 65

CHAPTER 6: HIGH BALLS 66

Drill 1: Jump to Catch Stationary Ball 67
Drill 2: Crossover-steps + Catch High Ball 68
Drill 3: Catch High Ball at the Near Post Against a Defender 69
Drill 4: Compete to Catch High Ball in a 2 Team Game 70
Drill 5: Touch Post and Run Through Consecutive Poles to Catch High Balls 71
Drill 6: Continuous High Ball Catches from Different Angles 72
Drill 7: Fast Reactions to Catch High Balls Over Mannequins to Right or Left 73
Drill 8: Kicking and Catching High Balls Over a Large Goal Game 74
Drill 9: Competing to Catch High Balls in a Dynamic 3 Zone Game 75
Drill 10: Catching High Balls Against Defender in the Box + Long Kick Out 76

CHAPTER 7: ONE v ONE 77

Drill 1: Blocking Close Up Shots in a Cone Channel 78
Drill 2: Diving Forward to Save at an Opponent's Feet 79
Drill 3: Move Forward to Attack the Ball and Save 80
Drill 4: Running Out of Goal to Save 1 v 1 Against an Opponent Running onto a Pass 81
Drill 5: Saving at Close Range with Opponents Moving in for Rebounds 82
The "Block Position" 83
Drill 6: Correct Technique for "Block Position" in a 1 v 1 Situation 84

©SoccerTutor.com   Goalkeeper Training Program - 120 Drills

Drill 7: "Block Position" in a 1 v 1 Situation using Mini Goals 85
Drill 8: Fast Reactions to Form "Block Position" to Left or Right 86
Drill 9: Practicing the "Block Position" in a 1 v 1 Duel Game with Mini Goals 87
Drill 10: Practicing All Techniques for 1 v 1 Situations in a 4 Cone Drill 88

CHAPTER 8: TECHNICAL SKILLS WITH THE FEET 89

Drill 1: Short One-Touch Passing on Left and Right Side with Both Feet 90
Drill 2: Directional First Touch Out in Front + Return Pass 91
Drill 3: Opening Up to Receive and Pass 92
Drill 4: Accurate Chip Passing 93
Drill 5: One-Touch Zig-Zag Passing Through Cones on the Move 94
Drill 6: Moving to Receive Back Passes and Play Out within the 6-Yard Box 95
Drill 7: Back Pass, One-Two and Chip Pass in a 4-GK Passing Drill 96
Drill 8: Passing/Receiving Ground and Aerial Passes in a 3-GK Line Passing Drill 97
Drill 9: One-Two Combinations with Short and Long Passing 98
Drill 10: "Wall Ball Game" with Passing Against Low Bench 99

CHAPTER 9: FOOTWORK 100

Drill 1: Movement in All Directions with Ankle Resistance Band 101
Drill 2: Sideways Movement and Catch with Jump 102
Drill 3: Awareness and Quick Movements in Different Directions within a Square + Catch 103
Drill 4: Side-steps and Jumps in All Directions within a Square + Catch 104
Drill 5: Speed and Coordination Training with a Ladder + Catch and Throw 105
Drill 6: Turn, Big Step + Small Steps to Receive a Pass 106
Drill 7: Quick Back-steps Towards Goal + Jump to Save 107
Drill 8: Sprinting with Different Types of Resistance 108
Drill 9: Sprint Out of the Penalty Area Towards the Ball and Accurate Chip Pass 109
Drill 10: Different Types of Footwork and Catching Techniques within a 6-Yard Box Circuit 110

CHAPTER 10: DISTRIBUTION 111

Drill 1: Practicing Various Distribution Techniques (Long Kick, Drop Kick, Rolling Ball, Overarm Throw) 112
Drill 2: Accurate Distribution Through Channels in a Competitive 1 v 1 Game 113
Drill 3: Hitting Targets: Rolling, Throwing and Kicking 114
Drill 4: Accurate Passing into Small Goals 115
Drill 5: Goal Kick, Drop Kick and Catch in a 3-GK Group 116
Drill 6: Catch, Throw Out, One-Two and Long Kick in a Dynamic Circuit 117
Drill 7: Accurate Overarm Throws to the Left, Right and Centre 118
Drill 8: "Piggy in the Middle" Distribution Game 119
Drill 9: Different Distribution Techniques in a 5-Part Points Game 120
Drill 10: Short and Long Distribution in a Circuit Points Game 121

CHAPTER 11: DRILLS WITH OUTFIELD PLAYERS 122

Drill 1: Catching Aerial Balls in the 6-Yard Box 123
Drill 2a: Throwing the Ball Out and Catching Headers in the 6-Yard Box 124

Drill 2b: Rolling the Ball Out and Saving First Time Shots After Lay-Off...................................125
Drill 3: 2 GKs (+2 Players) vs 2 Players in a Dynamic 2 Goal Possession Game.........................126
Drill 4: Dynamic Goalkeeper to Goalkeeper Rondo Possession Game.....................................127
Drill 5: Distribution and Catching within a Passing Combination Drill......................................128
Drill 6a: Sprinting Out of Goal to Win the Ball in a 1 v 1 Against an Oncoming Attacker..............129
Drill 6b: Sprinting Out of Goal to Close the Angle for an Oncoming Attacker...........................130
Drill 7a: 1 v 1 Against Attacker from Either Side..131
Drill 7b: Protecting the Goal Against 2 Attackers with the Help of 1 Defender..........................132
Drill 8: 4 v 1 / 8 v 2 Rondos with the Goalkeeper in the Middle...133
Drill 9: Saving First Time Shots from the Edge of the Penalty Area in a 2 Team Game.................134
Drill 10: Defending Crosses in a Dynamic 2 Zone 4 (+1) v 4 (+1) Small Sided Game...................135

CHAPTER 12: GOALKEEPER GAMES..136

Drill 1: Head and Catch Goalkeeper Circle Game...137
Drill 2: "Goalie Wars" Game...138
Drill 3: "Goalkeeper Squash" Game with Rebounder..139
Drill 4: Throw and Catch Goalkeeper Tennis Game...140
Drill 5: Goalkeeper Tennis Game with Volleys..141
Drill 6: End to End 2 Zone Rebounder Game...141
Drill 7: Goalkeeper Penalty Competition..143
Drill 8: Goalkeeper "One v One" Competition...144
Drill 9: Goalkeeper "Head Ball" Small Sided Game..145
Drill 10: Players vs Goalkeepers Small Sided Game..146

MEET THE AUTHOR

Maarten Arts
UEFA A Coaching Licence

maarten@peakelite.co.uk

- **Royal Union Saint Gilloise (Belgium) Goalkeeping Coach**
  (2018 - Present)

- **Al Wahda (Abu Dhabi) Head Goalkeeping Coach**
  (2017 - 2018)

- **Wadi Degla FC (Egypt) Head Goalkeeping Coach**
  (2015 - 2017)

- **Lierse SK (Belgium) Goalkeeping Coach**
  (2014 - 2015)

- **Saudi Arabia National Team Goalkeeping Coach**
  (2013 - 2014)

- **Umm Salal (Qatar) Goalkeeping Coach**
  (2010 - 2013)

- **FC Utrecht (Netherlands) Goalkeeping Coach**
  (1998 - 2009)

I am proud to present this Goalkeeper Training Program. Through many years coaching all around the world, I have created a full blueprint of **120 Drills** to produce top class goalkeepers.

This training program has proved to create better, all round goalkeepers at every level, from juniors up to top-level international goalkeepers. This book is not only about reproducing the drills in it, but it should also inspire you to create your own drills in the image of this program.

Being creative and surprising our goalkeepers with new drills and training elements is a huge part of our great job! I wish you all great success in your careers and I hope the drills in this book will help make your goalkeepers TOP Class.

This book has 12 chapters. Each of the 12 chapters includes 10 drills on a specific goalkeeping technique or topic:

1. CATCHING
2. FALLING
3. DIVING
4. PUNCHING
5. PARRYING
6. HIGH BALLS
7. ONE v ONE
8. TECHNICAL SKILLS WITH THE FEET
9. FOOTWORK
10. DISTRIBUTION
11. DRILLS WITH OUTFIELD PLAYERS
12. GOALKEEPER GAMES

GOALKEEPER TRAINING TIPS

1. In the drills displayed, when it says "Coach," this role can also be taken by another goalkeeper (GK).

2. Coaches and goalkeepers should have their gloves on when they enter the training pitch and during the during warm-up.

3. Warm-ups without the ball i.e. running, jumping and stretching, should be done by the goalkeepers themselves before the actual training starts.

4. If you work with a larger number of goalkeepers (4-8), try to still maintain a good overview by marking out the working areas all in the same line.

5. Let the goalkeepers work in pairs, so they will have many (more) ball touches. Only when training young goalkeepers (ages 7-10) does the Coach **need** to throw/play himself.

6. If there are odd numbers (3, 5 or 7), never have 1 goalkeeper working on his own. Instead, you can make a group of 3.

7. Work according to the 1-2-3 principle. Number 1 is the first action (e.g. catching a cross), number 2 is the distribution (throwing/passing the ball back) and number 3 is moving back into the correct position as quickly as possible.

8. Create drills where every goalkeeper is busy and challenged.

9. Train as much as possible with the ball and finish your training with a game.

10. Goalkeepers should pass and shoot as much as possible in training sessions, making sure to also use their weaker foot.

11. Use cones to force the goalkeepers to attack the ball.

12. When starting a new drill or when the goalkeepers are collecting balls, make them do this while running to allow for more effective training time.

13. Drink enough water and often, but only the Coach decides when to drink.

14. Ask your goalkeepers questions like "What did you learn today?" and "Why do you have to shout when a cross comes?" It helps them to think about the purpose of the drill and it gives the Coach a good idea of how successful he was in what he wanted to achieve from the session.

15. Visualise as much as possible.

16. Encourage the goalkeepers to work on their weaknesses before or after training, and even at home.

17. We are training to improve performances in competitive matches. The match is the final exam. You can check if what you trained has become automatic for your goalkeepers when you watch the matches.

18. It is essential to watch as many of the matches your goalkeepers play as possible. After the game, there should always be constructive feedback.

19. Make videos of training and/or matches and show them to your goalkeepers. You can analyse technique and performances together.

DRILL FORMAT

Each drill includes clear diagrams with supporting training notes:

- Name/Objective of Drill
- Description of Drill
- Variation or Progression (if applicable)
- Coaching Points

KEY

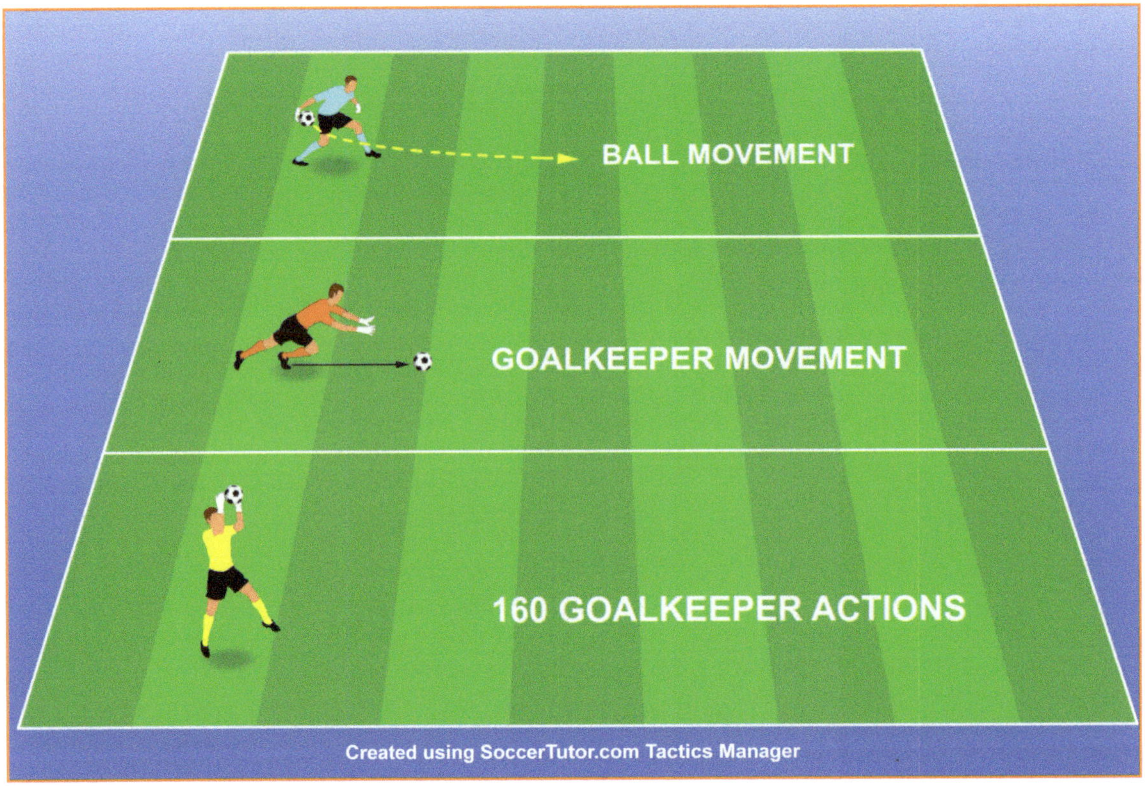

- BALL MOVEMENT
- GOALKEEPER MOVEMENT
- 160 GOALKEEPER ACTIONS

Created using SoccerTutor.com Tactics Manager

CHAPTER 1

CATCHING

CHAPTER 1: Catching

1. Catching the Ball in Front of Goal

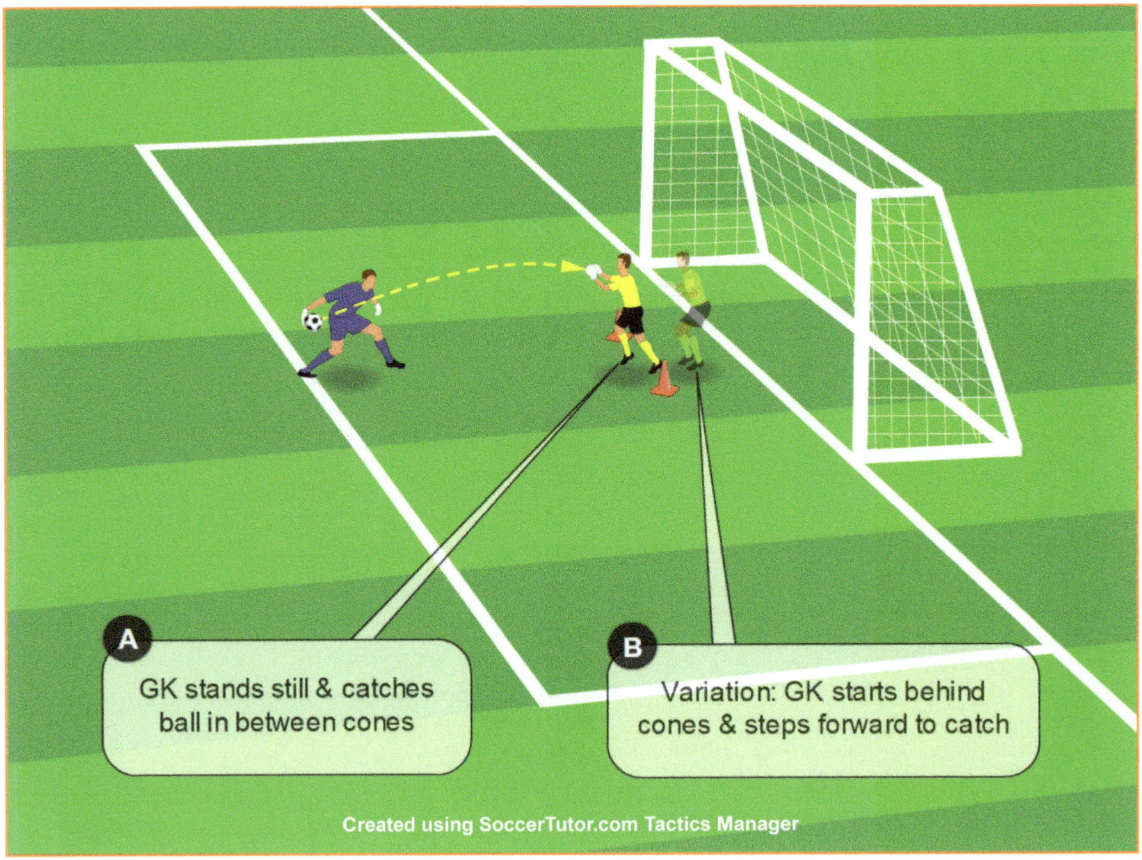

![Diagram: A - GK stands still & catches ball in between cones. B - Variation: GK starts behind cones & steps forward to catch]

Description

A. The GK stands in between the cones. The Coach throws the ball and the GK catches with outstretched arms in front of his body.

B. The GK stands behind the cones. The Coach throws the ball and the GK takes one step forward (in between the cones) and catches with outstretched arms in front of his body.

Coaching Points

1. Catch on top of the ball.
2. Arms should be fully outstretched in front.
3. Secure the ball by bringing it to the chest.
4. The fingers should be in a "W-Shape" when catching.

CHAPTER 1: Catching

2. Side-steps and Catch

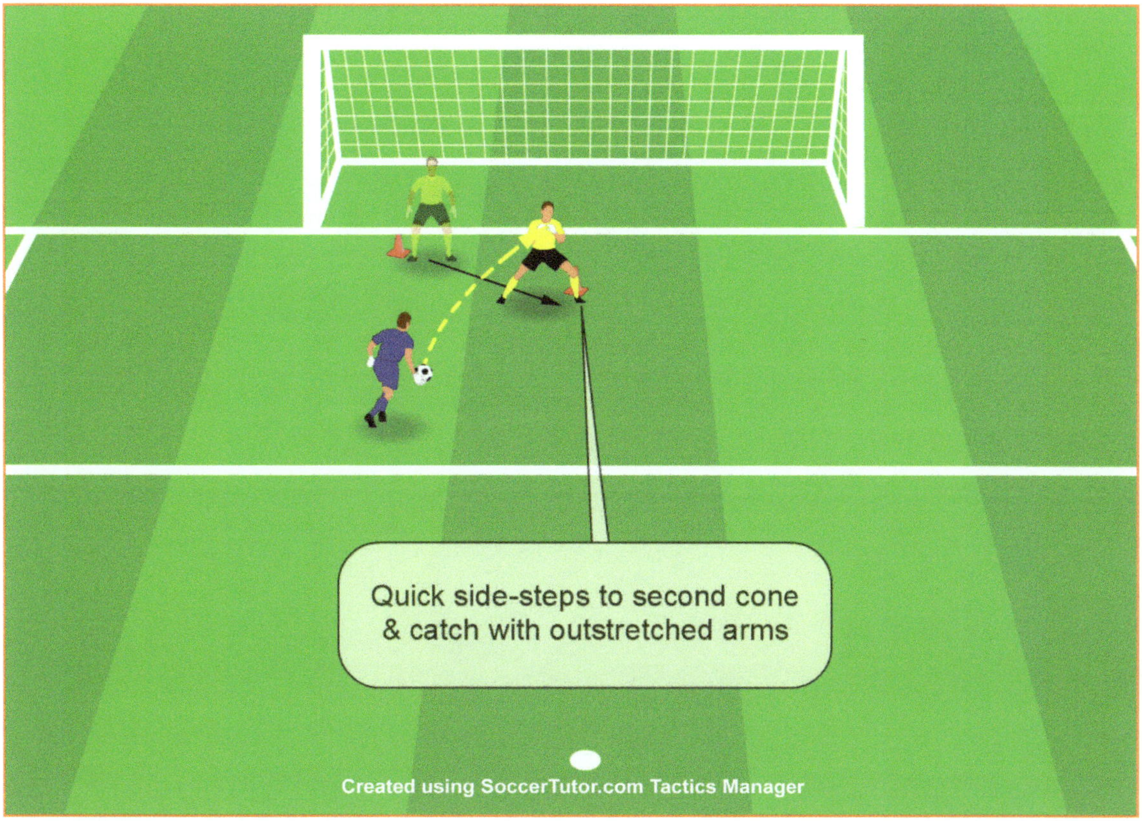

Quick side-steps to second cone & catch with outstretched arms

Description

- The GK starts on the cone near the post. The GK moves sideways (side-steps) and the Coach throws the ball towards the central cone.
- The GK catches the ball with outstretched arms in front of the cone.

Coaching Points

1. Start with 1 foot against the cone.
2. Move with quick steps.
3. Start with a high body position (upright) for faster movement.
4. The Coach should be in line with the GK when he throws the ball.
5. Arms should be completely straight (90-degree angle to the body).

CHAPTER 1: Catching

3. Catching After Quick Small Steps

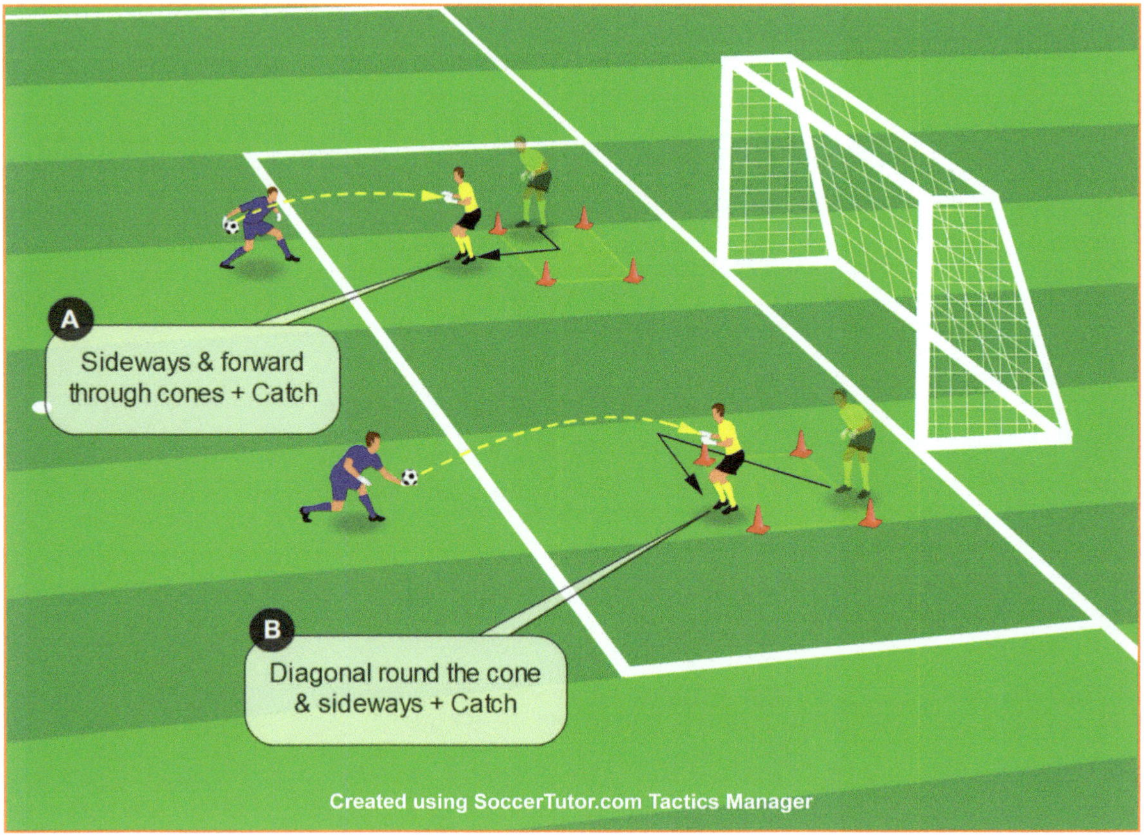

![Diagram]
A. Sideways & forward through cones + Catch
B. Diagonal round the cone & sideways + Catch

Created using SoccerTutor.com Tactics Manager

Description

A. The GK moves sideways (side-steps) with quick small steps between the cones, then moves forward and catches the ball in front of the cones.

B. The GK moves diagonally (side-steps) with quick small steps around a front cone and moves sideways (back inside) to catch the ball in front of the cones.

Coaching Points

1. No tension in the upper body - there should only be tension in the legs.
2. Start with a high body position (upright).
3. Do not put one leg over the other (cross) at the moment of catching.
4. The age/level of the GK determines whether the server should throw the ball or shoot.

CHAPTER 1: Catching

4. Catching After Turning from the Near Post

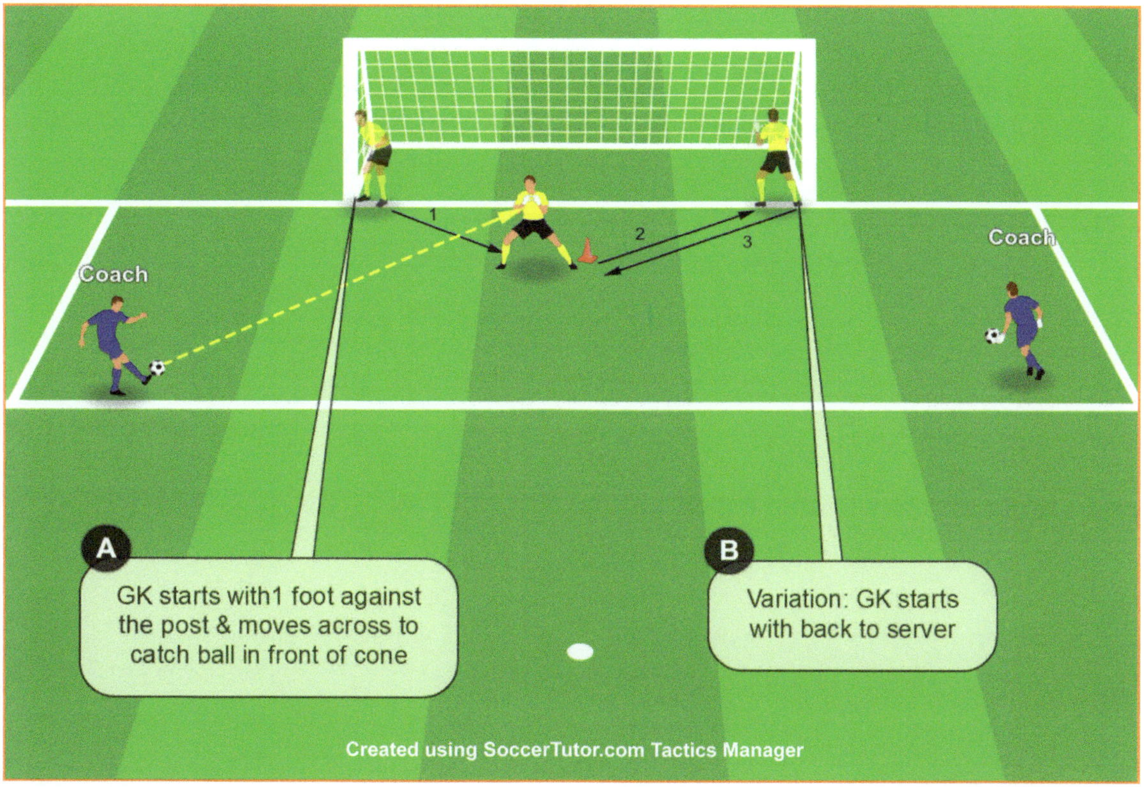

A. GK starts with 1 foot against the post & moves across to catch ball in front of cone

B. Variation: GK starts with back to server

Description

A. The GK starts with 1 foot against the post and the Coach throws or shoots the ball towards the central cone. The GK moves towards the central cone and catches the ball in front of it.

B. Variation: Repeat from the other side, but now the GK starts with his back to the server, so must turn, move towards the central cone and catch.

Coaching Points

1. Move with quick steps on the front part of the foot.
2. At the moment of catching, the body should be 100% open.
3. The server should throw the ball with 2 hands to have more control.

CHAPTER 1: Catching

5. Catching After Low Hurdle Jumps

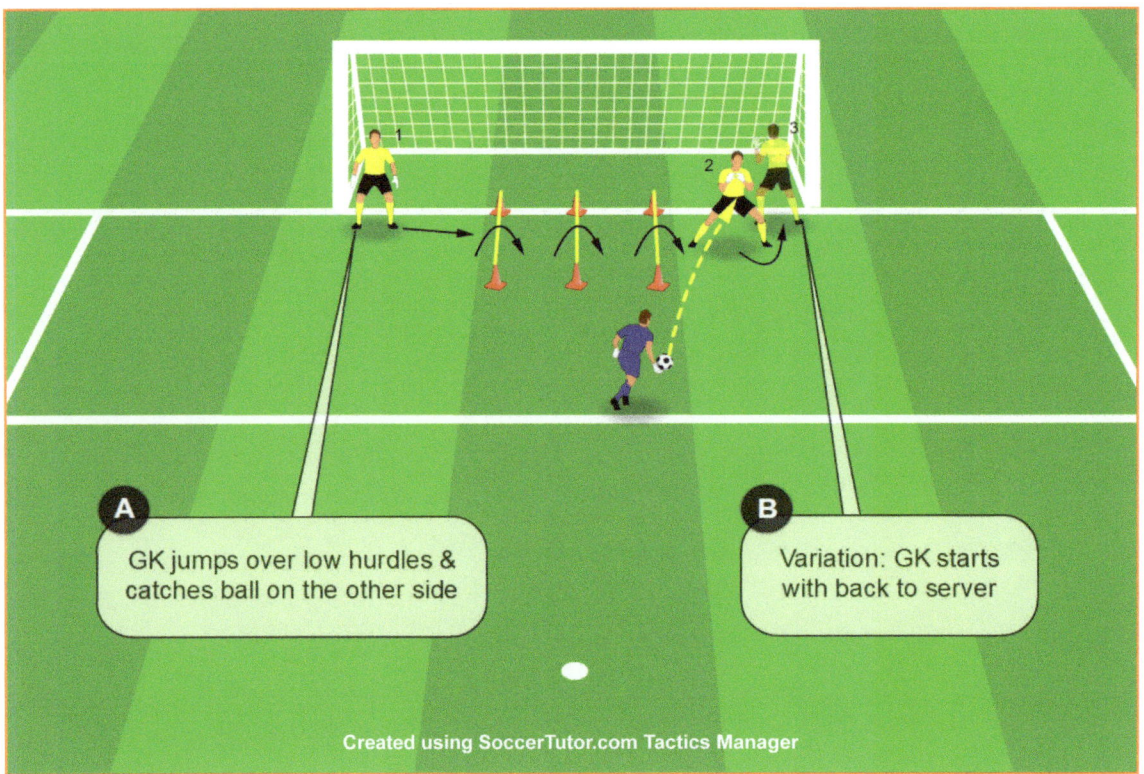

Description

A. The GK moves off the post, jumps over the 3 low hurdles (side-on position) and catches the ball on the other side.

B. Variation: Repeat from the other side, but now the GK starts with his back to the server, so must turn, move towards the centre, jump over the 3 low hurdles and catch the ball on the other side.

Coaching Points

1. Always keep your eyes on the ball.
2. First start with 1 hurdle, then gradually add more e.g. 3 in diagram example.
3. Try to keep the upper body in the same position throughout.
4. When the ball is moving, try to step forward to catch it as quickly as possible.

CHAPTER 1: Catching

6. Catching and Throwing with Slalom Through Poles

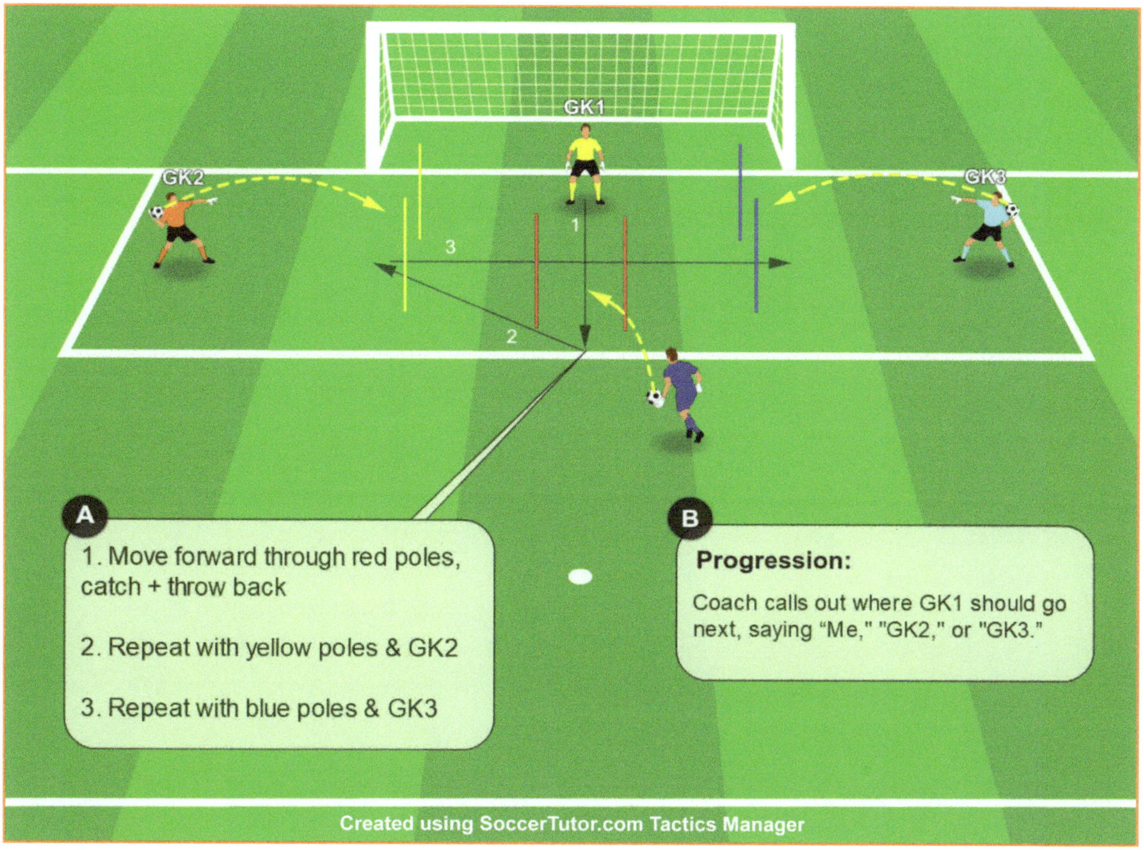

A
1. Move forward through red poles, catch + throw back
2. Repeat with yellow poles & GK2
3. Repeat with blue poles & GK3

B
Progression:
Coach calls out where GK1 should go next, saying "Me," "GK2," or "GK3."

Description

A. GK1 moves forward between the red poles. The Coach throws the ball up for him to catch and throw back. GK1 then moves in between the yellow poles to catch and throw back to GK2. Finally, he goes through the blue poles and repeats the same with GK3.

B. Progression: The Coach calls out where GK1 should go next, saying "Me," "GK2," or "GK3." For higher level players, have all the servers kick the ball instead of throwing.

Coaching Points

1. Always catch the ball in front of the poles.
2. Throw the ball back in a technically correct way, before moving to the next poles.
3. GK1 throws the ball back with 1 hand and the others throw with 2 hands.

CHAPTER 1: Catching

7. Catching with Quick Cone Touches

[Diagram showing goalkeeping drill setup with GK1, GK2, GK3 positions and numbered steps:
1. Touch blue cone
2. Move forward
3. Catch throw from GK2
4. Touch red cone
5. Move forward
6. Catch throw from GK3]

Description

- GK1 touches the cone on his right side (blue) and GK2 throws a ball up in the air.
- GK1 moves forward and catches the ball.
- After that, GK1 touches the other cone (red), moves forward and catches a ball from GK3.
- After a few repetitions, switch to touching the left cone.

Coaching Points

1. Always look at the ball (not at the cones).
2. Catch the ball as close to the thrower as possible.
3. Take small steps towards the cones.
4. Make sure there is no tension in the arms or shoulders when catching.

©SoccerTutor.com — Goalkeeper Training Program - 120 Drills

CHAPTER 1: Catching

8. Catching and Awareness Drill

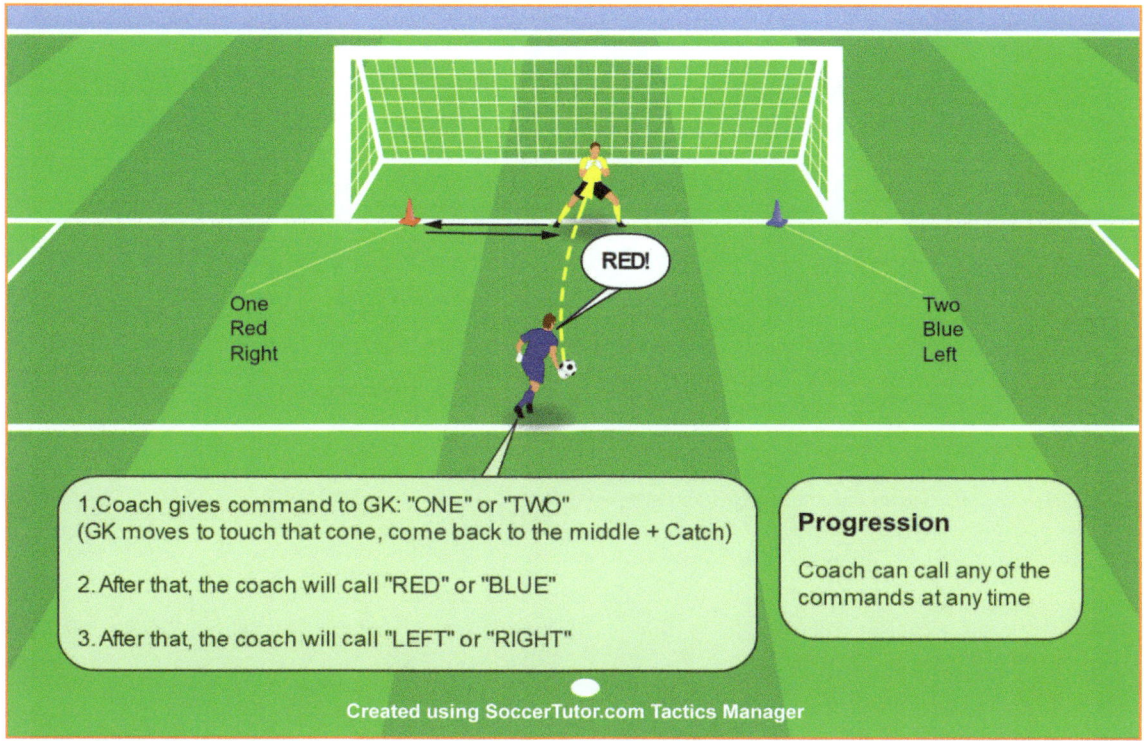

Description

1. The Coach gives a command to the GK: "ONE!" or "TWO!"
   The GK then has to go and touch that cone, come back to the middle and catch the ball.

2. After that, the Coach will call "RED!" or "BLUE!"

3. After that, the Coach will call "LEFT!" or "RIGHT!"

Progression: Once the GK is into the rhythm of the drill, the Coach can use any of the 6 commands at any time. The GK must react quickly with small steps and good technical catching.

Coaching Points

1. Concentrate on the command of the Coach: Do not move before the call.

2. Always look at the ball (not at the cones).

3. Move back to the middle along the goal line.

©SoccerTutor.com   Goalkeeper Training Program - 120 Drills

CHAPTER 1: Catching

9. Throwing/Kicking and Catching in a Continuous Circuit

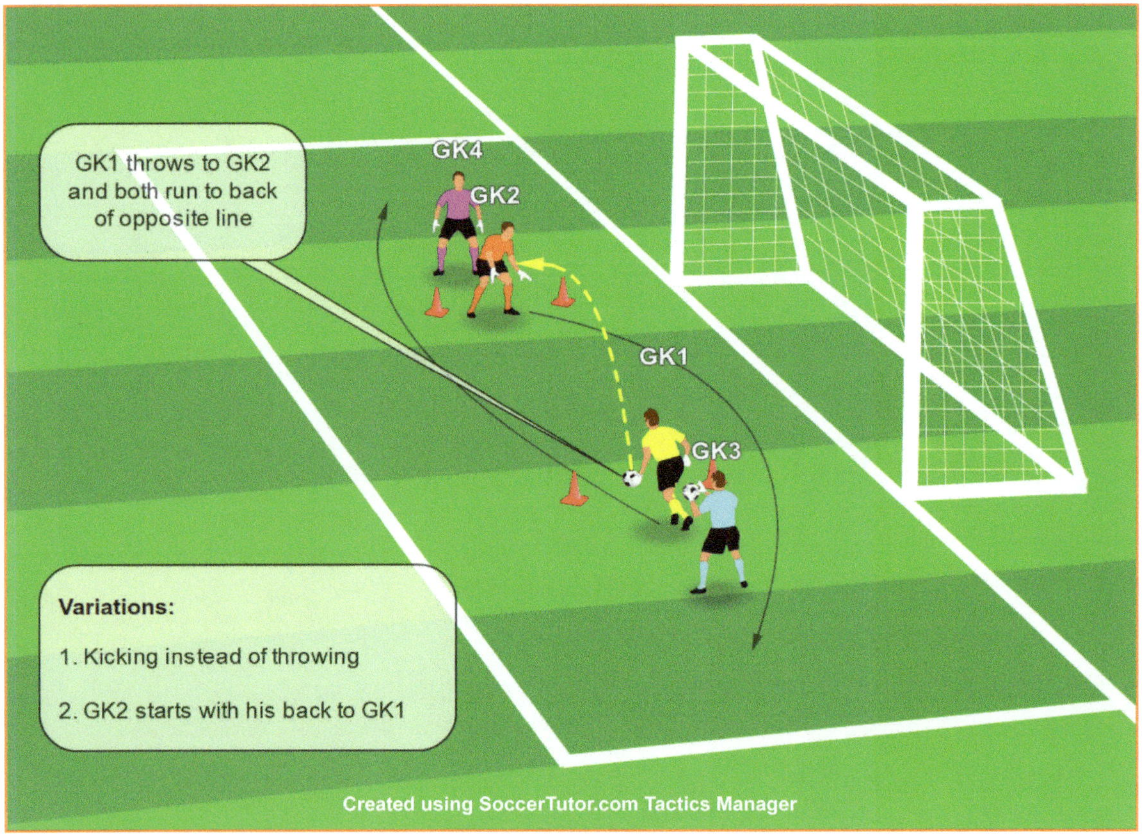

Description

- GK1 throws the ball to GK2.
- GK1 goes to the back of the opposite line and GK2 does the same.
- GK3 throws to GK4 and the same sequence runs continuously with all 4 goalkeepers.

Variations: (1) Instead of throwing the ball, the goalkeepers can kick the ball.
(2) The receiving GK starts with his back to the server.

Coaching Points

1. Make sure to make good quality throws.
2. If the level is good, make the distance between the cones larger.
3. After catching the ball, immediately start moving to the opposite line.

CHAPTER 1: Catching

10. Throwing and Catching in a 4 v 4 Possession Game within the 6-Yard Box

Description

- The blue team starts and tries to throw the ball to each other 10 consecutive times (to score 1 point).
- If the ball goes out of the 6-yard box, is touched by a player on the other team or falls to the ground, then the ball is given to the opposing team.
- You are not allowed to throw back to the player you received the ball from.

Variation: Play 5 v 4 with 1 neutral player, who plays with the team in possession.

Coaching Points

1. The Coach or one of the GKs counts the number of consecutive throws out loud.
2. The players should attack the ball when catching.
3. Don't walk with the ball.
4. Throw with 1 hand. If a GK uses 2 hands, then the ball is given to the other team.

CHAPTER 2

FALLING

CHAPTER 2: Falling

1. Falling Save at Close Distance

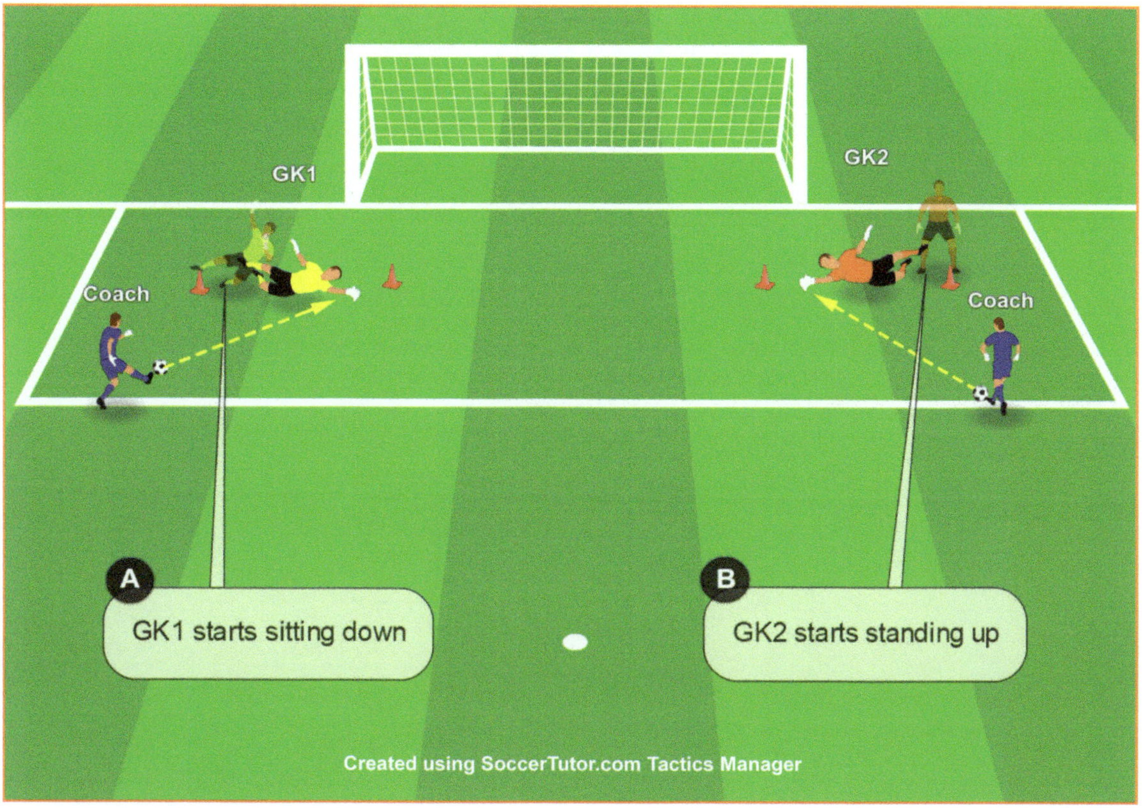

Description

A. The GK starts by sitting on the ground behind a cone. The Coach kicks the ball and the GK falls with outstretched arms towards the ball (through the cones).

B. The GK is now standing behind the cones and falls forward with outstretched arms through the cones.

Coaching Points

1. At first, practice with 1 outstretched arm to get the body in a straight line.
2. Shoulders should always be in front of the knees and feet.
3. The Coach starts in the same line as the GK.
4. When standing, body weight should be forward.

©SoccerTutor.com   Goalkeeper Training Program - 120 Drills

CHAPTER 2: Falling

2. Falling Saves to Left and Right

1. Ball kicked to right
2. Ball kicked to left

Description
- The GK starts between the cones and the Coach plays the ball to one side. The GK falls with outstretched arms to save. The ball is then played to the other side, with the GK reacting each time and falling with outstretched arms to save.

Variations: **(1)** The Coach can decide which side to play to at any time.

(2) The GK stands with his back to the Coach and waits for the call of "NOW" - the GK then turns and the Coach plays the ball to either side.

Coaching Points
1. The first steps have to be sideways, not forward.
2. Start in a low position.
3. Move the arm closest to the ball first, to close the gap under the body.
4. Priority: First think to **STOP** the ball and then **CATCH** the ball.

©SoccerTutor.com   Goalkeeper Training Program - 120 Drills

CHAPTER 2: Falling

3. Continuous Falling Saves from Opposite Sides

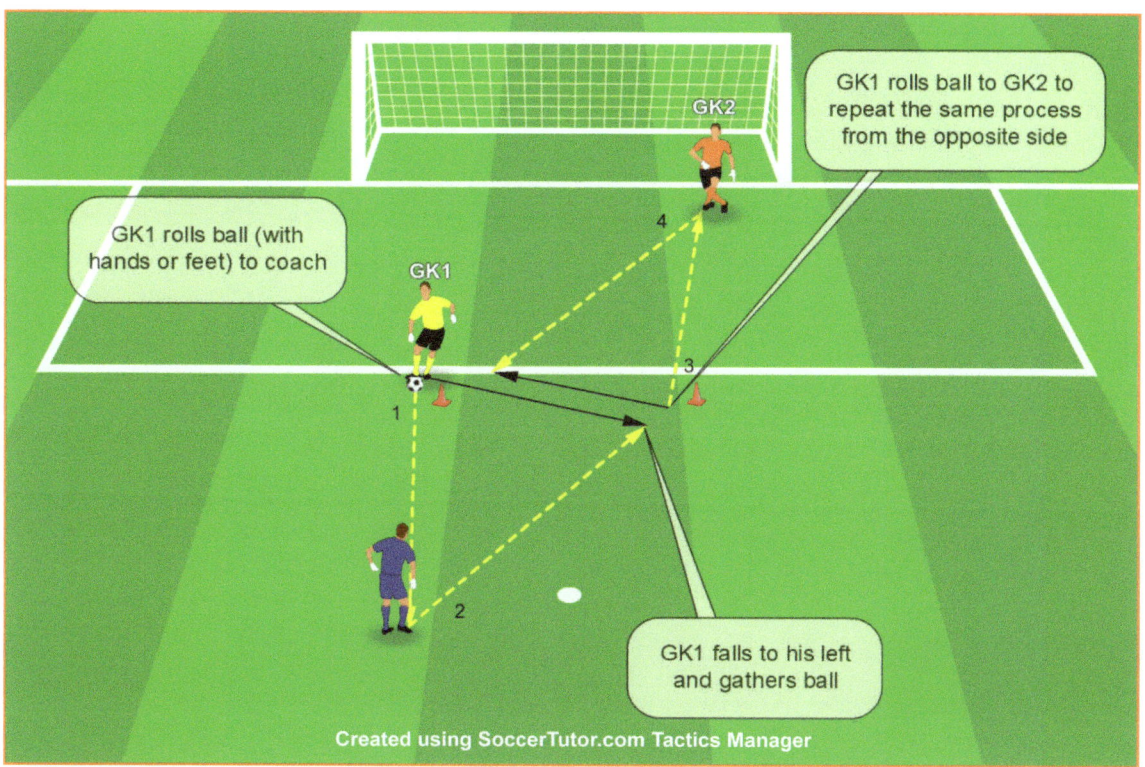

Description
1. GK1 rolls the ball to the Coach.
2. The Coach passes the ball to GK1's left side.
3. GK1 moves between the cones, falls down to his left and gathers the ball.
4. GK1 rolls the ball to GK2.
5. GK2 passes the ball to GK1's left side.
6. GK1 moves between the cones, falls down to his left and gathers the ball.

* After 3 repetitions, the Coach and GK2 adjust positions and GK1 falls to the right side (prevents training one side too long to avoid injury). After 6 repetitions, GK1 and GK2 swap.

Coaching Points
1. From his starting position, GK1 takes 1 step before attacking the ball.
2. This drill should be done at a high speed throughout.
3. A good quality roll from the GK means getting a good ball back.

CHAPTER 2: Falling

4. Jump Low Hurdle + Falling Save

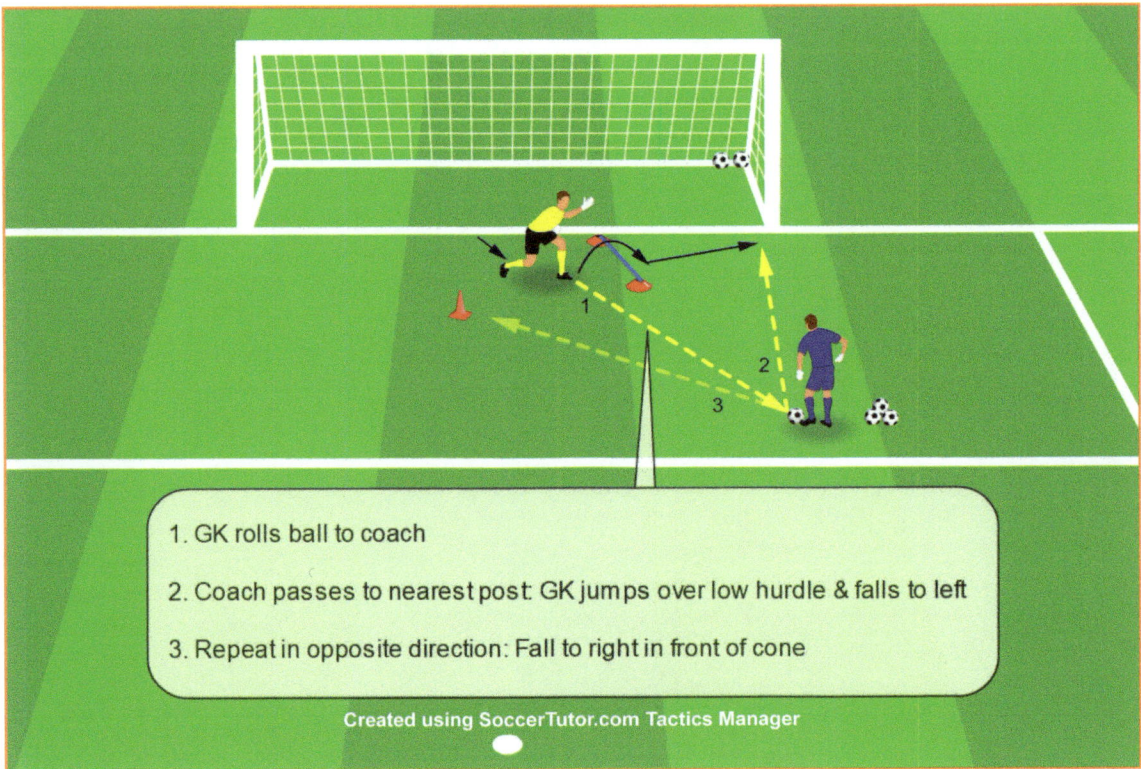

1. GK rolls ball to coach
2. Coach passes to nearest post: GK jumps over low hurdle & falls to left
3. Repeat in opposite direction: Fall to right in front of cone

Description

1. The GK rolls the ball to the Coach.
2. The Coach passes the ball to the nearest post. The GK jumps over the low hurdle, falls down to his left and gathers the ball.
3. Repeat in opposite direction: The GK starts by the post, jumps over the low hurdle and falls to the right side towards the cone.

Variation: The GK jumps 3 times back and forth over the hurdle, instead of once.

Coaching Points

1. Start close to the goal line.
2. Use the post as you would a cone: Try to get in front of it as much as possible.
3. This drill should be done at a high speed throughout.
4. After jumping over the hurdle, the first step should be sideways.

CHAPTER 2: Falling

5. Two Falling Saves in Quick Succession

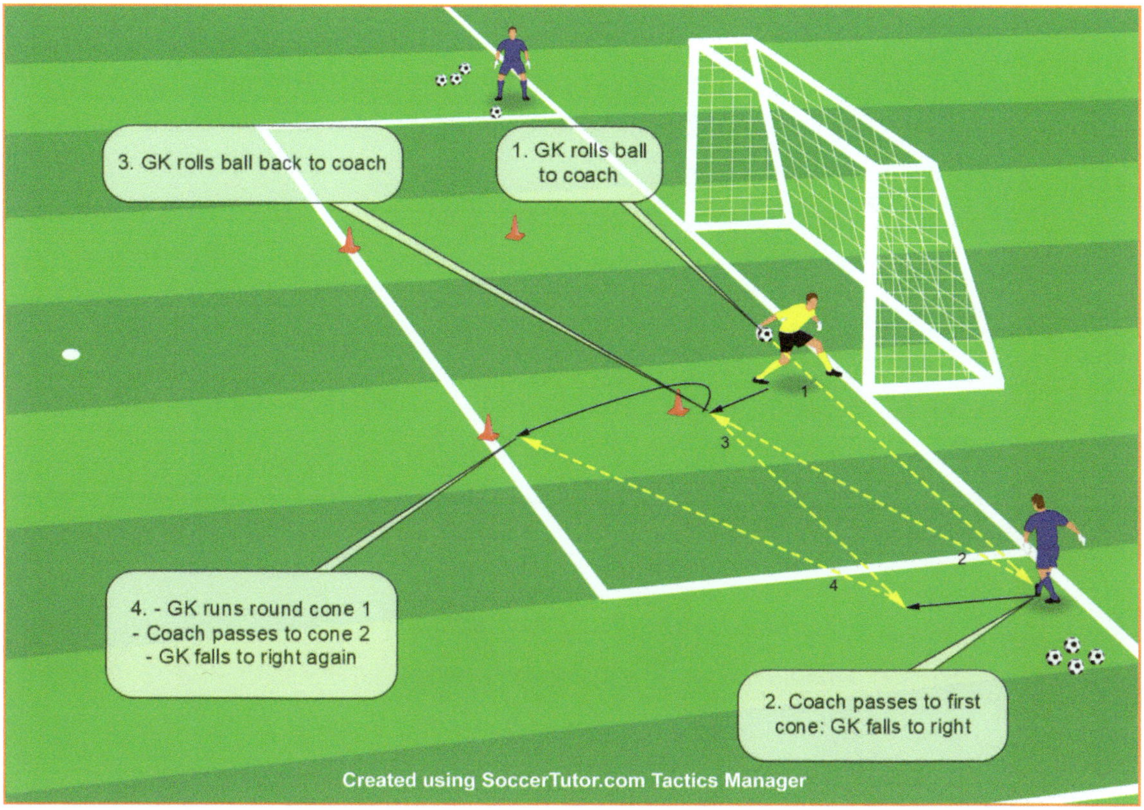

[Diagram:
1. GK rolls ball to coach
2. Coach passes to first cone: GK falls to right
3. GK rolls ball back to coach
4. - GK runs round cone 1
   - Coach passes to cone 2
   - GK falls to right again]

Description

1. The GK rolls the ball to the Coach.
2. The Coach passes the ball to the 1st cone. The GK falls to his right and gathers the ball.
3. The GK rolls the ball back to the Coach.
4. The GK runs around the 1st cone and back into position. The Coach passes the ball to the 2nd cone. The GK falls to his right again and gathers the ball.
5. Repeat the sequence on the other side.

Coaching Points

1. The GK starts in an "open" position
2. After rolling the 1st ball, take 1 step to come in line with the goal post.
3. Use a very low starting position, so that the hands are close to the ground.
4. After rolling the 1st ball back, keep your eyes fixed on the ball.

CHAPTER 2: Falling

6. Falling Saves and Awareness Drill

Description

1. The GK rolls the ball to the Coach.
2. The Coach calls out "RED!" or "BLUE!"
3. The GK has to react quickly and attack the ball (through the blue cones in the diagram example) to save.

- You can also use different commands such as "ONE!" or "TWO!" / "RIGHT!" or "LEFT!"

Progression: **(1)** Mix up the commands to make the drill more difficult.
(2) Have the GK start with his back to the Coach.

Coaching Points

1. The GK only takes 1 step and then attacks the ball.
2. Don't start too close to the cones.
3. Try to always stand back up without using the hands.
4. After rolling the ball back, get back into the starting position quickly.

CHAPTER 2: Falling

7. Changing Direction + Falling Save within a 4-GK Passing Combination

![Diagram]

Description

1. GK1 rolls the ball to GK2.
2. GK2 passes the ball for GK1 to run onto (Cone B).
3. GK1 passes to Cone C.
4. GK3 touches Cone D.
5. GK3 falls to Cone C to gather the ball. The drill starts again in the opposite direction, with GK3 rolling the ball to GK4.

Variation: GK1 can play a diagonal pass towards Cone D and GK3 touches Cone C first.

Coaching Points

1. GK2 and GK4 have to play their passes slowly for GK1 and GK3 to run onto.
2. When GK1 plays a diagonal ball, GK2 and GK4 have to move to the other side.
3. Wait as long as possible before touching the cone, prior to the falling save.

CHAPTER 2: Falling

8. Fast Reactions and Turning + Falling Save

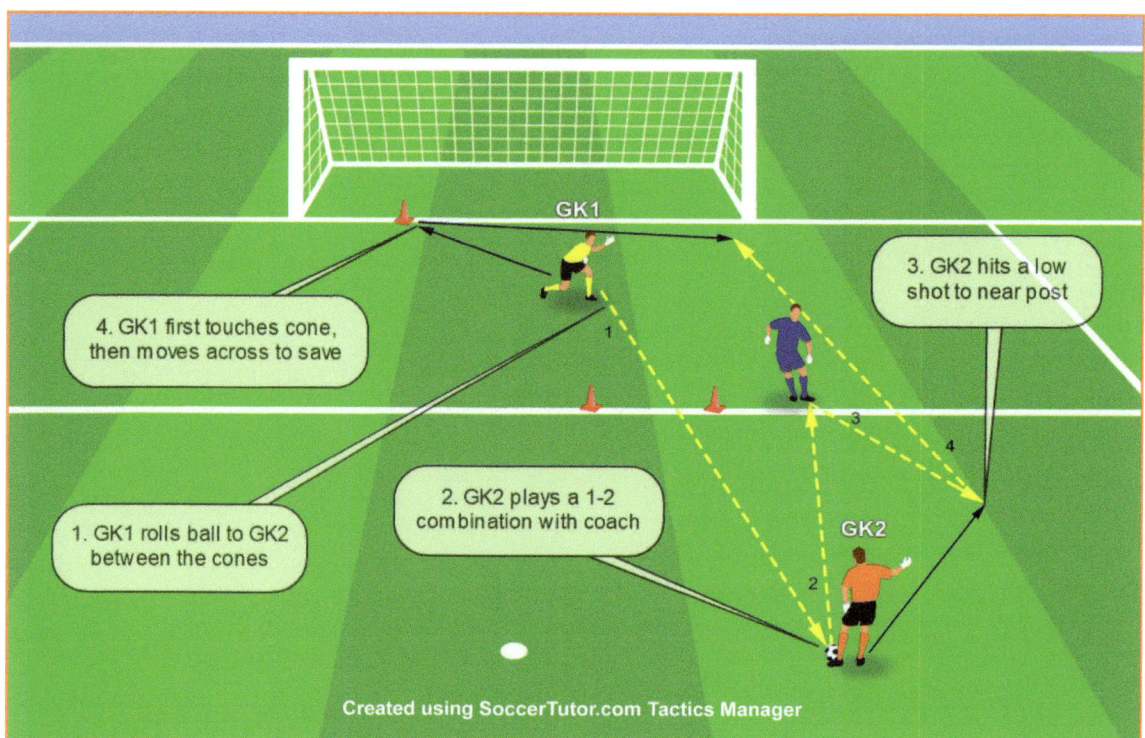

Description

1. GK1 rolls ball to GK2 between the cones.
2. GK2 plays a 1-2 combination with the Coach.
3. GK2 then hits a low shot to the near post.
4. GK1 has to first touch the cone on the goal line and then move across to save the shot.

Variation: GK2 shoots to the far post and GK1 has to touch the near post first.

Progressions

1. Remove the cone on the goal line: The GK touches the post, then saves at the other post.
2. The Coach and GK2 start closer to the goal line.

Coaching Points

1. GK1 rolls the ball in front of the goal line and then moves back to the cone.
2. After GK1 touches the cone, he moves sideways along the goal line.

©SoccerTutor.com   Goalkeeper Training Program - 120 Drills

CHAPTER 2: Falling

9. Falling Save at the Near Post from a Cross

Description

1. GK1 rolls the ball to the Coach, who plays a deep pass to the by-line.
2. GK2 sprints towards the ball and crosses it to the cone.
3. GK1 falls down and attacks the ball.
4. GK1 moves to the position of GK4, GK2 moves to GK3 and GK3 moves to GK1.

Coaching Points

1. GK1 should not get into a position at the near post too early.
2. Take up an extremely low starting position.
3. GK2 has to wait to sprint until the Coach plays the ball.

CHAPTER 2: Falling

10. Falling Saves to Defend the Bottom Corners

Description

- We have 2 small goals in a big goal. GK1 is in goal and the other 2 GKs are shooting from in between the cones, as shown.
- When the Coach behind the goal puts his hand up, GK2 or GK3 shoot into a small goal.
- GK1 saves the ball = 2 points.
- GK2 or GK3 score = 1 point.
- After 6 shots, rotate the positions (GK1 -> GK2 -> GK3 -> GK1). The GK with the most points after 3 rounds wins.

Coaching Points

1. GK1 starts with his feet behind the line.
2. First step sideways, then make a falling save to try and stop the ball.
3. If you don't hold onto the ball, always go after it immediately to avoid a rebound being scored.

©SoccerTutor.com   Goalkeeper Training Program - 120 Drills

CHAPTER 3

DIVING

CHAPTER 3: Diving

1. Diving to Side from Kneeling Position

![diagram: GK stretches his right leg & dives to catch ball; GK starts on 1 knee]

Description

1. The GK kneels (on 1 knee) behind Cone 1.
2. The Coach stands in front of him and throws the ball up towards Cone 2.
3. The GK stretches his right leg and dives to catch the ball.
4. After 3 dives, change sides so the GK is diving to his left.

Coaching Points

1. The Coach starts in line with Cone 1 and the GK.
2. After catching, make sure the ball touches the ground before any part of the body does.
3. Stand back up without using the hands.

CHAPTER 3: Diving

2. Falling with Ball in Hands and Maintaining Control

After catching, the GK breaks his fall by making sure the ball hits the ground first

Description

1. The GK starts with the ball in his hands and dives forward.
2. He breaks his fall by making sure the ball touches the ground first before any part of his body does. After that, the rest of the body will follow.
3. The GK stands up without using his hands.
4. Repeat in the opposite direction.

Coaching Points

1. Put the ball forward in front of you.
2. Higher level GKs: Throw the ball a little in front of you and then dive after it.

CHAPTER 3: Diving

3. Moving to One Side and Quickly Changing Direction to Make a Diving Save

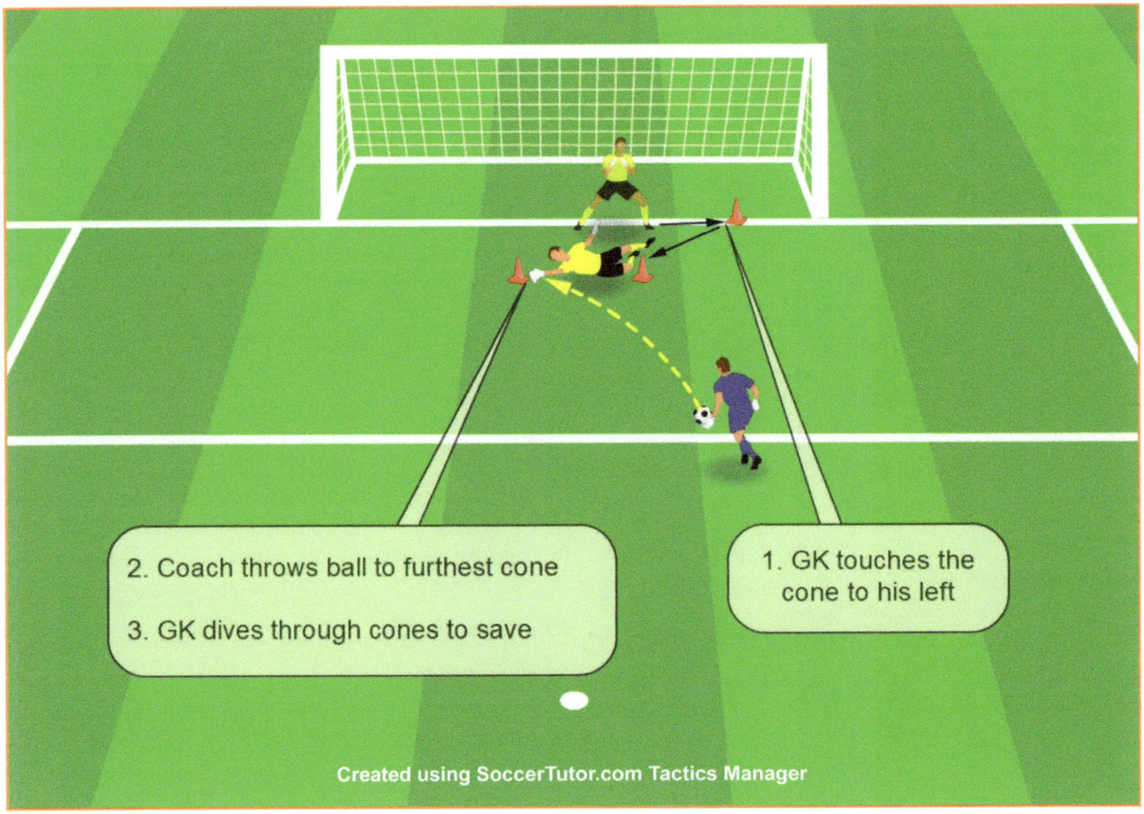

Description

1. The GK starts in the middle of the goal. He first makes quick (small) side-steps and touches the cone on the goal line.
2. As soon as the GK touches the cone, the Coach throws the ball to the furthest cone.
3. The GK dives through the 2 cones in front of him and attacks the ball as fast as he can.

Coaching Points

1. The GK starts in the middle of the goal, with his eyes fixed on the ball.
2. The GK does not stop after touching the cone: He moves forward immediately.
3. Jump before you cross the line between the cones.

CHAPTER 3: Diving

4. Changing Direction + Diving Over Rope

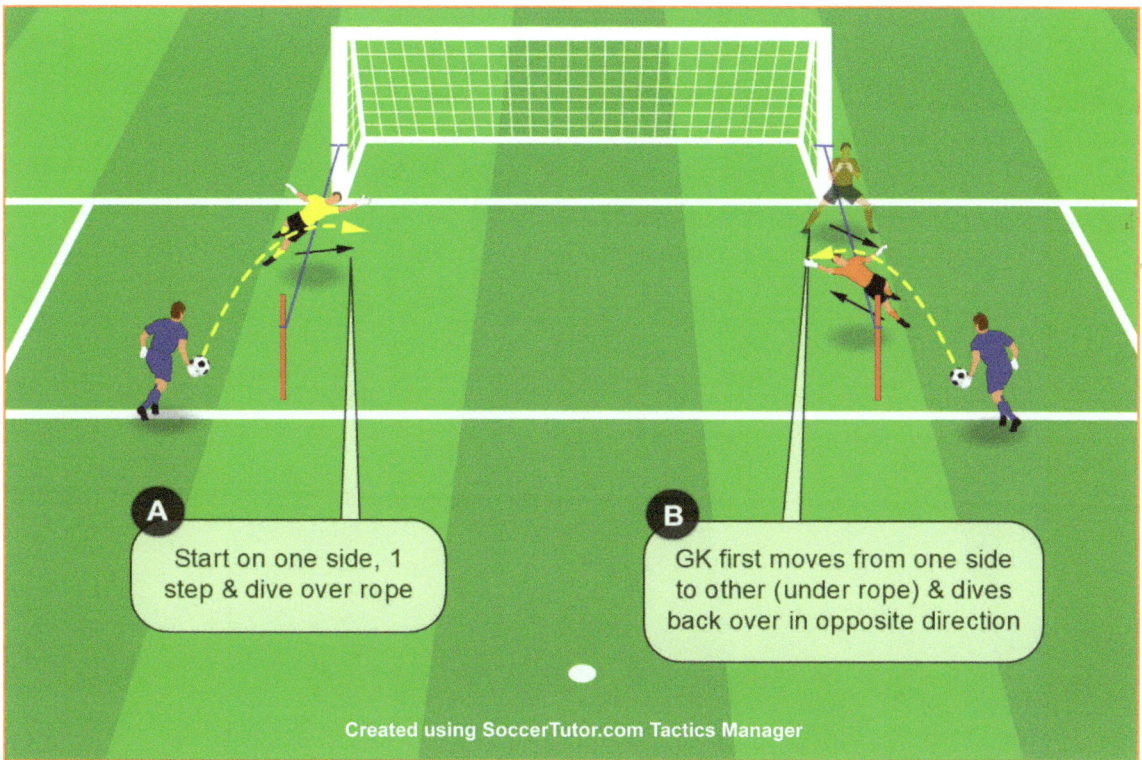

Description

A. Start on one side and with one step, dive over the rope.

B. The GK first moves from one side to the other (under the rope) and then dives back over the rope in the opposite direction.

Variations

1. Jump **OVER** the rope and then dive back **OVER** the rope in the opposite direction.
2. Use more balls, so the goalkeepers are continuously diving over the rope.

Coaching Points

1. The Coach stands on the same side as the GK starts.
2. The Coach does not throw the ball too high.
3. When going under the rope, make sure not to touch it.
4. This drill should be done at a high speed throughout.

CHAPTER 3: Diving

5. Diving Out of Goal to Grab the Ball

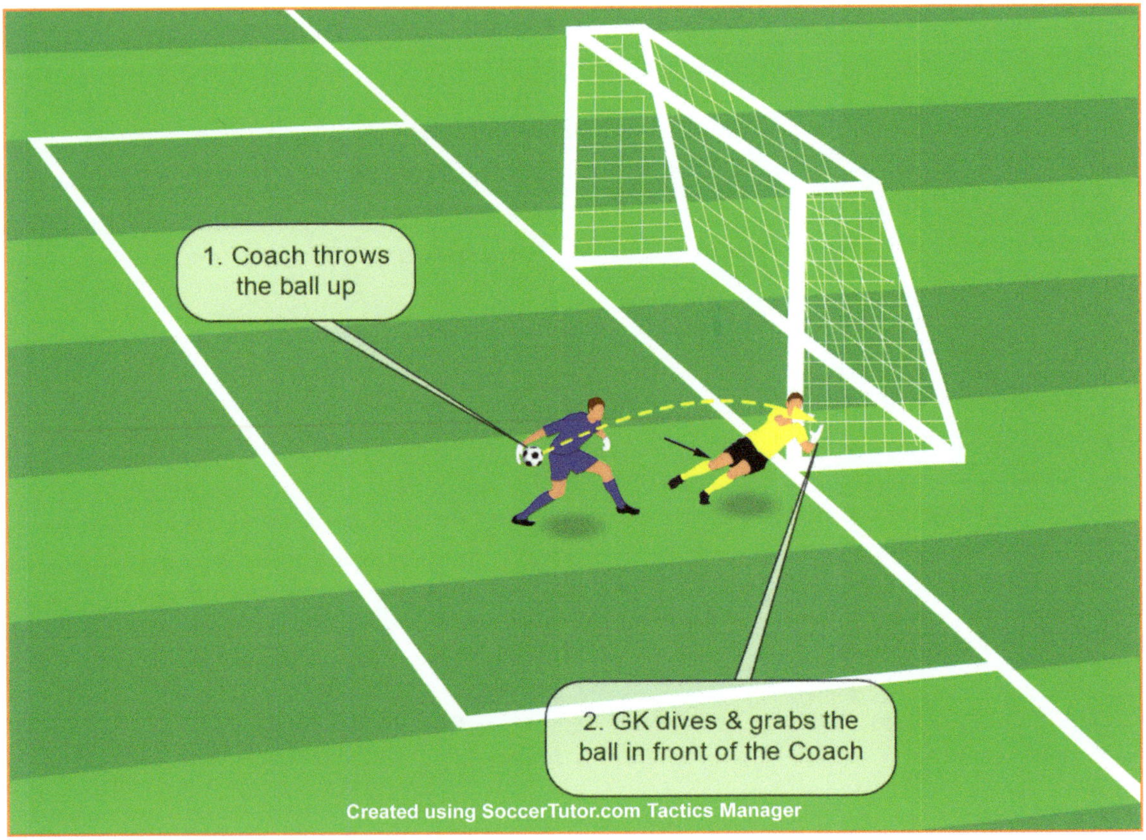

Description

1. The Coach stands just outside the near post with his back to the GK. The GK starts just inside the post.
2. The Coach throws the ball up wide of the post.
3. The GK dives forward (and to the side) to grab the ball in front of the Coach.

Variation: The Coach can let the ball bounce on the ground.

Progression: Higher level goalkeepers can start a little further back from the Coach.

Coaching Points

1. The GK starts in an "Open" position.
2. Dive in a straight line to the ball.

©SoccerTutor.com · Goalkeeper Training Program - 120 Drills

CHAPTER 3: Diving

6. Diving and Pushing the Ball Away from Danger

Description

1. GK1 is lying on the ground on his side.
2. The Coach throws the ball and GK1 hits it with his upper hand over GK2 to GK3. GK1 has to push his body upwards in order to attack the ball.

* Change the side and roles of the GKs often.

Variation: You can have GK1 starting on 1 knee or standing.

Coaching Points

1. Stay behind the ball.
2. Keep the elbow low.
3. GK1 moves back quickly into his starting position.

CHAPTER 3: Diving

7. Side-steps and Dive to Save in the Top Corner

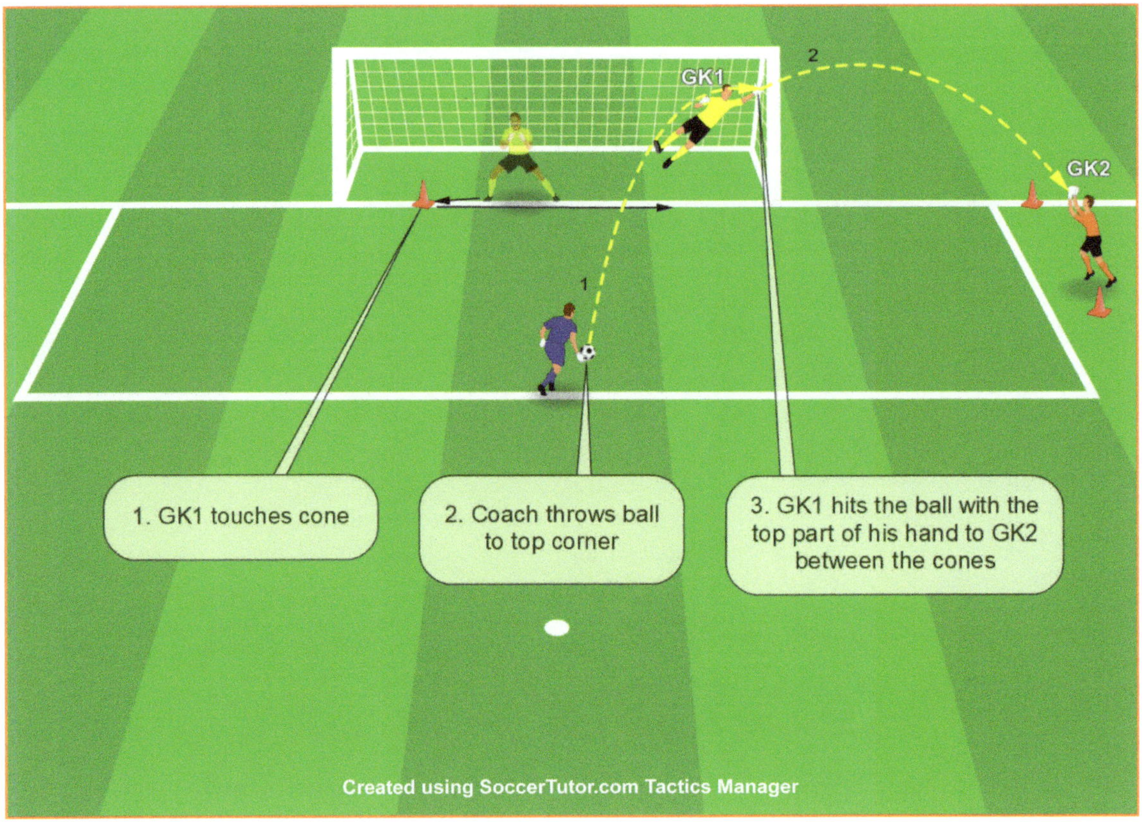

Description

1. GK1 touches the cone to his right and then moves to the left using fast footwork.
2. The Coach throws a ball towards the top corner.
3. GK1 hits the ball with the top part of his hand to GK2 between the cones.

Progression: The GK can decide to hit the ball away with 1 hand as shown in the diagram, or he can choose to catch the ball (higher difficulty).

Coaching Points

1. After touching the cone, stay close to the goal line (sideways movement).
2. GK1 has to play the ball directly into the hands of GK2.

CHAPTER 3: Diving

8. Back-steps and Dive to Tip Ball Over Crossbar

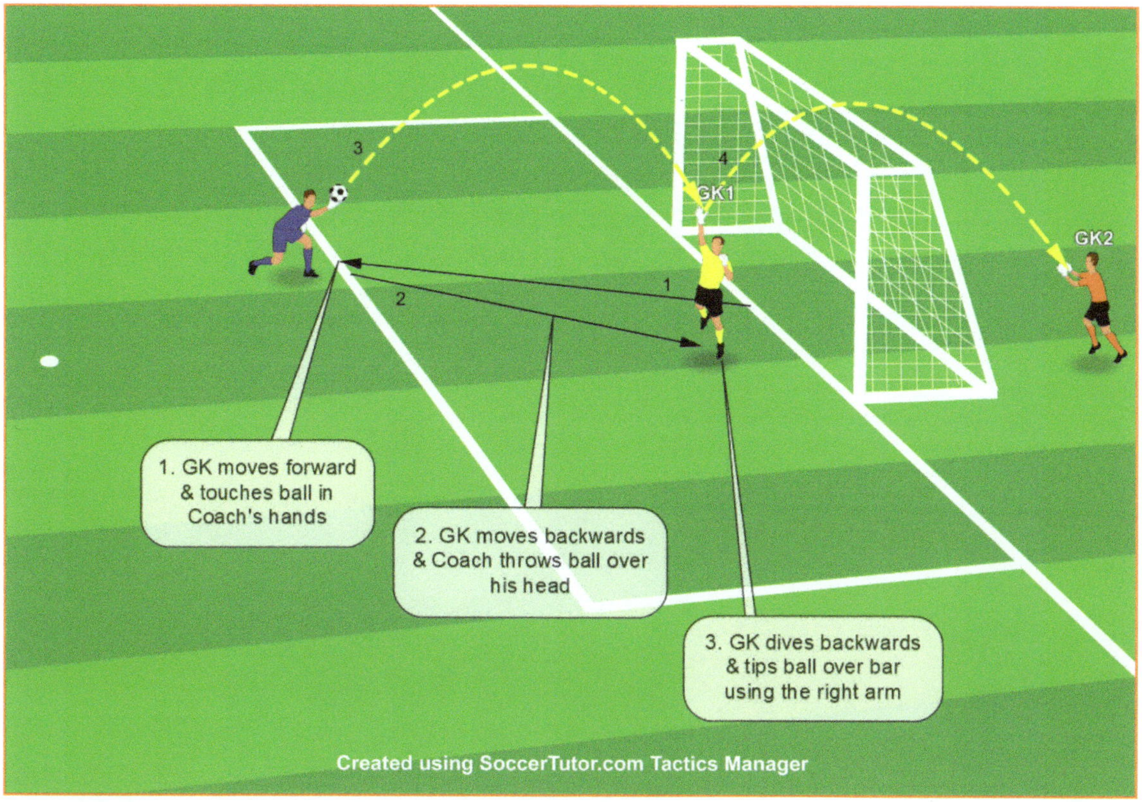

[Diagram of drill setup on soccer field]

Description

1. GK1 moves forward and touches the ball in the hands of the Coach.
2. GK1 then moves backwards at an angle and the Coach throws the ball over his head.
3. GK1 has to dive backwards and tip the ball over the crossbar to GK2 using his right arm. If the GK was running back at the opposite angle, he would use his left arm.

Coaching Points

1. The first step back after touching the ball in the Coach's hands is a crossover-step.
2. The GK must move back towards the goal line as quickly as possible.
3. The last step before the jump is a big powerful step.

CHAPTER 3: Diving

9. Diving to Save Free Kicks with Mannequin Wall

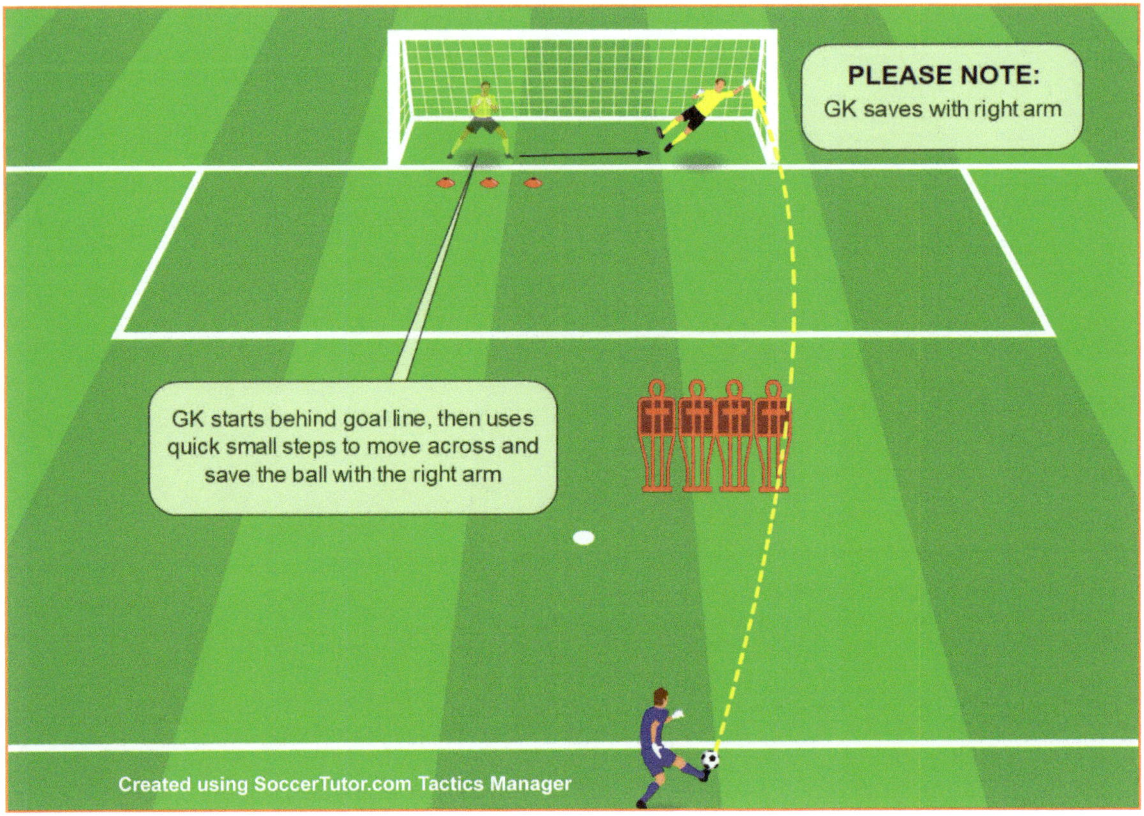

![diagram]

GK starts behind goal line, then uses quick small steps to move across and save the ball with the right arm

PLEASE NOTE: GK saves with right arm

Created using SoccerTutor.com Tactics Manager

Description

- The GK starts behind the line and the Coach shoots over the mannequin wall.
- The GK uses quick small steps to move across to the left and save with the right arm.
- **PLEASE NOTE:** The diagram shows the GK using the left arm to save, but he must use the right arm. If the GK was moving towards his right, he would use his left arm to save.
- The GK stays close to the goal line and behind the cones.

Variation: The Coach can shoot in the opposite corner and players can shoot free kicks.

Coaching Points

1. No gambling: Trust your starting position.
2. Check your position by looking at the top corner of the near post.
3. If possible, try to catch the ball. If you parry it, push it to the side and away from goal.

©SoccerTutor.com · Goalkeeper Training Program - 120 Drills

CHAPTER 3: Diving

10. Jumping On and Off Bench + Over Rope to Make a Diving Save

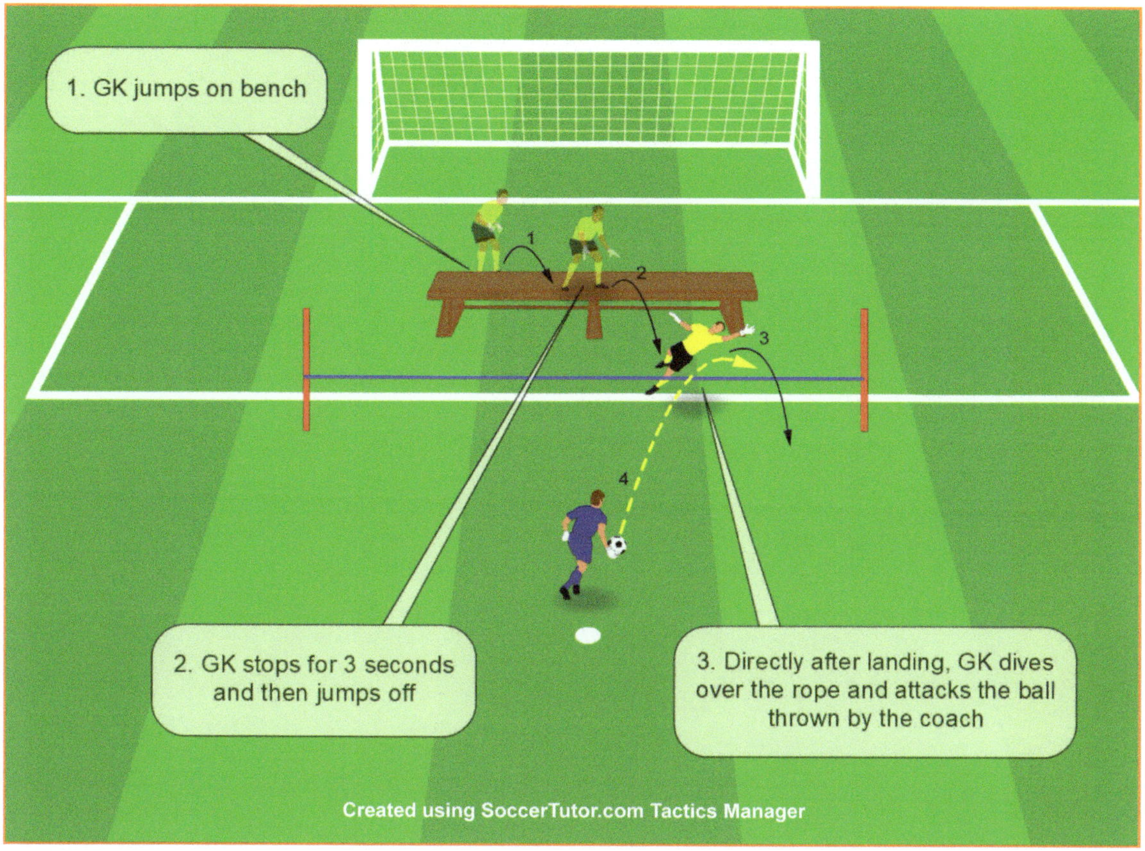

![Diagram with annotations: 1. GK jumps on bench; 2. GK stops for 3 seconds and then jumps off; 3. Directly after landing, GK dives over the rope and attacks the ball thrown by the coach]

Description

1. The GK jumps on the bench with his legs at a 90-degree angle (low position).
2. The GK stops for 3 seconds and jumps off.
3. The Coach throws the ball when the GK lands after jumping from the bench. Directly following the landing, the GK dives over the rope and attacks the ball.

Coaching Points

1. This is plyometric training to improve explosive power.
2. No more than 6 repetitions per set (8 repetitions for higher level GKs).
3. Change sides every time.
4. Make sure the GK gets enough rest time between sets.
5. No more than 3 sets.

©SoccerTutor.com   Goalkeeper Training Program - 120 Drills

CHAPTER 4

PUNCHING

CHAPTER 4: Punching

1. Training the Correct Angle and Position of Hands in a Basic Stationary Punching Drill

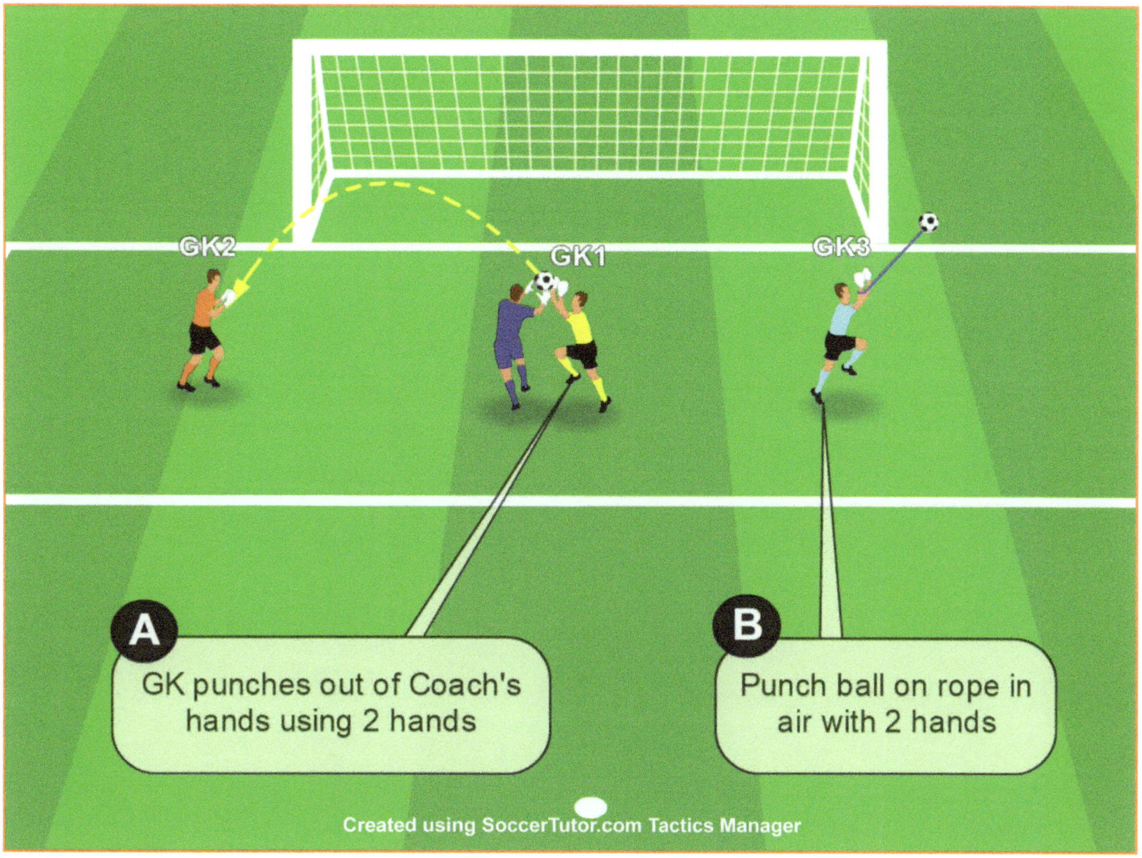

Description

A. The Coach holds the ball up and GK1 punches the ball with 2 hands to GK2.

B. This can also be practiced on your own, as shown with GK3 using a ball on a rope.

Variation: Punch with 1 hand.

Coaching Points

1. First practice without a jump. Progress to include a jump.
2. When punching with 2 hands, keep the elbows together so that the top of the hands will automatically be in line.
3. Weak hand: Keep the elbow low.

CHAPTER 4: Punching

2. Punching from Sitting, Kneeling and Standing Positions

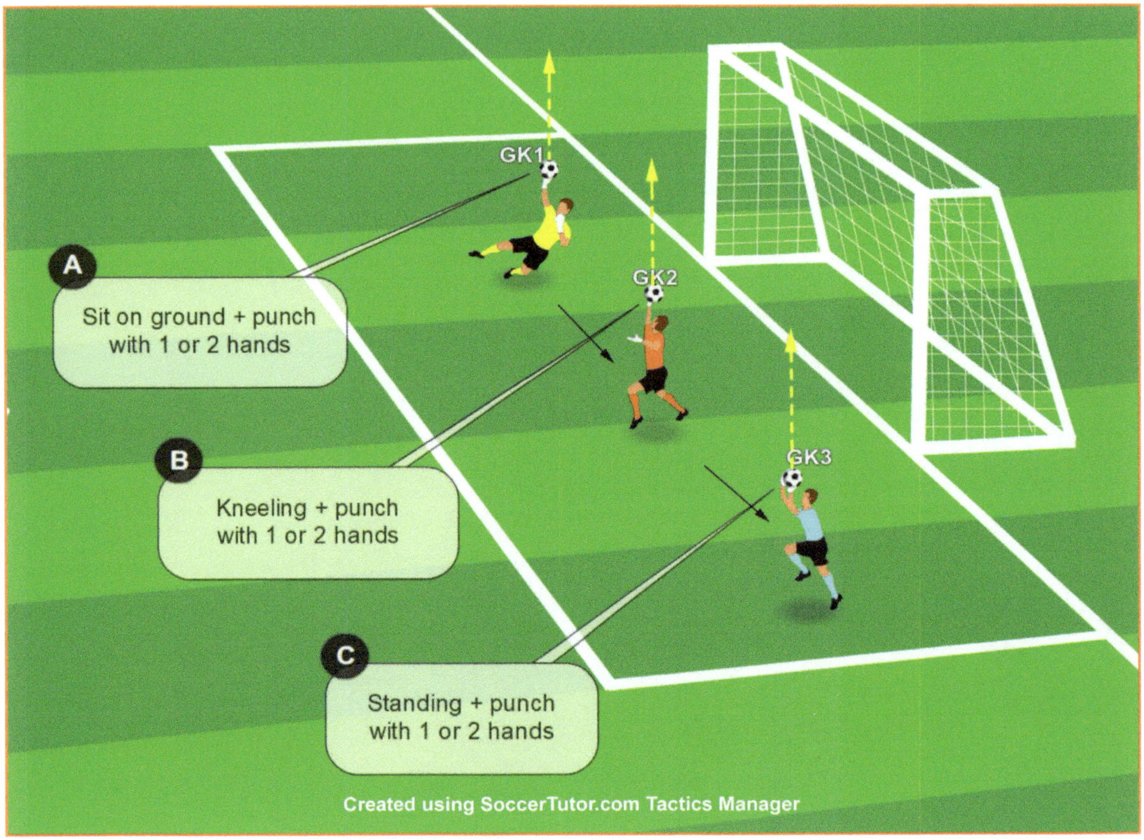

Description

Progress this drill through 3 steps (A -> B -> C):

A. GK1 sits on the ground and punches the ball in the air with 1 or 2 hands.

B. GK2 kneels on the ground and punches the ball in the air with 1 or 2 hands.

C. GK3 is standing and punches the ball in the air with 1 or 2 hands.

Coaching Points

1. The ball should be punched precisely through the middle.
2. When the ball goes sideways, it means you have punched under the ball too much.
3. When the ball goes down, it means you have punched on top of the ball too much.
4. Keep the elbows together.

CHAPTER 4: Punching

3. Throw, Punch and Catch in a 3-GK Juggling Group

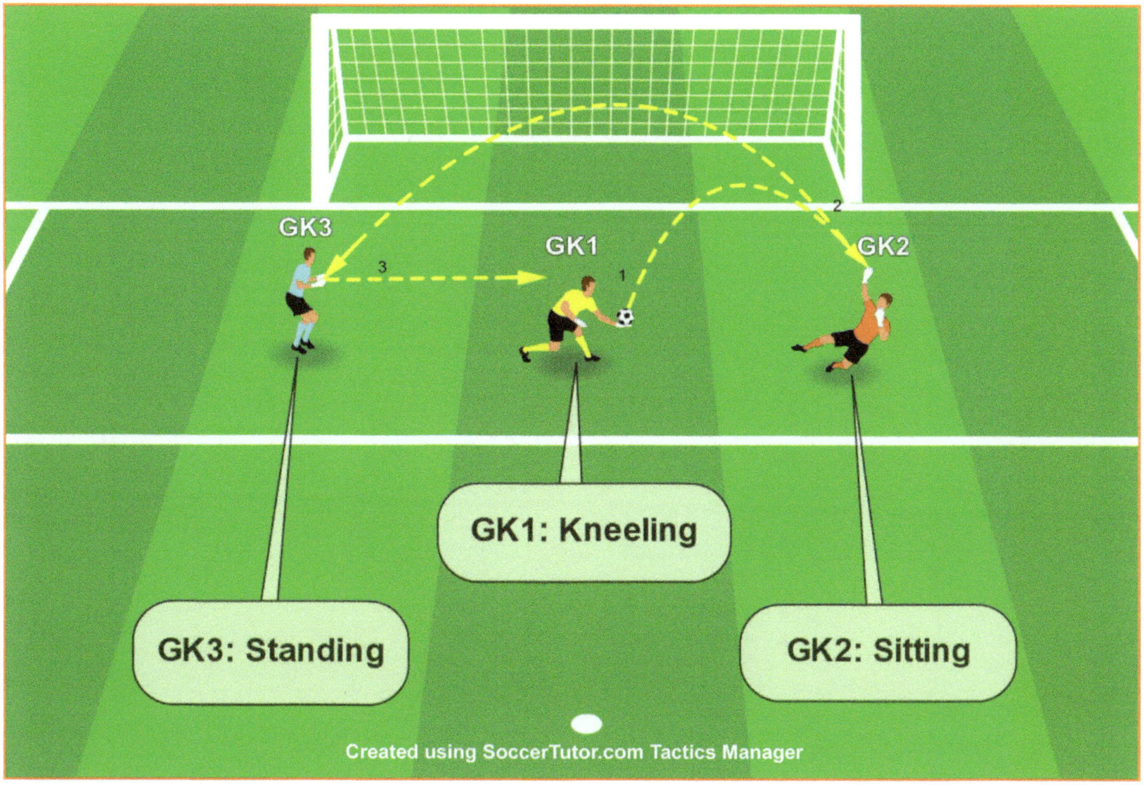

Description
1. GK1 is kneeling and throws the ball to GK2.
2. GK2 is sitting on the ground and punches the ball over the head of GK1 to GK3.
3. GK3 is standing and catches the ball, then throws it to GK1.

Progressions
1. Before punching, GK2 does a sit-up.
2. Work with 2 balls.

Coaching Points
1. GK1 has to throw the ball at head height.
2. Punch the ball with a quick powerful touch.
3. Always open and close the hands.

CHAPTER 4: Punching

4. Punching Over Mannequins from a Stationary Position

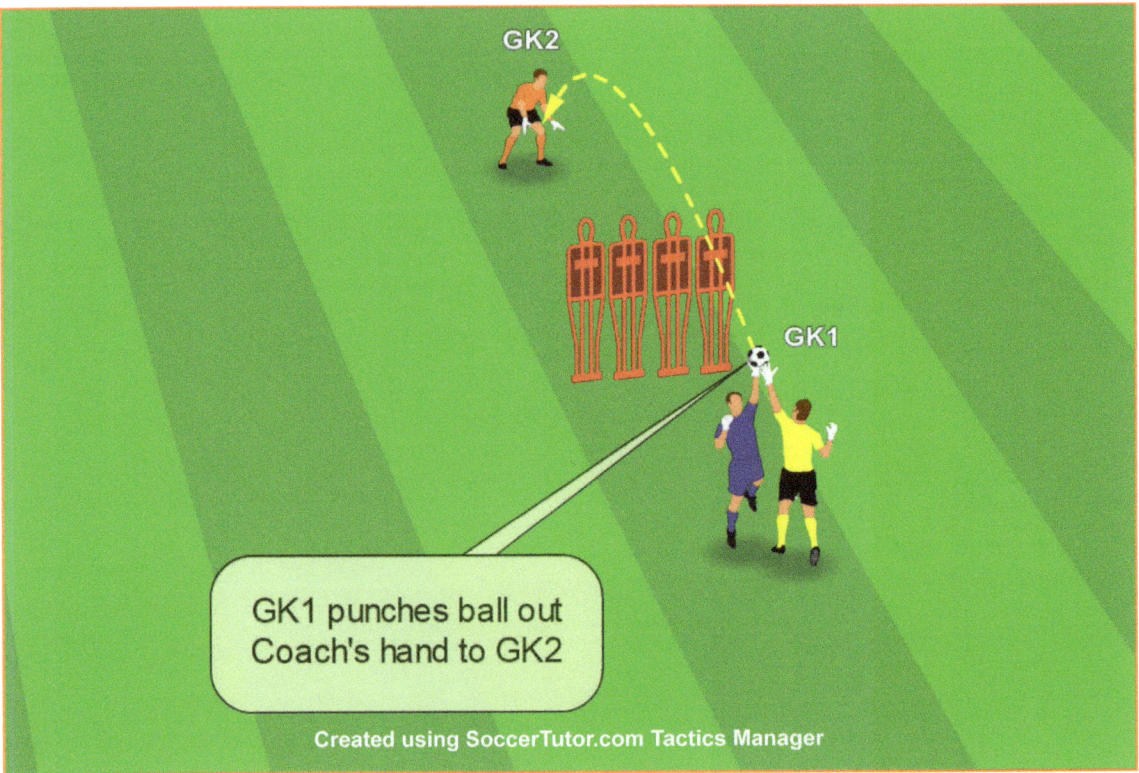

Description
1. The Coach holds the ball up with 1 hand.
2. GK1 punches the ball out of the Coach's hand and over the mannequins to GK2.

Progressions
1. GK1 takes a few steps towards the Coach and punches the ball.
2. The Coach tosses the ball up and GK1 jumps to punch the ball.

Coaching Points
1. Hit the ball with your arms at 3/4 length (slightly bent arms).
2. Move to and from the ball with quick small steps.
3. GK2 has to catch the ball at the highest possible point.
4. Weak hand: Keep the elbow low.

CHAPTER 4: Punching

5. Punching Over Mannequins in a Continuous Throwing Circuit

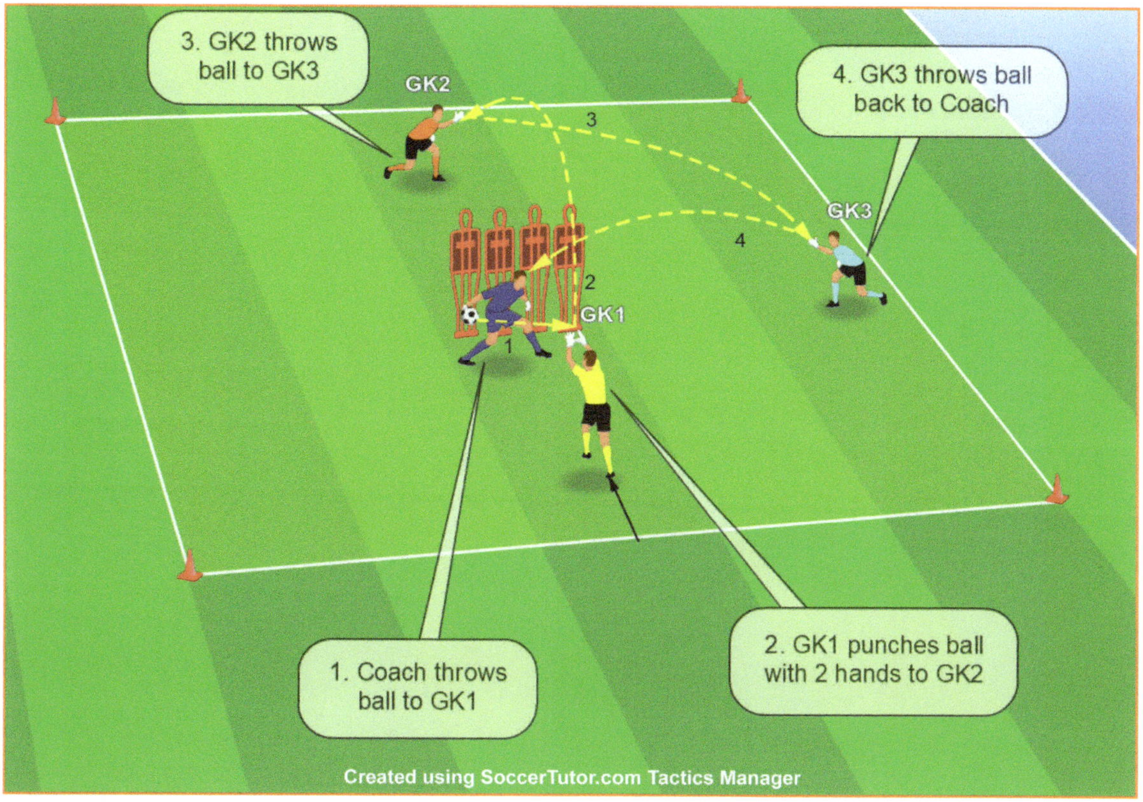

Description
1. The Coach throws the ball to GK1.
2. GK1 punches the ball with 2 hands over the mannequins to GK2.
3. GK2 catches and throws the ball to GK3.
4. GK3 throws the ball back to the Coach.

Progressions
1. GK1 punches with 1 hand.
2. Increase the speed of the drill.
3. Work with 2 balls. As the Coach throws to GK1, GK2 throws a second ball to GK3.

Coaching Points
1. GK1 has to call out "Keeper" before he punches the ball.
2. Position the mannequins more to the side, so GK1 has to turn his body.

CHAPTER 4: Punching

6. Punching the Ball while Holding Another Ball in a 3-GK Juggling Group

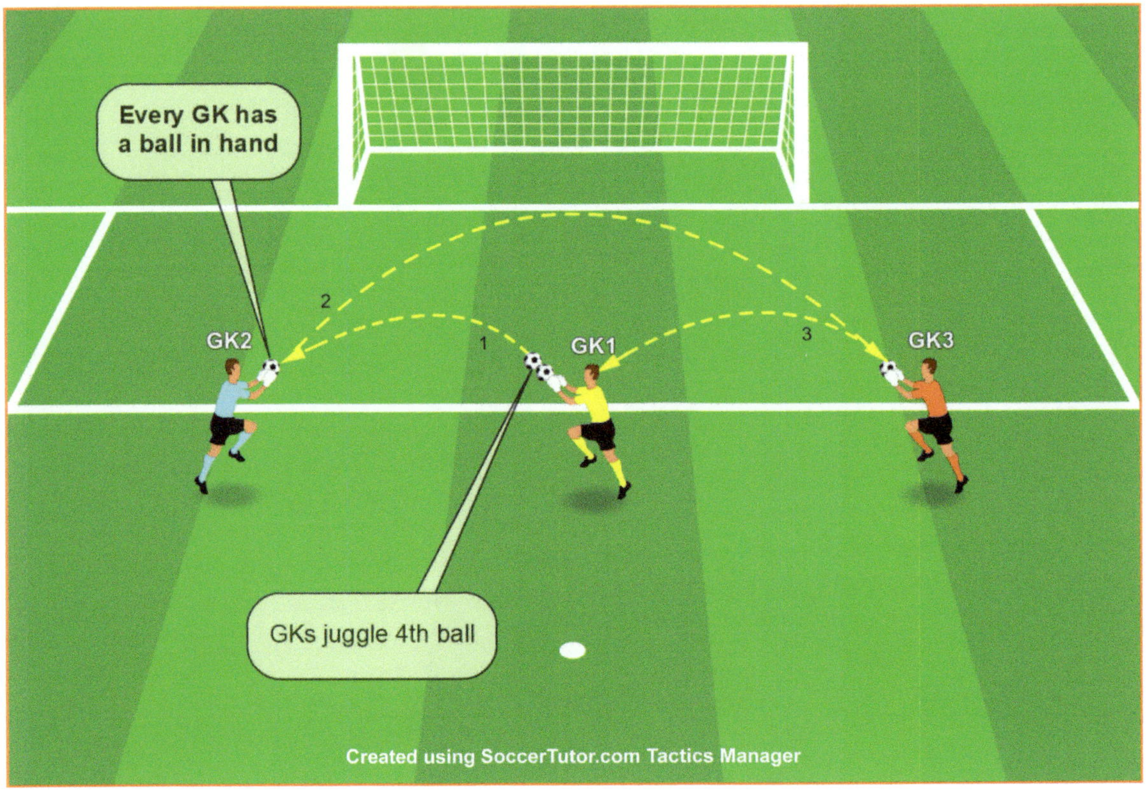

Description

1. Each GK has a ball in their hands. GK1 punches a 4th ball to GK2.
2. GK2 punches this ball over the head of GK1 to GK3.
3. GK3 punches the ball back to GK1.
4. GK1 punches back to GK3, GK3 punches over the head of GK1 to GK2 etc.

* Count the amount of successful consecutive punches. After every mistake, rotate the positions so a new GK goes in the middle.

Progression: After punching the ball over the GK in the middle, change positions with the middle GK.

Coaching Points

1. Make sure the distances between the GKs isn't too large.
2. Play the balls high, so the next GK can move under the ball.

©SoccerTutor.com — Goalkeeper Training Program - 120 Drills

CHAPTER 4: Punching

7. Accurate Punching with Alternate Hands from a Sitting Position

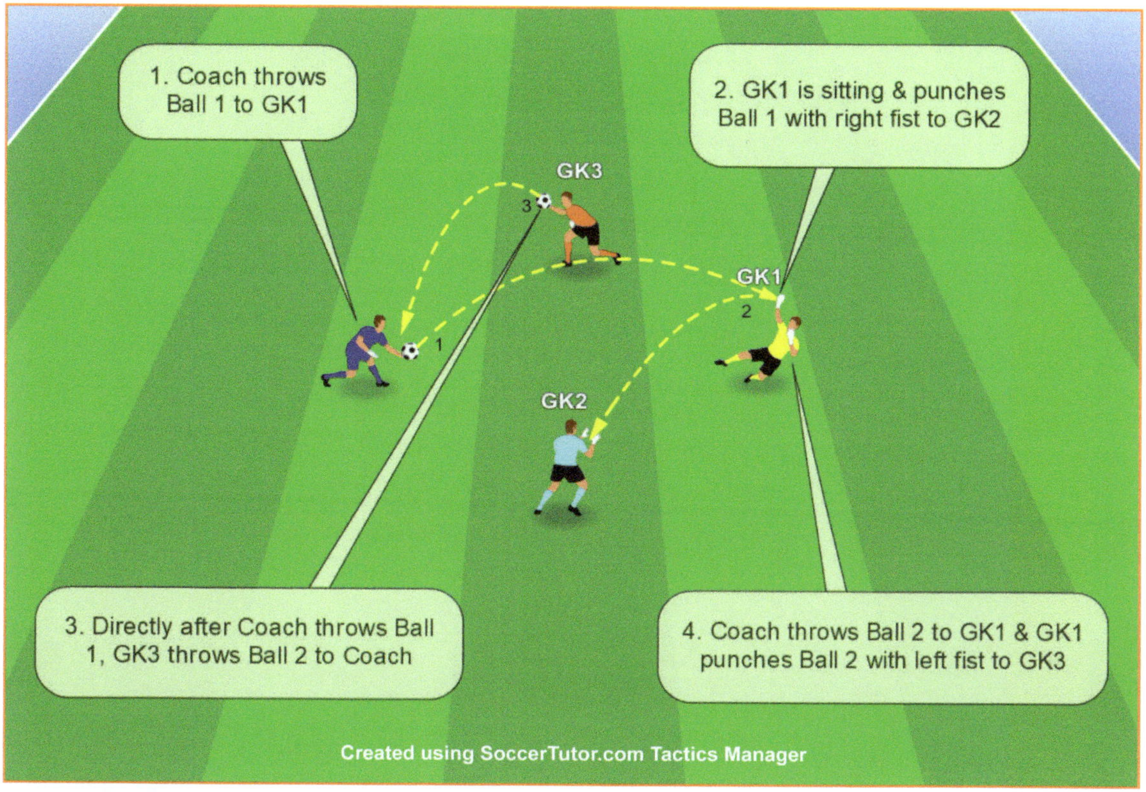

[Diagram showing the drill with GK1, GK2, GK3 and Coach positions, with the following labels:
1. Coach throws Ball 1 to GK1
2. GK1 is sitting & punches Ball 1 with right fist to GK2
3. Directly after Coach throws Ball 1, GK3 throws Ball 2 to Coach
4. Coach throws Ball 2 to GK1 & GK1 punches Ball 2 with left fist to GK3]

Description

1. The Coach throws Ball 1 to GK1.
2. GK1 is sitting and punches Ball 1 with his right fist to GK2.
3. After the Coach throws Ball 1, GK3 immediately throws Ball 2 to the Coach.
4. The Coach now throws Ball 2 to GK1 and GK1 punches the ball with his left fist to GK3.

Progressions

1. As the Coach throws the ball, he calls out whether to punch the ball to GK2 or GK3.
2. Before punching, GK2 does a sit-up.

Coaching Points

1. GK1 is sitting on his backside with knees bent.
2. GK1 has to call out "Keeper" before he punches the ball.

CHAPTER 4: Punching

8. Punching the Ball Away from Goal to Alternate Sides

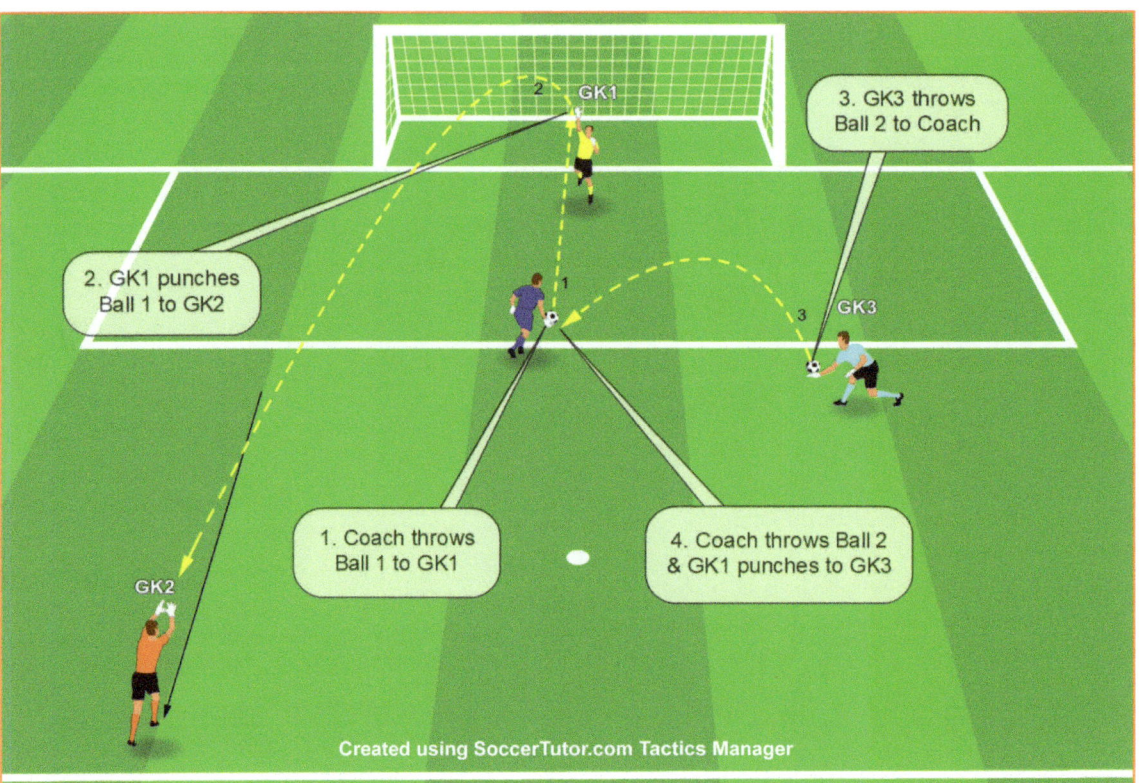

Description

1. The Coach throws Ball 1 to GK1.
2. GK1 punches Ball 1 to GK2 using both fists. GK2 must react, move and catch the ball.
3. After the Coach throws Ball 1, GK3 immediately throws Ball 2 to the Coach.
4. The Coach now throws Ball 2 to GK1 and GK1 punches the ball with both fists to GK3.

Progression: GK1 punches with 1 fist: Right fist to GK2 and left fist to GK3.

Coaching Points

1. The ball has to be punched out at a good height.
2. Try to punch the ball high and as far away as possible.
3. GK1 has to call out "Keeper" as quickly as he can, before punching the ball.
4. GK2 and GK3 use the high ball catching technique and call out "Keeper" when the ball is in the air.

CHAPTER 4: Punching

9. Quick Footwork and Punching the Ball Over the Crossbar

(Diagram)
1. GK 1 touches cone & moves back into position
2. Coach throws a high ball over GK1, who punches the ball over the crossbar to GK2
3. GK2 catches ball & throws back to Coach

Description

1. GK1 moves to the cone, touches it and then moves back into position.
2. The Coach throws a high ball. GK1 punches the ball over the crossbar to GK2.
3. GK2 catches the ball and throws it back to the Coach.

Progression: Work with 2 balls. GK2 throws a 2nd ball to the Coach immediately after the Coach throws the 1st ball to GK1.

Coaching Points

1. Before you punch the ball, you first let it pass you slightly. This is so you can get the right angle and body position to punch the ball up and over the crossbar.
2. Hit the ball with a quick powerful touch (punch).

CHAPTER 4: Punching

10. Punch Ball Small Sided Game with Large Goals

Description

- We play a small sided game inside the penalty area with 2 large goals. Each team has 1 GK in the goal and 3 outside.
- A GK in goal starts and throws the ball to one of his teammates. That GK has to punch the ball. After that, the 2nd ball can be caught.
- If the ball is caught, that GK must throw it up to themselves and punch it to a teammate.
- You can only score by punching the ball.

Progressions

1. The GKs have to punch with 1 fist.
2. Catching is not allowed, so every ball has to be punched throughout the game.

Coaching Points

1. When in possession, GKs should move wide to make use of all the space.
2. After losing the ball, all GKs on that team move inside to protect the goal.
3. Call out your name before catching/punching. If not, the ball goes to the other team.
4. Change the GK who is in the goal after every goal scored, or after 2 minutes.

©SoccerTutor.com   Goalkeeper Training Program - 120 Drills

CHAPTER 5

PARRYING

CHAPTER 5: Parrying

1. Parrying the Ball Away from Goal

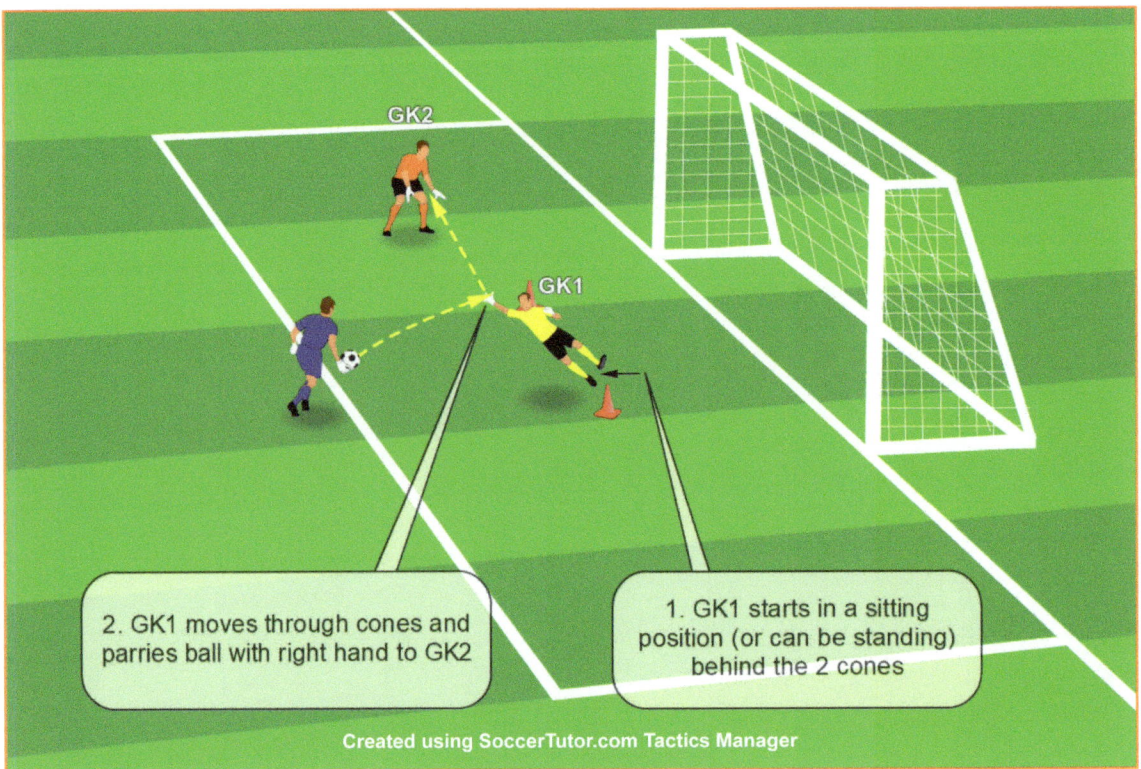

Description

1. GK1 starts in a sitting position (or can be standing) behind the 2 cones. The Coach rolls or throws a low ball to the furthest cone.
2. GK1 moves through the cones and parries the ball with his right hand to GK2.

Coaching Points

1. GK1's arm must be fully outstretched to parry the ball.
2. First the arm goes out, then the rest of the body will follow.
3. Touch the ball with the fingers (not the palm of the hand).
4. When standing, use a very low starting position with bent knees.

CHAPTER 5: Parrying

2. Parrying the Ball to Alternate Sides from a Sitting Position

Description
1. The Coach has 2 balls. He throws Ball 1 to GK1.
2. GK1 parries Ball 1 away with the top part of his hand/s to GK2.
3. GK2 throws Ball 1 to GK3, who moves behind the Coach to the other side of the goal.
4. The Coach throws Ball 2 to GK1 and GK3 gives Ball 1 back to the Coach.
5. GK1 parries Ball 2 away with the top part of his hand/s to GK4.
6. GK 4 throws the ball to GK3.

Coaching Points
1. GK1 has to turn his head and see the ball go into the hands of GK2 or GK3.
2. GK1 has to change the line of the ball completely, parrying to the left or right.
3. The distance between all GKs has to stay the same throughout the drill.

CHAPTER 5: Parrying

3. Dive and Parry + Get Up to Save Second Ball

![Diagram: Coach shoots ball low: GK parries 1st ball, runs around the cone & parries 2nd ball]

Description
- The GK rolls the 1st ball to the Coach.
- The Coach shoots the 1st ball low at Cone 1.
- The GK parries the ball, gets up, runs around Cone 1 and moves towards Cone 2.
- The Coach shoots the 2nd ball low at Cone 2 and the GK must parry it away again.

Variation: The GK parries the 1st ball and decides whether to parry or catch the 2nd ball.

Progression: After parrying the 2nd ball, go after the ball and gather it.

Coaching Points
1. Keep your eyes fixed on the ball at all times throughout the drill, even when running around Cone 1.
2. Attack the ball as much as possible, parrying away out in front of the cones.

CHAPTER 5: Parrying

4. Quick Side-steps, Dive Low and Parry Away

GK1 rolls ball to coach, touches cone to right & moves back to centre

Coach shoots & GK1 parries to GK2 between the cones

Created using SoccerTutor.com Tactics Manager

Description

1. GK1 rolls the ball to the Coach.
2. With quick side-steps, GK1 touches the cone to his right and then moves back to the centre of the goal.
3. The Coach shoots a low ball towards the bottom corner and GK1 parries the ball away to GK2 in between the cones.

Variation: GK1 can decide whether to parry the ball away or catch it.

Coaching Points

1. Make sure the steps to the cone and back to the middle are short and quick.
2. Move along the goal line, in order to stay behind the ball.
3. Parry the ball away from goal and to the side.
4. GK2 starts in the middle of the cones (and behind), then falls down to save the ball.

CHAPTER 5: Parrying

5. Quick Side-steps, Dive High and Parry Away in a Dynamic Goalkeeper Circuit

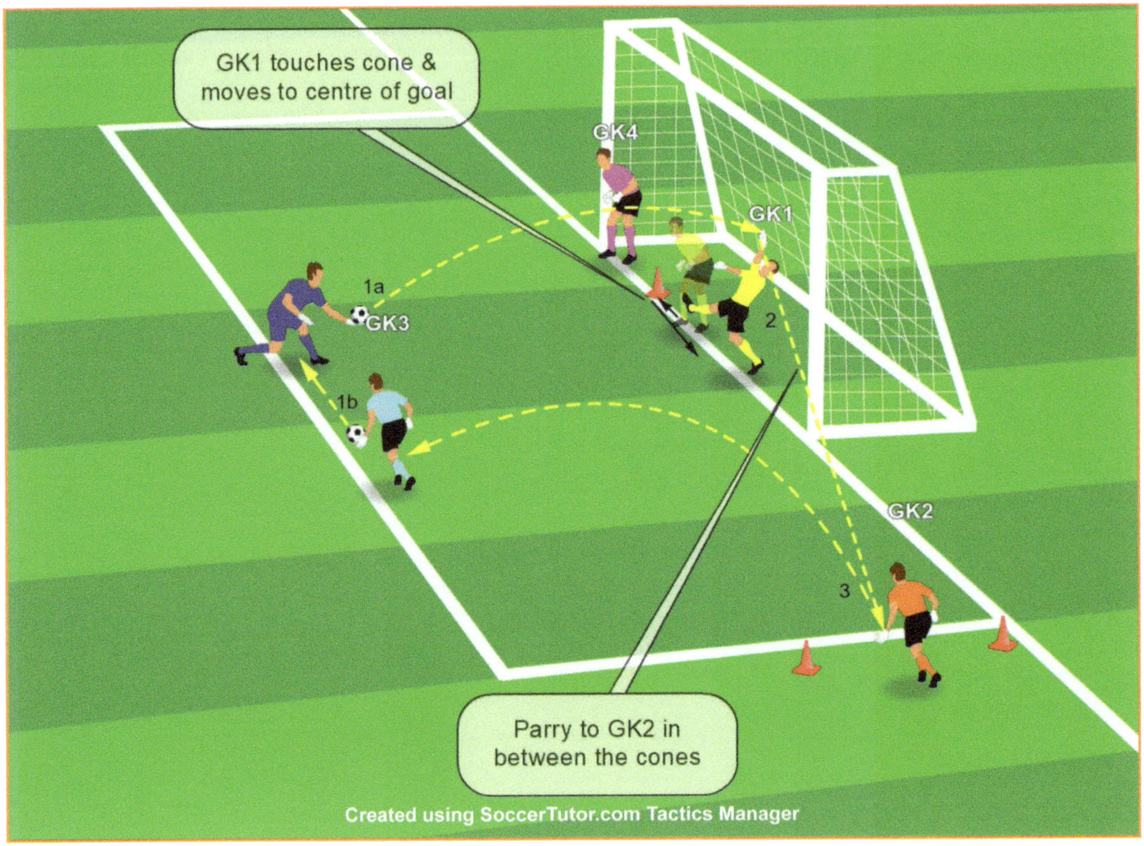

Description
1. GK1 touches the cone to his right and moves back towards the centre.
2. The Coach throws Ball 1 to the top corner.
3. Immediately after the Coach has thrown Ball 1, GK3 gives him Ball 2.
4. GK1 parries Ball 1 away with the top part of his hand to GK2 in between the cones.
5. GK2 throws Ball 1 to GK3. GK1 and GK4 switch positions.
6. The drill continues with the Coach throwing Ball 2 and GK4 now parrying away.

* After 6 balls (3 turns each for GK1 and GK4), GK1 and GK4 switch positions with GK2 and GK3.

Coaching Points
1. Every goalkeeper has a role and has to concentrate at all times throughout the drill.
2. GK1 steps back behind the line to make space for GK4.
3. GK4 can already get in position when GK1 goes for the ball.

CHAPTER 5: Parrying

6. Parrying Shots Away from Goal with 2 Hands

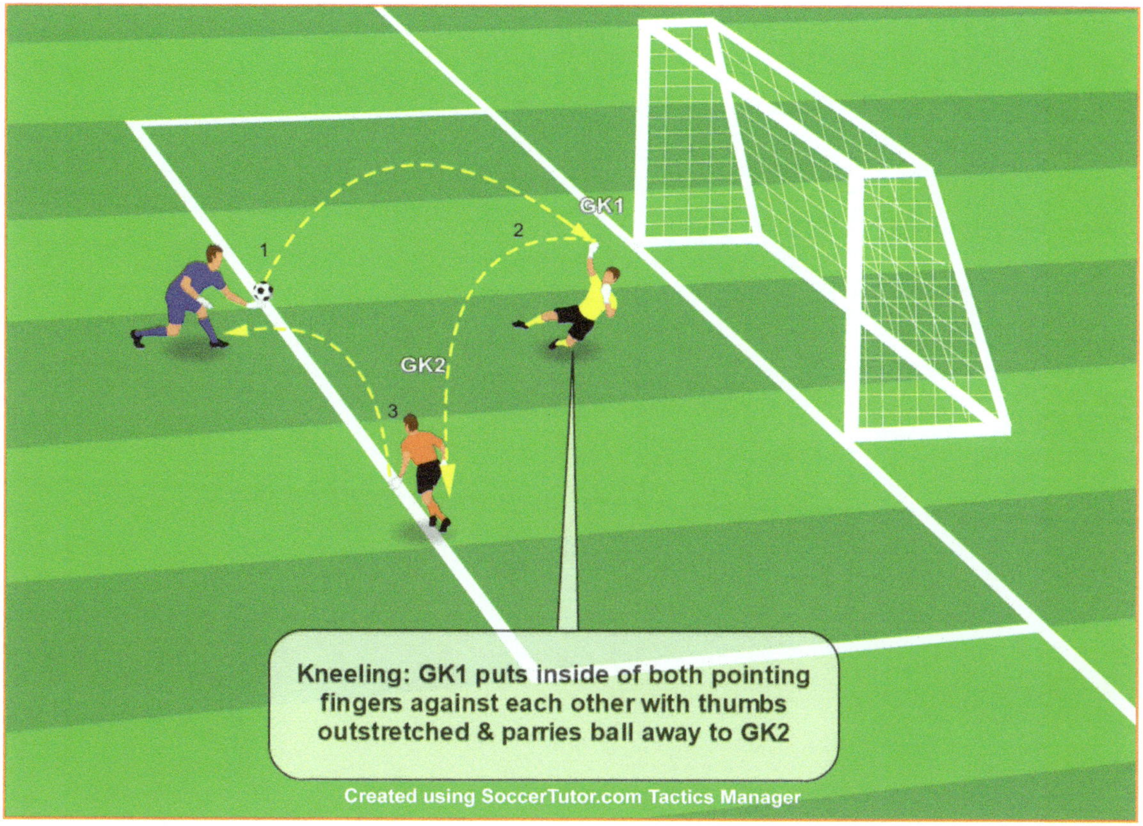

![Diagram showing kneeling GK1 parrying ball to GK2 with caption: Kneeling: GK1 puts inside of both pointing fingers against each other with thumbs outstretched & parries ball away to GK2]

Description
- GK1 is kneeling and the Coach throws the ball up in the air.
- GK1 puts the inside of both index fingers (closest to the thumb) against each other, with the thumbs outstretched. This creates a big surface (open hands) to parry the ball away.
- GK1 parries the ball to GK2 and GK2 throws the ball back to the Coach.

Variation: GK1 is standing and you can have the Coach volley (shoot) the ball.

Progression: GK1 can choose whether to parry the ball away or catch it.

Coaching Points
1. Parry the ball with the palms of the hands away from goal and to the side.
2. This technique allows the goalkeeper a bigger surface area than with the fists.
3. Parry the ball with your arms at 3/4 length (slightly bent arms).

CHAPTER 5: Parrying

7. Quick Sprint Forward, then Back + Parry Over the Crossbar

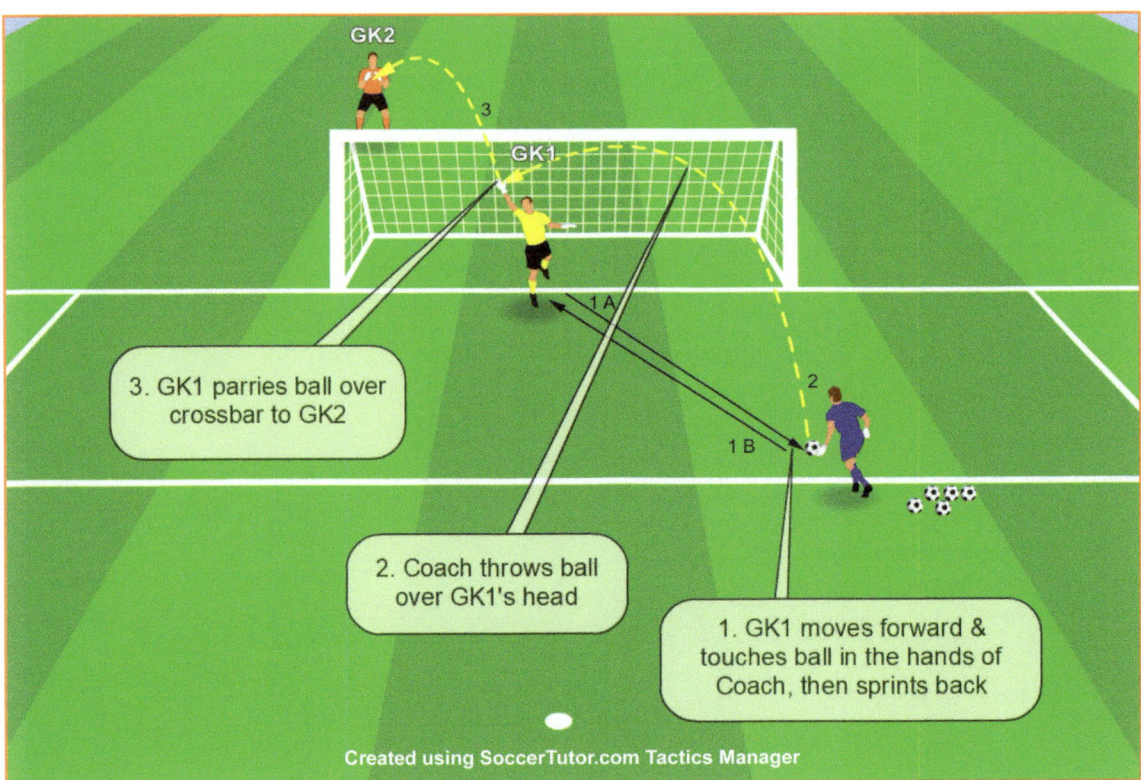

Description

1. GK1 moves forward and touches the ball in the hands of the Coach and sprints back.
2. The Coach throws the ball over GK1's head towards the far corner of the goal.
3. GK1 must quickly get back and parry the ball over the crossbar to GK2, using the top part of his hand.

Variation: The Coach throws the ball towards the nearest corner (right corner in diagram) and GK1 parries the ball away with the lower part of the hand.

Coaching Points

1. Always run back to the goal facing the biggest part of the goal.
2. GK1's first step back towards goal should be a crossover-step.
3. Put the hand under the ball and lift it over the crossbar.
4. When the ball is travelling towards the nearest corner (the variation), don't turn your body halfway. Instead, focus on quickly getting back to the goal line first.

CHAPTER 5: Parrying

8. Quick Side-steps and Parry the Ball Over the Crossbar at an Angle

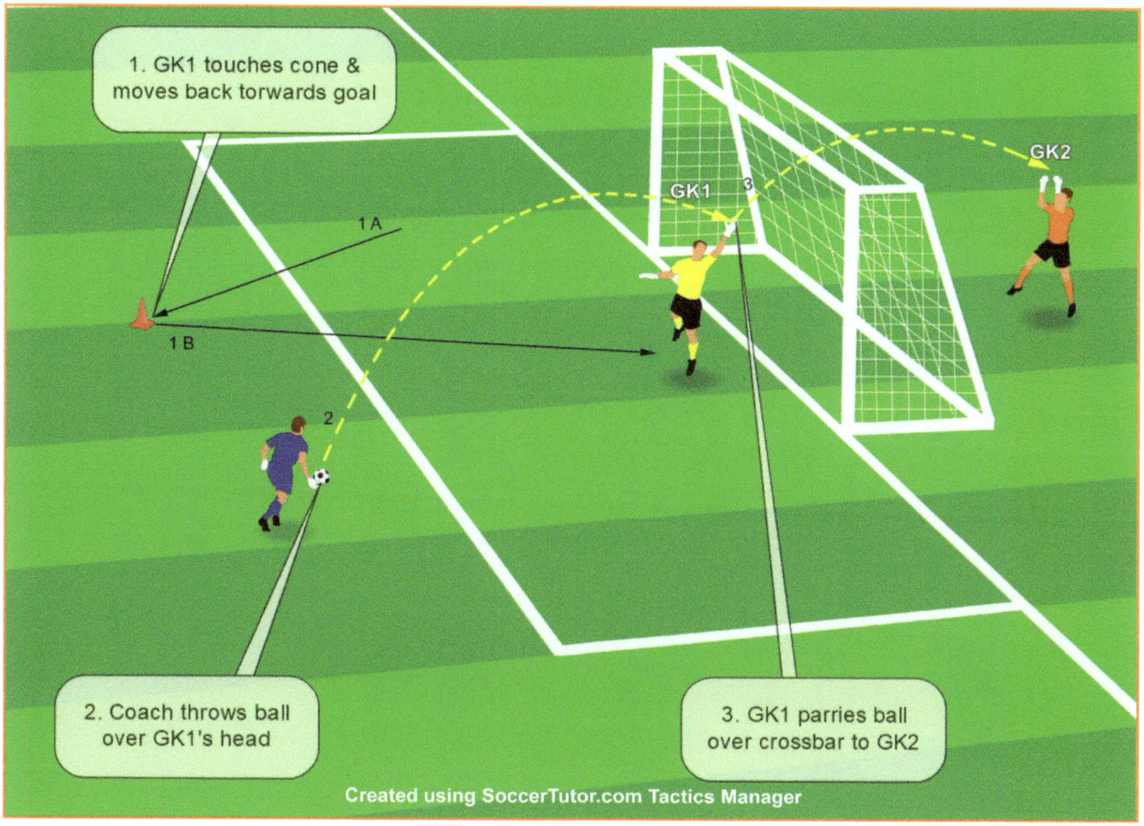

Description

1. GK1 touches the cone (1A) and moves sideways back towards the goal line (1B).
2. The Coach throws the ball over GK1's head.
3. GK1 parries the ball with the top part of his hand over the crossbar to GK2.

Coaching Points

1. The first step after touching the cone is a crossover-step.
2. GK1 must first allow the ball to go past him, so he can get under it and push it over the crossbar.
3. Use the speed and direction of the ball to comfortably clear the goal and parry to GK2.
4. Stay behind the ball when parrying it over the crossbar.

CHAPTER 5: Parrying

9. Diving and Parrying Shots to the Top or Bottom Corners

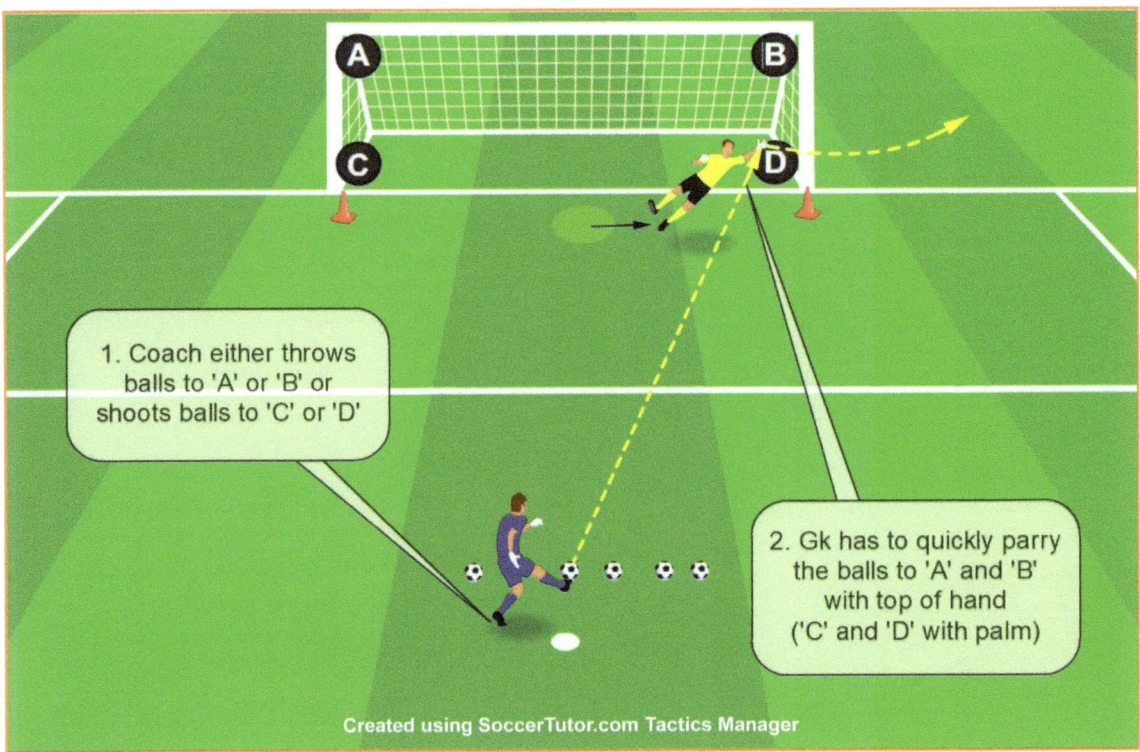

Description

- The Coach has a few balls on the ground in front of him.
- He can throw the balls to positions A and B (top corners) or he can shoot to positions C and D (bottom corners).
- The GK has to react quickly to save and parry the balls away from goal.
- Saves in the top corners should be made with the top part of the hand and saves in the bottom corners should be made with the lower part of the hand (palms).
- After each shot, the GK always returns to his starting position in the middle of the goal.

Coaching Points

1. The 2 cones are there to encourage the GK to move off the goal line and attack the ball.
2. This drill should be done at a high speed throughout.
3. After the save, move quickly back to the start position so you're ready for the next shot.
4. The GK should save a maximum of 6 shots in a row before rest is needed.

©SoccerTutor.com   Goalkeeper Training Program - 120 Drills

CHAPTER 5: **Parrying**

10. Continuous Quick Footwork and Parrying the Ball Over the Crossbar with 2 Goals

Description

1. GK1 goes around the red cone (1A), touches the blue cone (1B) and moves back towards the goal line (side-steps).
2. The Coach throws a ball over his head and GK1 parries the ball over the crossbar to GK2.
3. GK1 goes back around the red cone (1A) and does the same on the other side, parrying the ball over the crossbar of the 2nd goal to GK3.

Coaching Points

1. All steps must be small: No crossover-steps after touching the blue cone.
2. Use both hands, depending on the direction of the ball.
3. The goals should be very close together, as shown in the diagram.
4. The ball should be parried up and into the hands of GK2 and GK3.

CHAPTER 6

HIGH BALLS

CHAPTER 6: **High Balls**

1. Jump to Catch Stationary Ball

1. Coach holds ball in top of his hands

2. GK jumps with 1 step between cones & takes it out of Coach's hands

Description

1. The Coach holds the ball in the top of his hands.
2. The GK jumps with 1 step between the cones and takes it out of the Coach's hands.
- Train jumping off both legs.

Progression: The Coach can throw a high ball from short range for the GK to catch. When the ball leaves the hands of the Coach, the GK shouts "Keeper."

Coaching Points

1. Start with 2 feet on the goal line.
2. Don't take extra steps: Just 1 step to go to the ball.
3. Use the whole surface of the foot that you jump off with.
4. Catch on top of the ball: Your arms will be automatically stretched.

©SoccerTutor.com Goalkeeper Training Program - 120 Drills

CHAPTER 6: High Balls

2. Crossover-steps + Catch High Ball

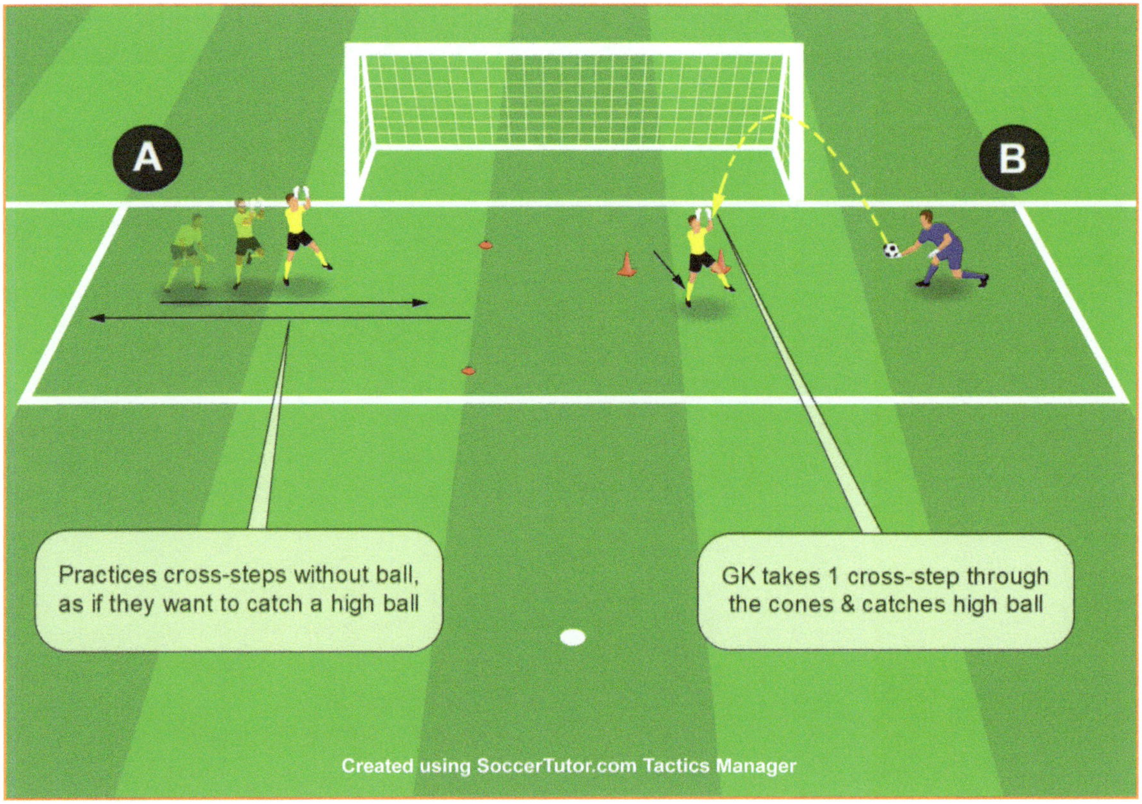

[Diagram: Practices cross-steps without ball, as if they want to catch a high ball. | GK takes 1 cross-step through the cones & catches high ball]

Description

A. The GKs practice crossover-steps without the ball, as if they are going to catch a high ball. Practice both sides.

B. The GK takes 1 crossover-step through the cones. The Coach throws a high ball up for the GK to catch out in front of the cones.

Coaching Points

1. These steps can be trained in the warm-up before the training session.
2. Right and left foot steps/jumps should be of the same quality.
3. Call out "Keeper" when the Coach throws the ball up.
4. Jump off from the line between the cones.

CHAPTER 6: **High Balls**

3. Catch High Ball at the Near Post Against a Defender

![drill diagram]

1. Coach throws a high ball between the near post & GK2
2. GK1 throws ball back to Coach & moves to GK2's position, while GK2 goes to back of line
3. GK3 moves to GK1 position to catch the next ball

Description

1. The Coach throws a high ball between the near post and GK2. GK1 must shout "Keeper" when the ball leaves the hands of the Coach.
2. After catching the ball, GK1 throws it back to the Coach and moves to the position of GK2. GK2 moves to the back of the line behind GK4.
3. GK3 moves to the position of GK1 and catches the next ball from the Coach.

Variations: **(1)** Have 2 GKs at the near post and GK1 has to go between them.
(2) You can also use mannequins. Put them close together so the GK has to make contact.

Coaching Points

1. It is important that the GK is trained in catching while making contact with other players.
2. When you put another GK in front, the quality of the catching should remain the same.
3. Start close to the near post, so you only need 1 step (higher level = start further away).

CHAPTER 6: High Balls

4. Compete to Catch High Ball in a 2 Team Game

1 GK from each team competes to catch high ball

Description

- The 2 teams are split into pairs and compete to catch the high ball thrown by the Coach. The player that catches the ball scores 1 point for his team.
- After the 3 pairs compete once or twice, change sides.
- If a GK catches the ball but does not shout (name or "Keeper") before he catches it, the point goes to the other team.

Variation: Have different starting positions: Push-up, sitting, back turned to Coach etc.

Coaching Points

1. In this drill, the GKs have to show courage.
2. "Tipping" is not allowed: Both GKs must try to catch the ball.
3. If the ball falls on the ground, play on until one of the 2 GKs has the ball in 2 hands.
4. Try to make pairs of equal level, height and weight.

CHAPTER 6: High Balls

5. Touch Post and Run Through Consecutive Poles to Catch High Balls

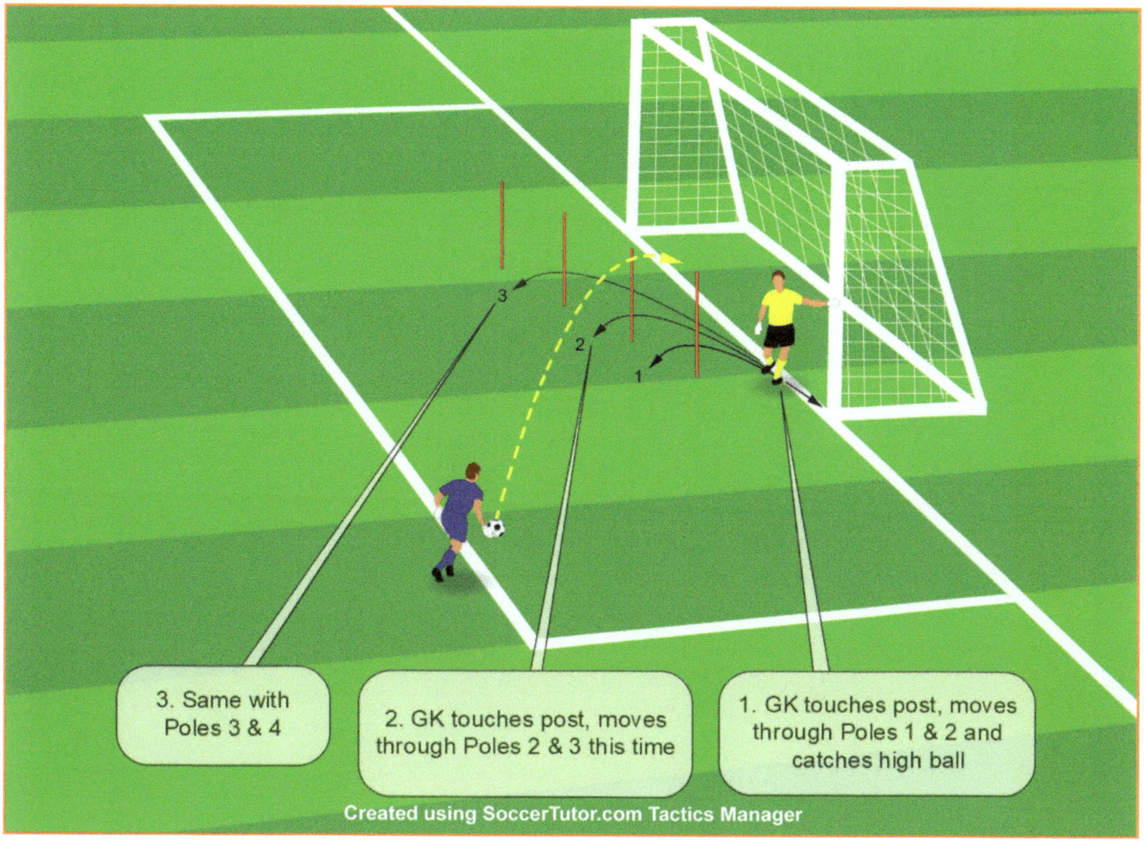

![drill diagram]

3. Same with Poles 3 & 4

2. GK touches post, moves through Poles 2 & 3 this time

1. GK touches post, moves through Poles 1 & 2 and catches high ball

Created using SoccerTutor.com Tactics Manager

Description

1. GK touches the post, moves through Poles 1 & 2 and catches the high ball.
2. GK touches the post, moves through Poles 2 & 3 and catches the high ball.
3. GK touches the post, moves through Poles 3 & 4 and catches the high ball.

Variation: After touching the post, the Coach gives commands for what poles the GK has to move through.

Progression: Position another GK in front of the poles to provide a challenge.

Coaching Points

1. Before crossing the line between the poles, the GK has to call out "Keeper."
2. Move slowly to the post and then speed up after touching the post.
3. Jump off before crossing the line between the poles.

©SoccerTutor.com   Goalkeeper Training Program - 120 Drills

CHAPTER 6: **High Balls**

6. Continuous High Ball Catches from Different Angles

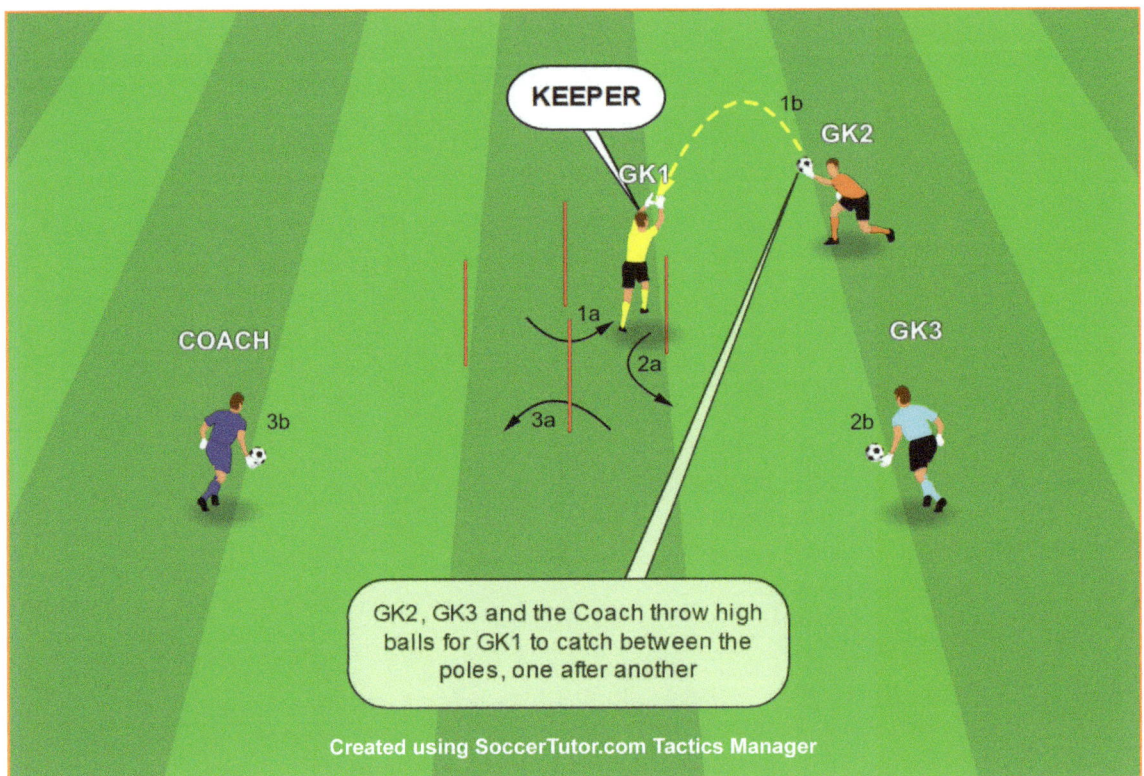

Description

- GK2, GK3 and the Coach take turns to throw a high ball into the space between the poles, one after each other.
- GK1 has to choose the right way to attack the ball and catch it.

Progression: The Coach can command who throws the ball and GK1 has to quickly react to be in the right position to catch the next high ball.

Coaching Points

1. Before crossing the line between the poles, the GK has to call out "Keeper."
2. GK1: No panic, first focus on the command of the Coach.
3. Catch the ball using as few steps as possible.
4. The last step before catching the ball should be big.

CHAPTER 6: High Balls

7. Fast Reactions to Catch High Balls Over Mannequins to Right or Left

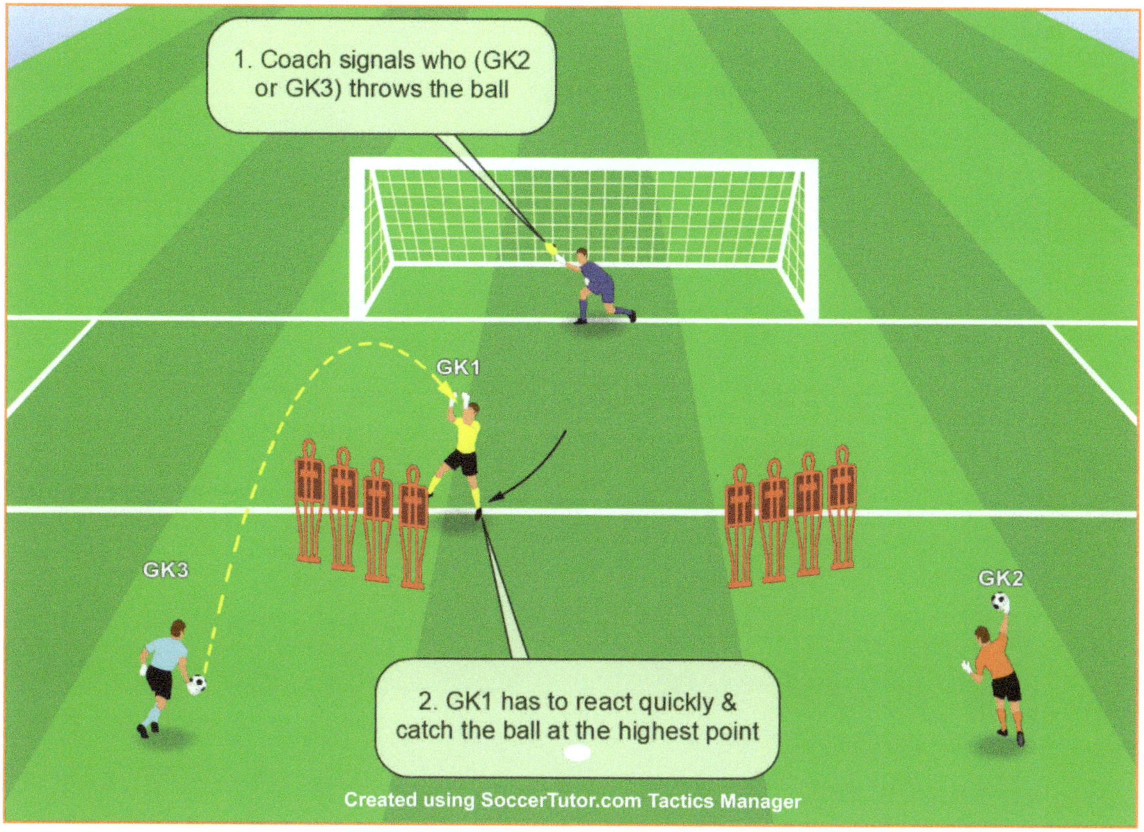

Description

- The Coach stands on the goal line. GK2 and GK3 are ready to throw their balls over the mannequins.
- The Coach puts out his arm to signal who (GK2 or GK3) throws the ball. GK1 must react quickly, move to that side and catch the ball at the highest point.

Variation: GK2 and GK3 can kick the ball with a volley or from the ground.

Progression: Position the mannequins further out, so the GK has to cover a larger distance before catching the high ball.

Coaching Points

1. GK1 starts a few yards in front of the goal line and changes the jump off leg every time.
2. GK2 and GK3 must throw the ball just over the mannequins and not too close to the goal.

©SoccerTutor.com — Goalkeeper Training Program - 120 Drills

CHAPTER 6: High Balls

8. Kicking and Catching High Balls Over a Large Goal Game

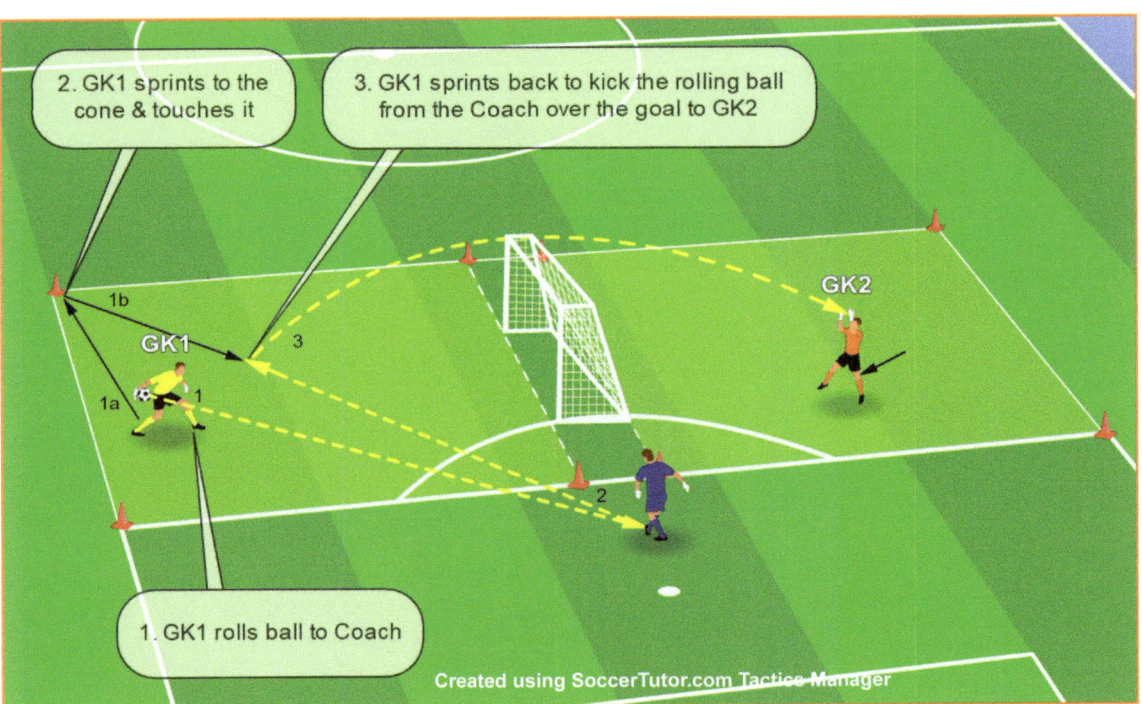

Description

1. GK1 rolls the ball to the Coach.
2. GK1 sprints to the cone behind him and touches it.
3. GK1 then sprints back to the middle and kicks the rolling ball from the Coach over the goal to GK2.

Game Rules: **(1)** Each successful catch scores 1 point.

(2) GK2 shouts "Keeper" before the ball goes over the goal, otherwise GK1 scores 1 point.

(3) If the ball goes out (or not over the goal), then GK2 scores 1 point.

(4) If the ball touches the ground in GK2's area, then GK1 scores 2 points.

Variation: Play 2 v 2.

Progression: Play all balls using the weaker foot.

Coaching Points

1. Play a slow ball to the Coach, so you have more time to go and touch the cone.
2. Bring every ball to the chest after catching and before rolling the ball to the Coach.

CHAPTER 6: High Balls

9. Competing to Catch High Balls in a Dynamic 3 Zone Game

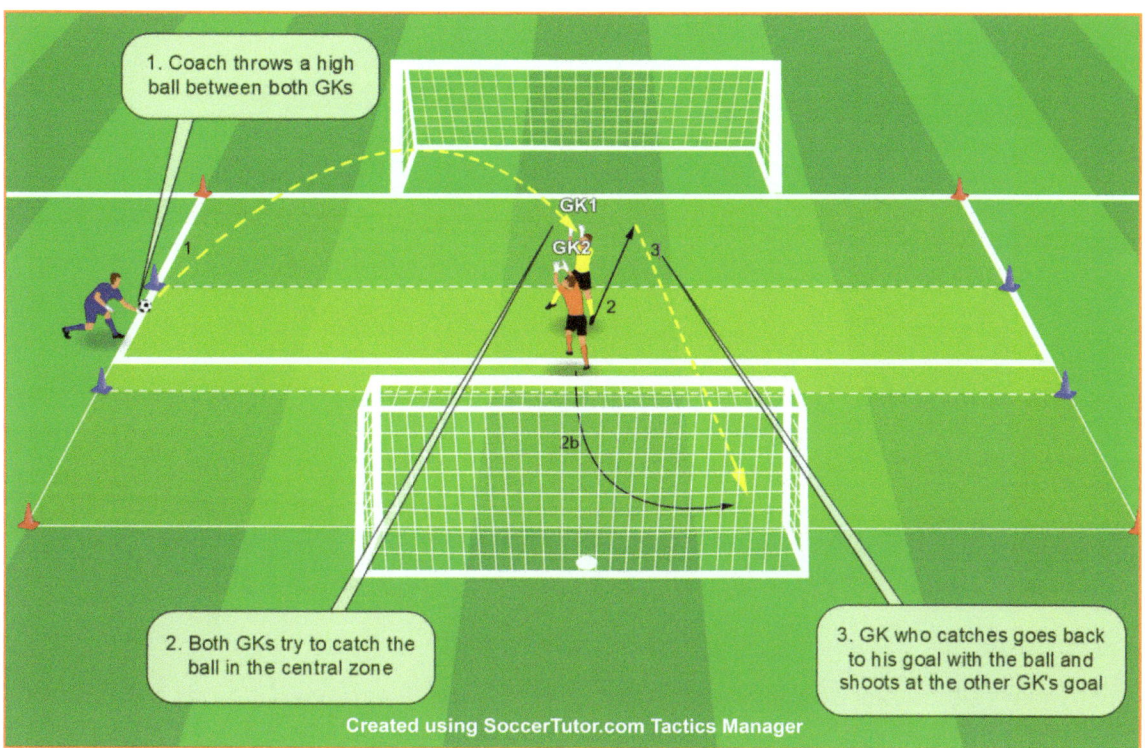

Description

1. The Coach throws a high ball between both GKs in the central zone.
2. Both GKs try to catch the ball in the central zone. The GK who catches scores 1 point.
3. The GK who catches the ball goes back to his goal with the ball. He then shoots, trying to score in the other GK's goal. If they score, they get 1 point.

* GKs have to shout "Keeper" before catching, otherwise the point goes to the other GK. Change sides after every 2 throws. The loser of the game has to do 10 push-ups.

Variations

1. Try scoring with a 1 v 1 instead of shooting.
2. Try scoring with a throw.

Coaching Points

1. Courage is needed to compete with another GK and catch the ball.
2. Depending on the angle of the throw, use the correct leg to jump off.

©SoccerTutor.com — Goalkeeper Training Program - 120 Drills

CHAPTER 6: High Balls

10. Catching High Balls Against Defender in the Box + Long Kick Out

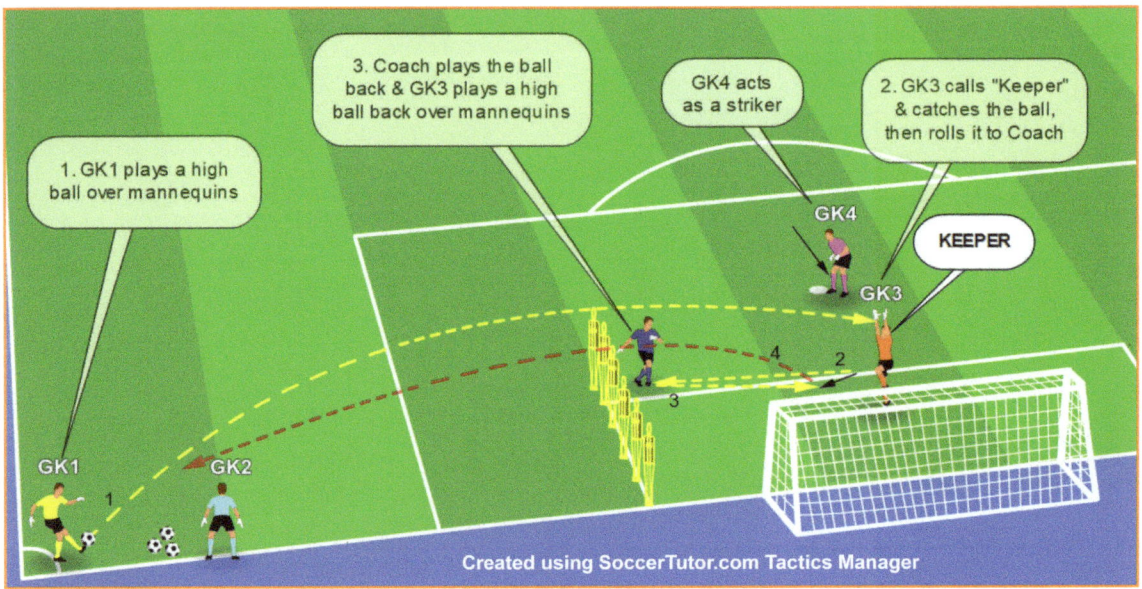

Description

1. GK1 plays a high ball over the mannequins and into the 6-yard box. GK4 acts as a striker in front of GK3.

2. GK3 shouts "Keeper" before the ball crosses over the mannequins and catches the ball.

3. After GK3 catches the ball, he rolls it to the Coach. The Coach passes the ball back to GK3, who plays a high ball back over the mannequins to GK1.

4. GK1 and GK2 switch positions, as do GK3 and GK4. The drill continues.

Variations

1. For lower age/level, remove the mannequins and throw the ball instead of kicking.

2. This drill can be done with just 2 GKs (no striker or spare man).

3. Position the mannequins in a more central position.

Progressions

1. GK3 plays the ball over the mannequins with his weaker foot.

2. Add mannequins on the other side by the far post.

CHAPTER 7

ONE v ONE

CHAPTER 7: One v One

1. Blocking Close Up Shots in a Cone Channel

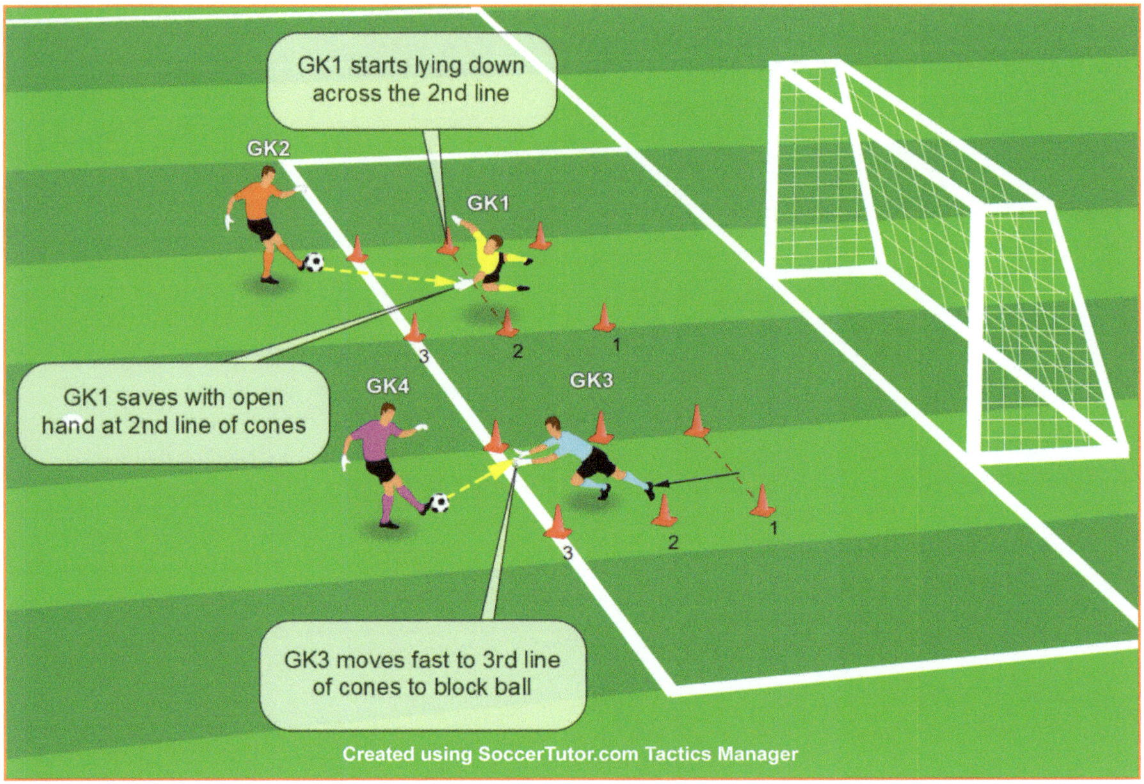

[Diagram: GK1 starts lying down across the 2nd line; GK1 saves with open hand at 2nd line of cones; GK3 moves fast to 3rd line of cones to block ball]

Description

- GK1 is lying in a straight line between the cones (2nd line of cones). GK2 kicks the ball at GK1. At the same time GK2 kicks the ball, GK1 blocks the ball with open hands.

- GK3 is sitting on the ground behind the cones and moves forward to block the ball (3rd line of cones) as soon as GK4 kicks it.

- For both variations, you can also have GK1 or GK3 standing in a ready-low position to block the ball.

Coaching Points

1. Block the ball in an aggressive way: Go to the ball with high speed.
2. Eyes should be open and on the ball at all times.
3. GK3 feels much stronger than GK4 because they can block with their whole body, whereas GK4 just uses their leg.

©SoccerTutor.com   Goalkeeper Training Program - 120 Drills

CHAPTER 7: One v One

2. Diving Forward to Save at an Opponent's Feet

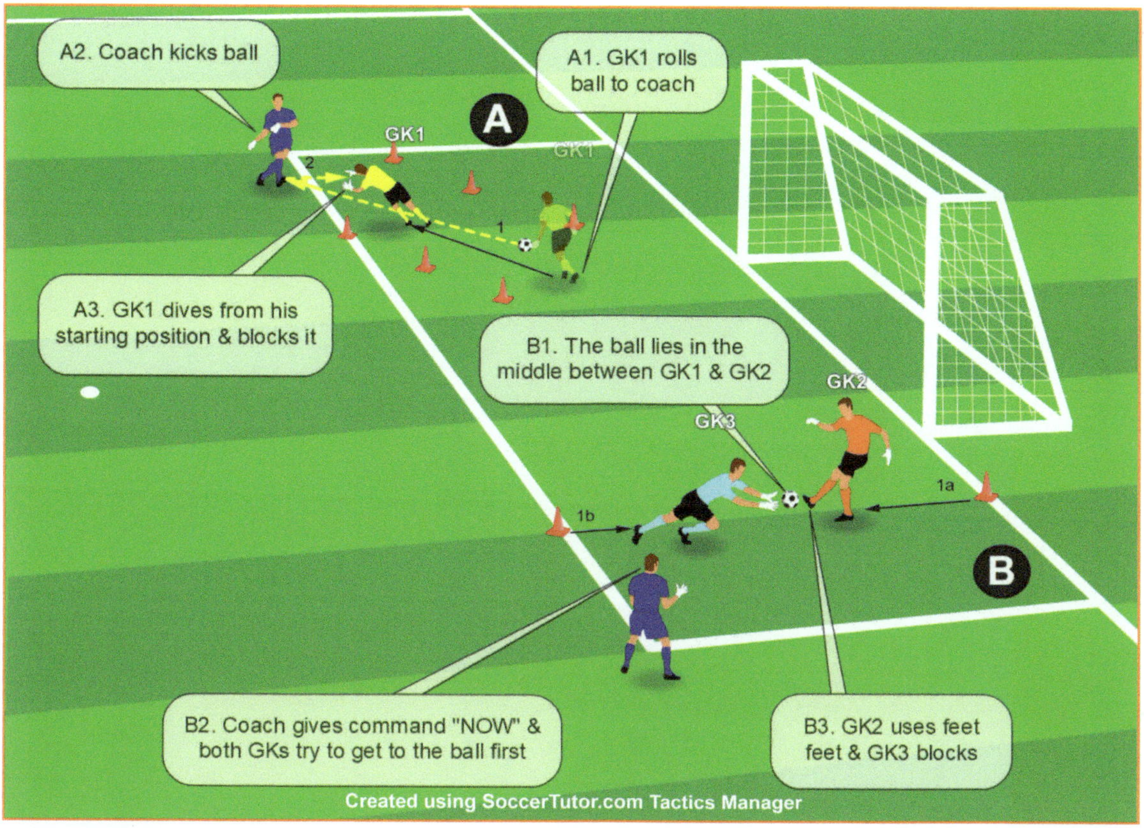

Description

A. **(1)** GK1 rolls the ball to the Coach. **(2)** The Coach kicks the ball. **(3)** GK1 dives from his starting position and blocks it. **(4)** Repeat with GK1 starting a few yards behind the first line of cones and trying to block the ball there.

B. **(1)** The ball lies in the middle between GK1 and GK2. **(2)** The Coach gives a command of "NOW" and both GKs try to get to the ball first. **(3)** GK2 only can only touch the ball with his feet and GK3 can block it with any part of the body.

Coaching Points

1. At the moment of contact, the body should be in a straight line.
2. Block with 2 hands.
3. GK3's body should be in a straight line, as in the previous drill.
4. GK3 should take as few steps as possible (ideally just 1).

©SoccerTutor.com   Goalkeeper Training Program - 120 Drills

CHAPTER 7: One v One

3. Move Forward to Attack the Ball and Save

[Diagram showing the drill setup with GK1 in goal, coach to the side, cones arranged in front of goal, and GK2 positioned behind]

1. GK1 rolls the ball to the coach
2. Coach plays ball in direction of the cones
3. GK1 has to attack the ball through the cones

Progression: You can add GK2 (or more GKs) to put pressure on GK1

Description
1. GK1 rolls the ball to the Coach.
2. The Coach kicks the ball in the direction of the cones to the GK's left (right next time).
3. GK1 has to attack the ball through the cones.

Progressions
1. The Coach can decide to kick the ball to the right or left (GK1 must react quickly).
2. Have GK2 (or more GKs) put pressure on GK1 and jump over him.

Coaching Points
1. Don't gamble: GK1 has to wait until the ball is played.
2. Never call out (shout) when you go for a 1 v 1 (you are warning the striker). In a real game situation, only shout when there is also a defender close to the ball.

CHAPTER 7: One v One

4. Running Out of Goal to Save 1 v 1 Against an Opponent Running onto a Pass

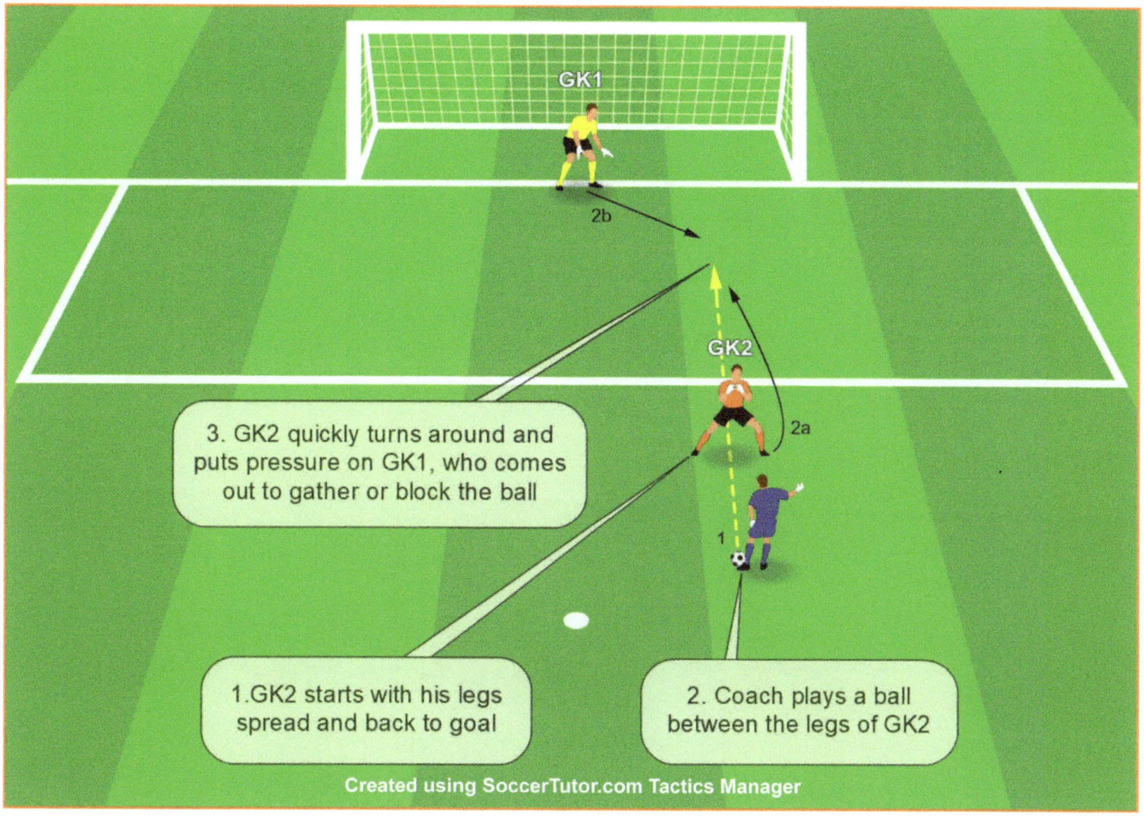

![diagram]

Description

1. GK2 starts with his legs spread and his back to goal.
2. The Coach passes the ball between the legs of GK2.
3. GK2 quickly turns around and puts pressure on GK1, who comes out of goal to quickly gather or block the ball.

Variation: The Coach chooses whether to shoot at goal or pass the ball between the legs of GK2. This means that GK1 has to watch and be ready for different situations.

Coaching Points

1. Starting position: Both feet on the goal line.
2. GK1 has to wait until the ball is played and then go in a straight line to the ball.
3. GK2 jumps over GK1.
4. If possible, gather the ball into the chest.

©SoccerTutor.com   Goalkeeper Training Program - 120 Drills

CHAPTER 7: One v One

5. Saving at Close Range with Opponents Moving in for Rebounds

[Diagram:
- 1. GK1 rolls ball to the coach
- 2. Coach shoots to one side (left or right)
- 3. GK2 & GK3 put pressure on GK1, who comes out to gather or block the ball]

Description

1. GK1 rolls the ball to the Coach and moves off his line.
2. The Coach shoots to one side (left or right).
3. GK2 and GK3 put pressure on GK1, who comes out to gather or block the ball. Both GK2 and GK3 jump over GK1.
4. All GKs rotate positions (GK1 -> GK2 -> GK3 -> GK1).

Coaching Points

1. GK1 has to show courage.
2. GK1 needs quick thinking and fast reactions.

©SoccerTutor.com   Goalkeeper Training Program - 120 Drills

CHAPTER 7: One v One

THE "BLOCK POSITION"

The **"Block Position"** is used in **One v One** situations to block the attacker's path to goal and create as large a block as possible, while also making sure the ball can never go under the leg.

These are the key instructions:

- **Left Leg:** The foot should be lined up in the direction of the ball.

- **Right Leg:** The knee should be close to the ground but never touching it. Turn the leg sideways and cover as much space as possible. The space between the 2 legs should be small, so the shortest path to the goal is closed.

- **Left Hand:** Close to the ground, protecting the space next to the left foot.

- **Right Hand:** In front of the body and higher, so you can attack a ball that is played to that side of the goal.

- **Head:** Never turn your head away, as your body will then also turn. Keep your eyes on the ball.

©SoccerTutor.com — Goalkeeper Training Program - 120 Drills

CHAPTER 7: One v One

6. Correct Technique for "Block Position" in a 1 v 1 Situation

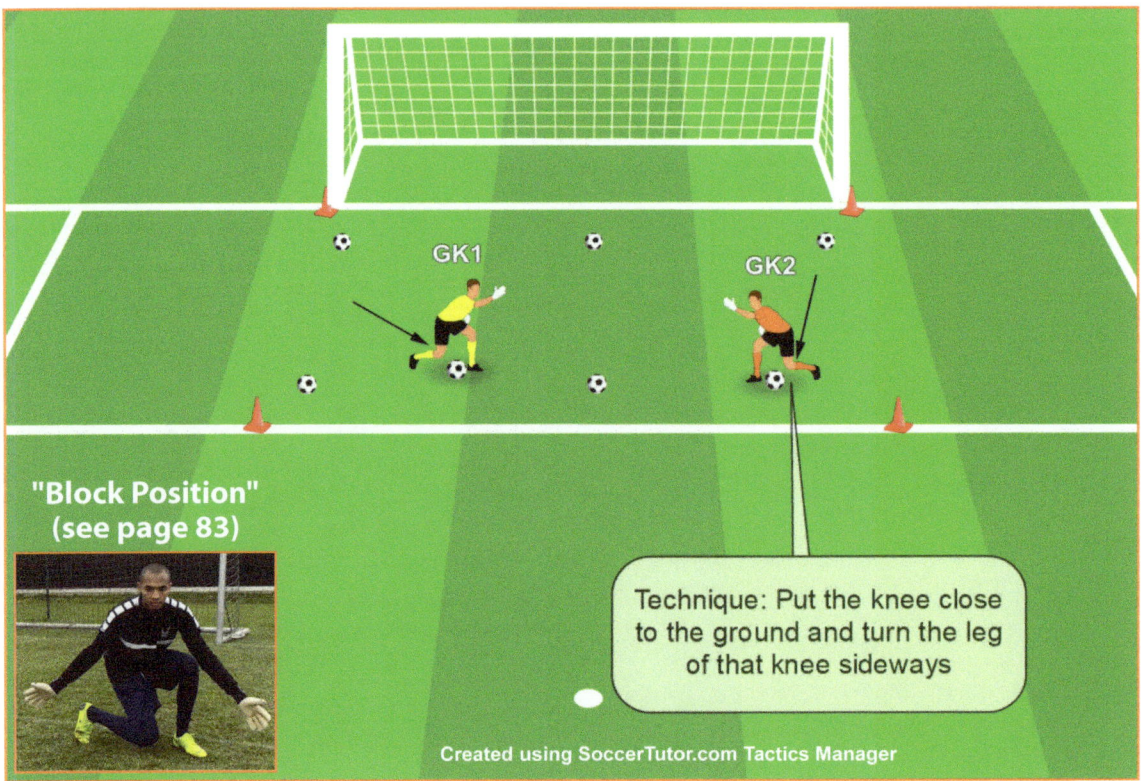

Description

- The GKs move freely in the space marked out by the cones and move behind 1 ball at a time. When they move close to a ball, they put their knee close to the ground and turn the leg of that knee sideways.

- They are practicing the proper block position technique for a 1 v 1 situation, making sure the ball can never go under that leg - see page 83 for full details.

- Change legs all the time.

Variation: Coach gives commands for what leg to use and where to go (number each ball).

Coaching Points

1. Never put the knee on the ground, because your movement is then limited.
2. Train until both legs go down in the same way.
3. Don't look down at the ball. Look up as if a player is approaching for a 1 v 1.
4. The step towards the ball is a big step.

©SoccerTutor.com   Goalkeeper Training Program - 120 Drills

CHAPTER 7: One v One

7. "Block Position" in a 1 v 1 Situation using Mini Goals

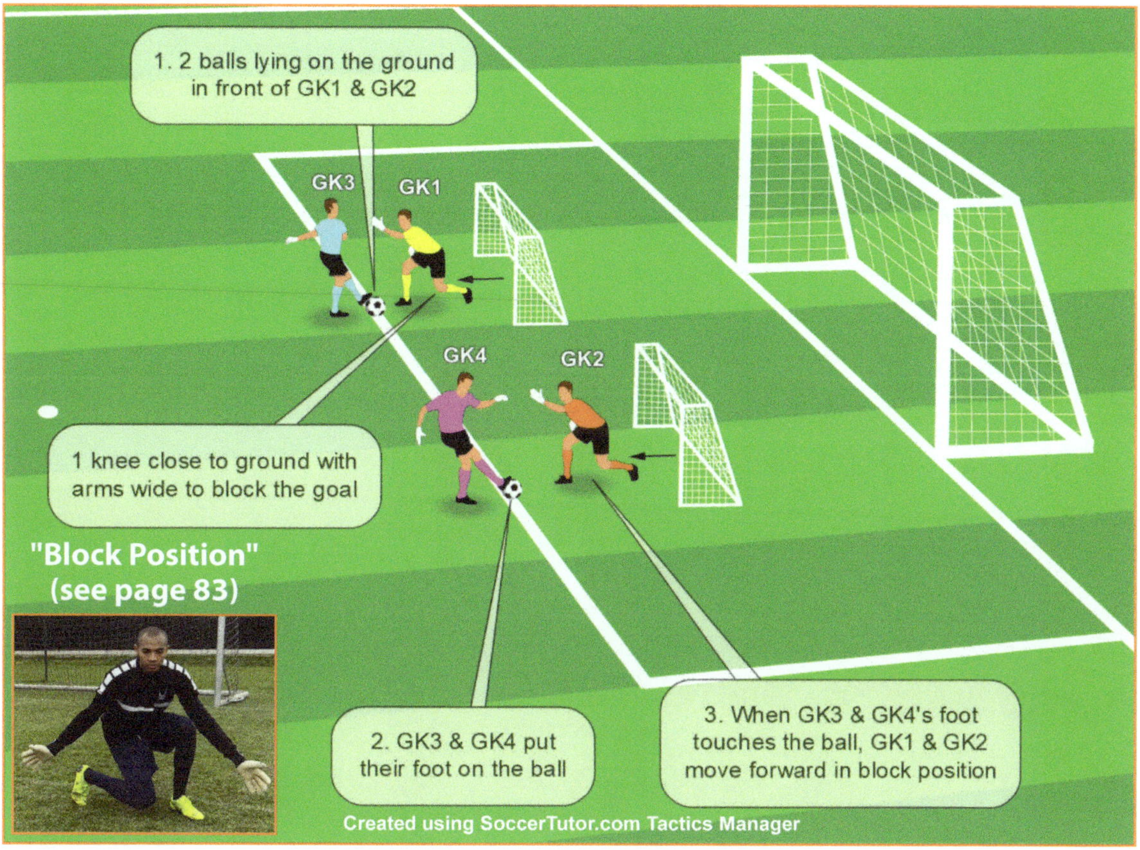

Description

1. There are 2 balls lying on the ground in front of GK1 and GK2.
2. GK3 and GK4 put their foot on the ball.
3. GK1 and GK2 move forward in the block position (change the leg each time).

Variation: GK3 and GK4 shoot, trying to score in the mini goals (not just put foot on ball).

Coaching Points

1. The hands should be close to the ground (outside the legs) to cover a large space.
2. The upper body should be straight.
3. Move towards the ball as far as possible, to block the goal.
4. If the ball comes off the body while blocking, go after the ball and try to gather it.

©SoccerTutor.com   Goalkeeper Training Program - 120 Drills

CHAPTER 7: One v One

8. Fast Reactions to Form "Block Position" to Left or Right

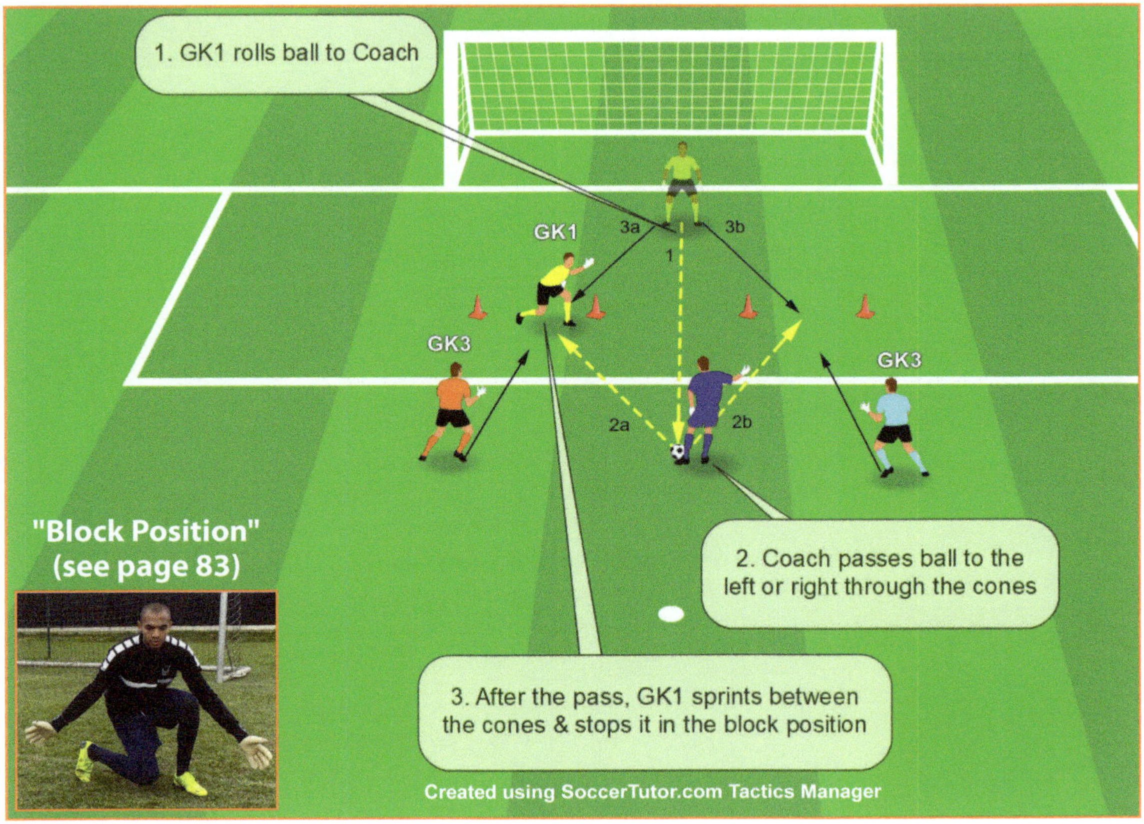

Description

1. GK1 rolls the ball to the Coach.
2. The Coach can pass to the left or the right through the cones.
3. After rolling the ball out, GK1 sprints between the cones and forms the block position to stop the shot of the Coach. GK2 or GK3 move forward to apply pressure to GK1.
4. All GKs rotate positions (GK1 -> GK2 -> GK3 -> GK1).

Variations: **(1)** Left side can be block position and the right can be attack ball with hands.
(2) Have the Coach shoot through the cones as well.

Coaching Points

1. GK1 has to use as few steps as possible to go get the ball.
2. Keep the options open (block or go with hands) until the last second.
3. GK1 can start with 1 foot in front of the other.

©SoccerTutor.com   Goalkeeper Training Program - 120 Drills

CHAPTER 7: One v One

9. Practicing the "Block Position" in a 1 v 1 Duel Game with Mini Goals

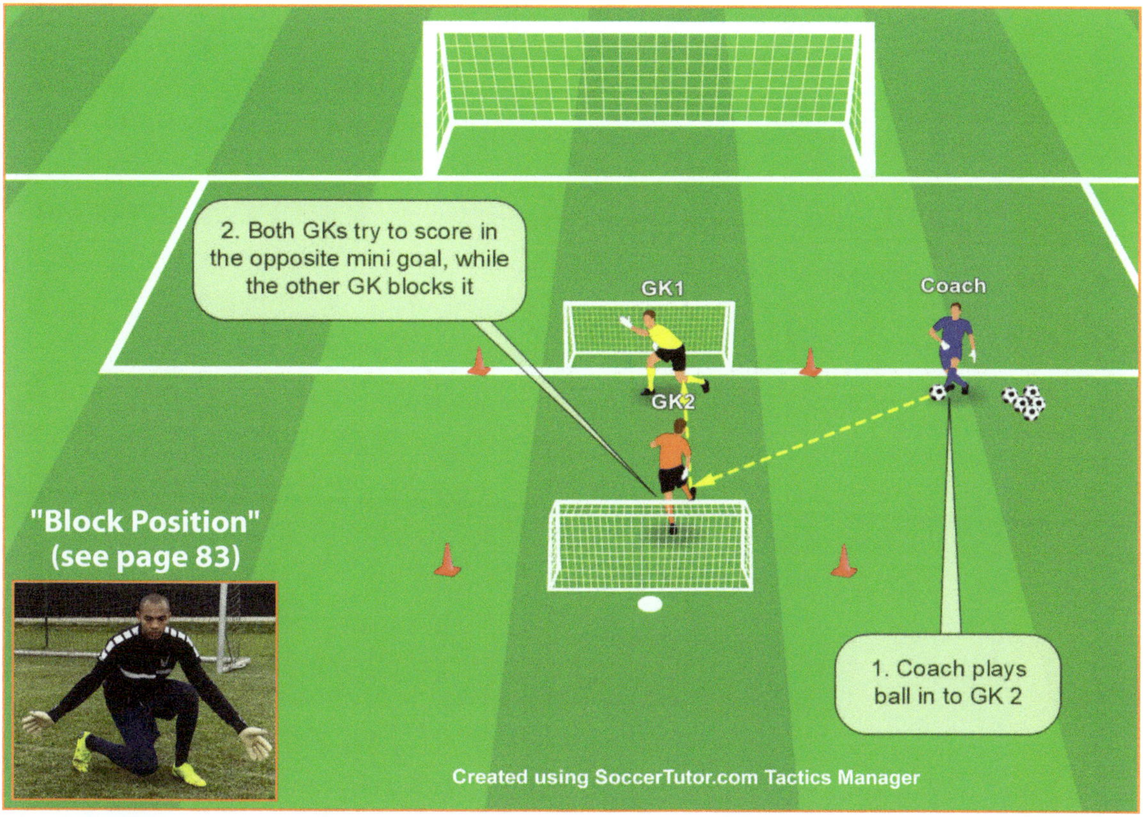

Description

1. The coach starts by passing the ball into GK2.
2. GK2 tries to score and GK1 tries to block. The game continues with both GKs trying to score, with the other one using the block position to defend their goal.

* If a goal is scored or the ball goes out of play, both GKs go back towards their goals and we restart with the Coach's pass to GK1.

Variation: Play with 2 teams. After every goal, the next GK of that team comes on.

Coaching Points

1. High intensity game: Many balls in a small area.
2. Try to get as close to the ball as possible when blocking.
3. Shoot as often as you can.

CHAPTER 7: One v One

10. Practicing All Techniques for 1 v 1 Situations in a 4 Cone Drill

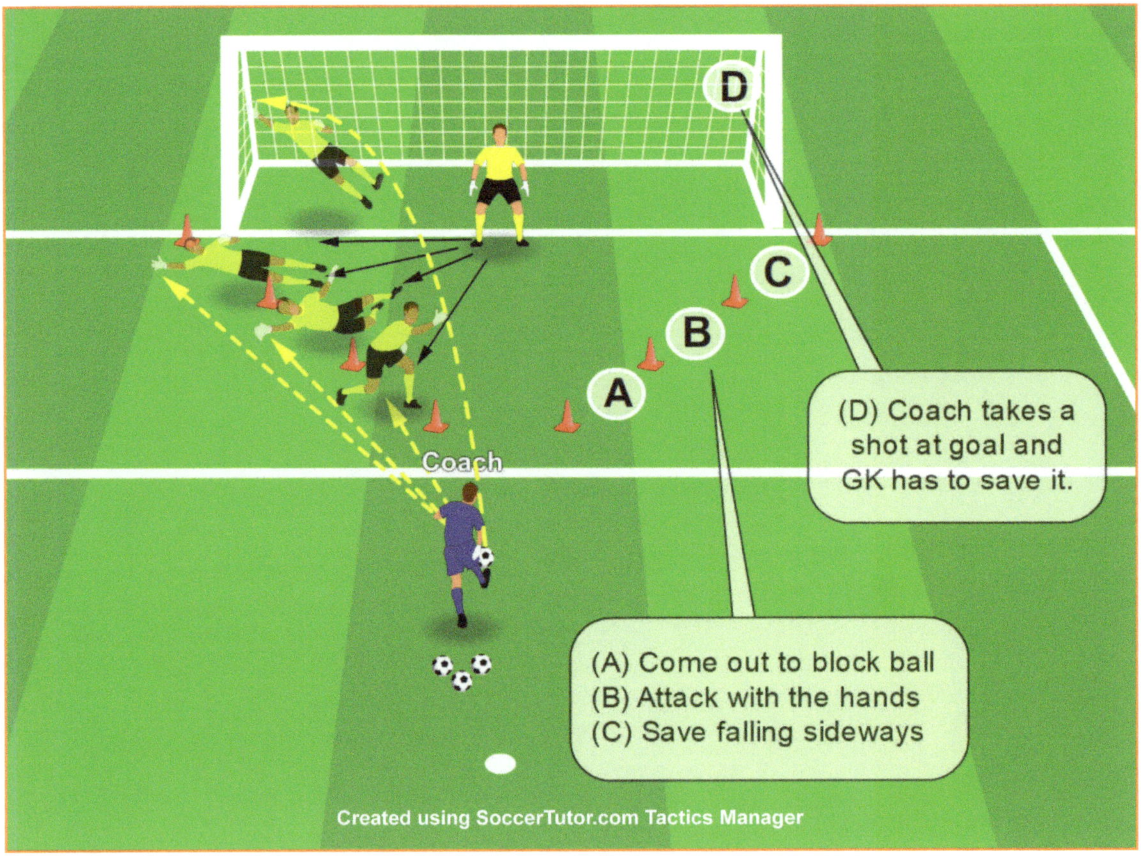

Description

The Coach can either play on the left or right side and has 4 options:

A. The Coach kicks the ball between the first 2 cones. The GK comes out to block the ball.

B. The Coach kicks the ball between the 2nd and 3rd cones. The GK comes out to attack the ball and save with the hands.

C. The Coach kicks the ball between the 3rd and 4th cones. The GK saves it falling sideways.

D. The Coach shoots at goal. This prevents the GK from gambling and moving forward too early, as he must be prepared for all eventualities.

Progression: Same exercise without the cones, but with 2 extra GKs who provide pressure from both sides.

Coaching Point: The GK has to wait until the last moment to react and commit.

CHAPTER 8

TECHNICAL SKILLS WITH FEET

CHAPTER 8: Technical Skills with Feet

1. Short One-Touch Passing on Left and Right Side with Both Feet

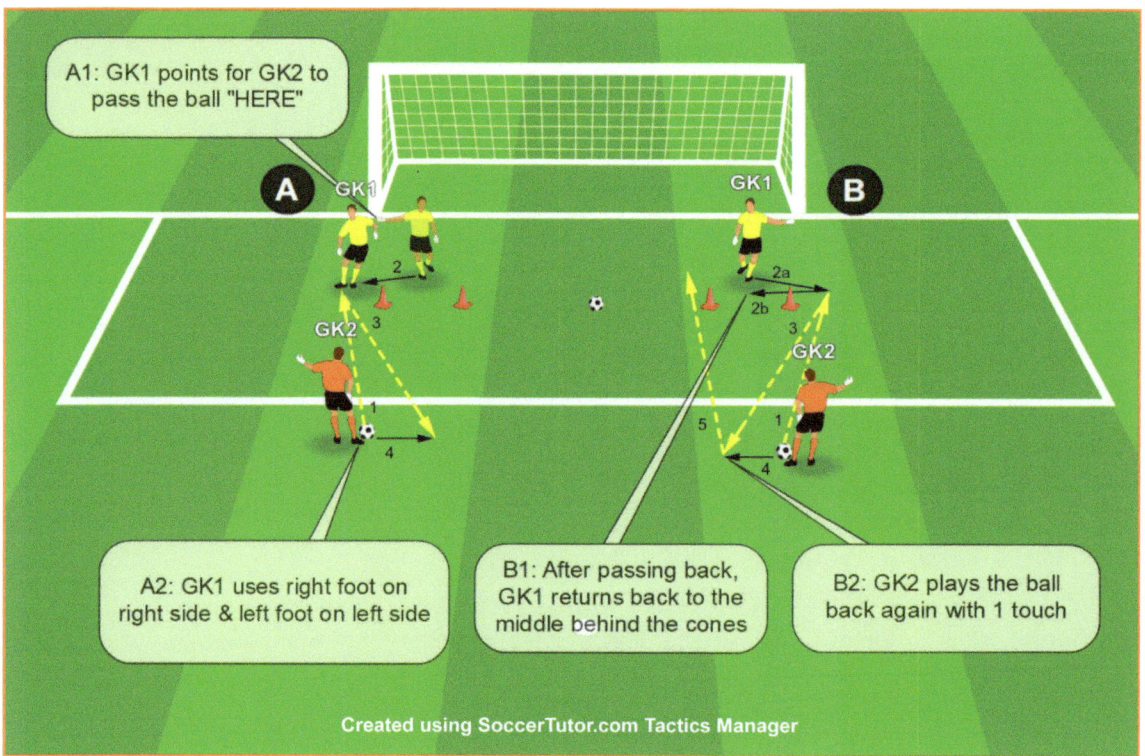

Description

A1. GK1 asks for the ball by pointing at the ground with his hand to where he wants it played and giving the command "HERE."

A2. GK2 passes the ball and GK1 uses 2 touches: 1 to control and 1 to pass back. On the right side, GK1 only uses his right foot. On the left side, GK1 only uses his left foot.

B1. As a variation to A1, GK1 uses 1 touch to pass back to GK2 and then moves quickly back to the middle (behind the cones).

B2. GK2 then plays the ball on the other side using 1 touch. This creates a very high speed 1 touch passing drill.

Coaching Points

1. GK1 has to ask for the ball directly after he passes it back to GK2.
2. GK1 has to stand on the balls of his feet, just as if he is expecting a shot.
3. GK2 has to take care to pass along the ground to GK1.

©SoccerTutor.com   Goalkeeper Training Program - 120 Drills

CHAPTER 8: **Technical Skills with Feet**

2. Directional First Touch Out in Front + Return Pass

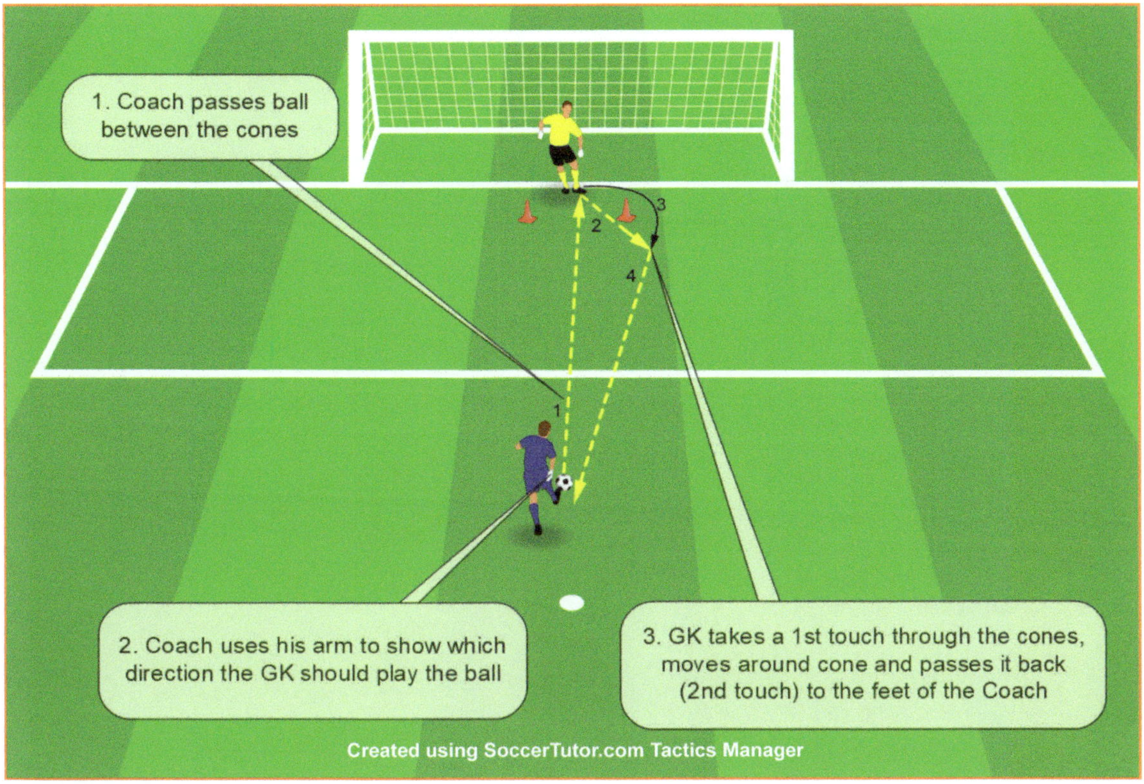

[Diagram: 1. Coach passes ball between the cones. 2. Coach uses his arm to show which direction the GK should play the ball. 3. GK takes a 1st touch through the cones, moves around cone and passes it back (2nd touch) to the feet of the Coach]

Description

1. The Coach passes the ball between the cones.
2. The Coach uses his arm to show which direction the GK should take his 1st touch.
3. The GK takes a 1st touch through the cones, moves around the cone and passes the ball back (2nd touch) to the feet of the Coach.

Variations: **(1)** The Coach can shout "left" or "right."
(2) The GK can chip the ball into the hands of the Coach (instead of a ground pass).

Coaching Points

1. The GK must not play the ball too far to one side, as he should be able to reach the ball with 2 steps.
2. After passing, immediately move back into the starting position.
3. Always play the ball back to the strong foot of the receiver.

CHAPTER 8: Technical Skills with Feet

3. Opening Up to Receive and Pass

Description

1. GK1 plays a low pass between the cones to GK2 with the right foot.
2. GK2 asks for the ball "HERE," controls the ball with his 1st touch and passes the ball through the cones to GK3 with his 2nd touch (both touches with right foot).
3. GK3 controls the ball and passes (right foot) it to GK1 to restart the same sequence.
4. Play clockwise instead of anti-clockwise and have the GKs use their left foot only.

Variations

1. All 3 GKs play using 1 touch passes.
2. Play with 2 balls: GK1 and GK3 both start with a ball.
3. GK2 plays a chip pass for GK3 to catch, who then rolls the ball to GK1.

Coaching Points

1. When GK2 controls the ball, the 1st touch should be in the direction he wants to play.
2. GK2 should ask for the ball as soon as GK3 has played his pass, so GK1 has more time.
3. Play every ball with the inside of the foot.

©SoccerTutor.com   Goalkeeper Training Program - 120 Drills

CHAPTER 8: Technical Skills with Feet

4. Accurate Chip Passing

Description
1. GK1 rolls the ball under the rope to GK2.
2. GK2 plays the ball back (first time) over the rope with the inside of the foot.

Variations
1. Make the distance bigger.
2. After GK1 rolls the ball, he jumps over the rope to apply pressure to GK2.
3. GK2 plays the ball with the instep (upper part of the foot).

Coaching Points
1. GK2 uses both feet to play the ball back.
2. GK2 should open his arms and lean his upper body back. Also, the last step before playing the ball should be big.
3. When using your weaker foot (e.g. left), put the left arm on your upper body to force the right arm to go out. This helps the GK to become balanced.

CHAPTER 8: Technical Skills with Feet

5. One-Touch Zig-Zag Passing Through Cones on the Move

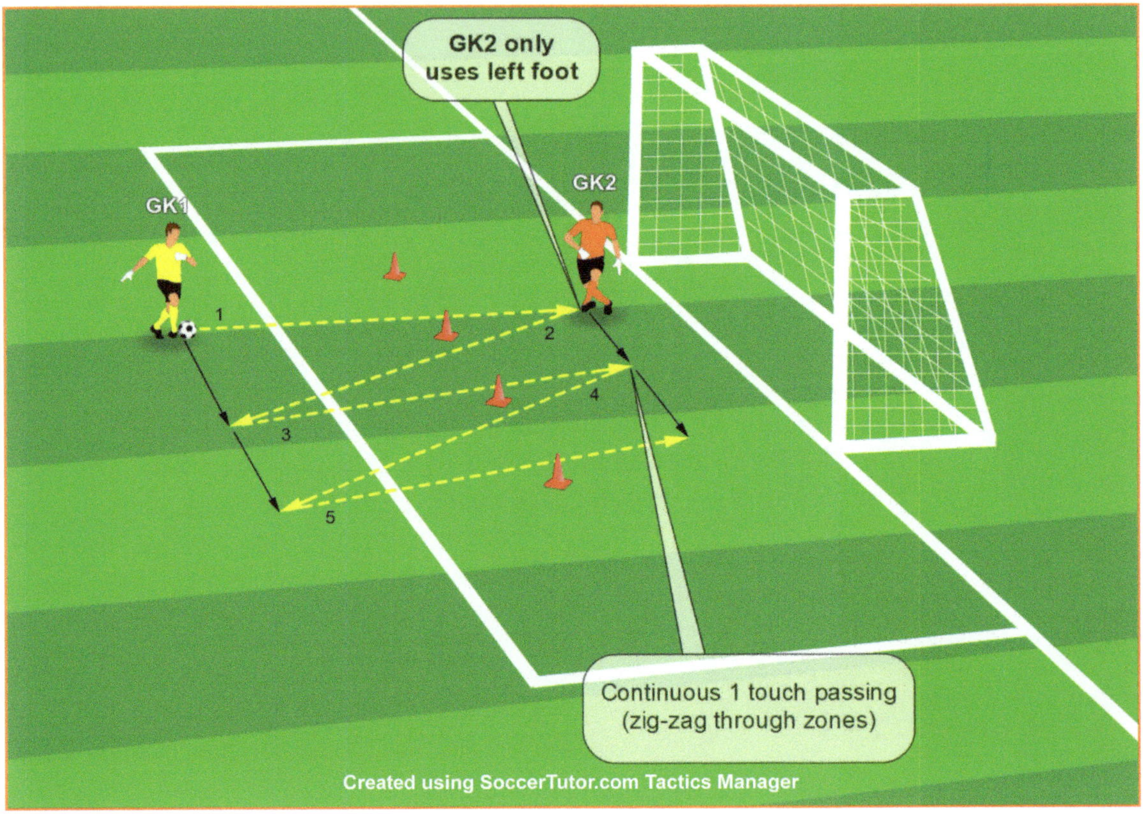

[Diagram: GK1 (yellow) and GK2 (orange) positioned in front of goal with cones arranged in zig-zag pattern. Callouts: "GK2 only uses left foot" and "Continuous 1 touch passing (zig-zag through zones)". Passes numbered 1–5.]

Description

- GK1 starts with the 1st pass. GK1 and GK2 play 1 touch passes through the cones as they move along, as shown in the diagram.
- GK1 only uses his right foot and GK2 only uses his left foot.
- After receiving the 5th pass at the end, GK2 restarts in the opposite direction. Now, GK1 only uses his left foot and GK2 only uses his right foot.
- Switch sides after every 2 rounds.

Coaching Points

1. Ball speed should be low. Increase the speed as the GKs become more confident.
2. Turn the inside of the foot open to play a straight ball with no bounces.
3. After passing, the GKs should ask for the ball "HERE."
4. Short distance = 100% concentration needed.

©SoccerTutor.com   Goalkeeper Training Program - 120 Drills

CHAPTER 8: Technical Skills with Feet

6. Moving to Receive Back Passes and Play Out within the 6-Yard Box

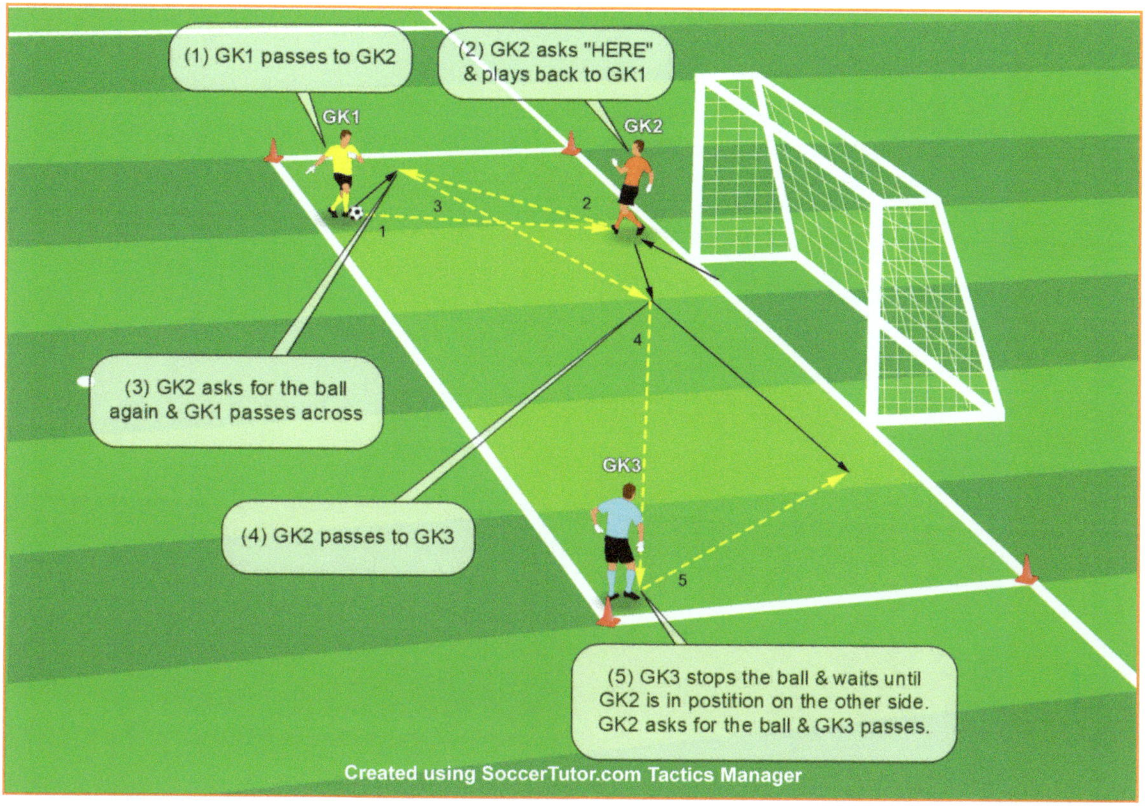

(1) GK1 passes to GK2

(2) GK2 asks "HERE" & plays back to GK1

(3) GK2 asks for the ball again & GK1 passes across

(4) GK2 passes to GK3

(5) GK3 stops the ball & waits until GK2 is in postition on the other side. GK2 asks for the ball & GK3 passes.

Created using SoccerTutor.com Tactics Manager

Description

(1) GK1 passes to GK2 near the post. **(2)** GK2 asks for the ball "HERE" and passes back to GK1. **(3)** GK2 asks for the ball again and GK1 passes across the body of GK2. **(4)** GK2 passes to GK3 on the other side. **(5)** GK3 stops the ball and waits until GK2 is in position and asks for the ball. GK3 finishes the sequence with the pass to GK2 outside the post.

GK2 only uses 1 foot throughout the sequence. Change the foot used after every sequence. All GKs rotate positions (GK1 -> GK2 -> GK3 -> GK1) after every sequence.

Progressions: (1) Make the 4th pass (from GK2 to GK3) a chip pass. **(2)** Add a 4th GK.

Coaching Points

1. Always make sure a back pass is directed wide of the goal.
2. Ask for the ball close to goal line, to create the largest distance between GK and striker.
3. When you ask for the ball: Stay open, so you can see the whole pitch.
4. After asking for the ball: Look to the other side, to see if you can play the ball there.

©SoccerTutor.com   Goalkeeper Training Program - 120 Drills

CHAPTER 8: Technical Skills with Feet

7. Back Pass, One-Two and Chip Pass in a 4-GK Passing Drill

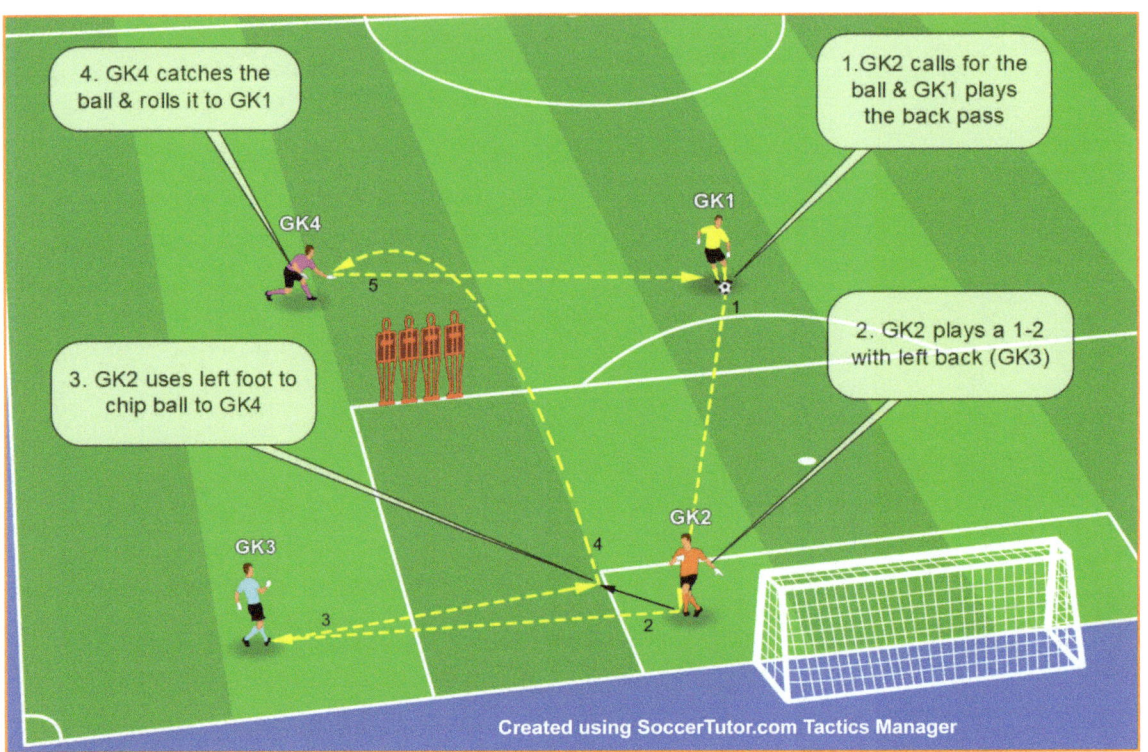

Description

1. GK2 asks for the ball and GK1 plays a back pass to start the drill.
2. GK2 plays a 1-2 combination (using left foot) with GK3, who is acting as a left back.
3. GK2 plays a left footed chip pass over the mannequins and into GK4's hands.
4. GK4 catches the ball and rolls it to GK1. The drill is repeated.

Variations: **(1)** Play on the right side using only the right foot. **(2)** 1 touch passing only. **(3)** 2 balls: GK1 and GK4 both start with a ball.

Progression: GK2 plays the ball over a big goal in a more central position.

Coaching Points

1. From an open position (see the whole pitch), GK2 turns his body and passes to GK3.
2. Before receiving the ball back from GK3, again turn and open the body shape.
3. GK2 should play the ball into the hands of GK4, not just over the mannequins.

CHAPTER 8: Technical Skills with Feet

8. Passing/Receiving Ground and Aerial Passes in a 3-GK Line Passing Drill

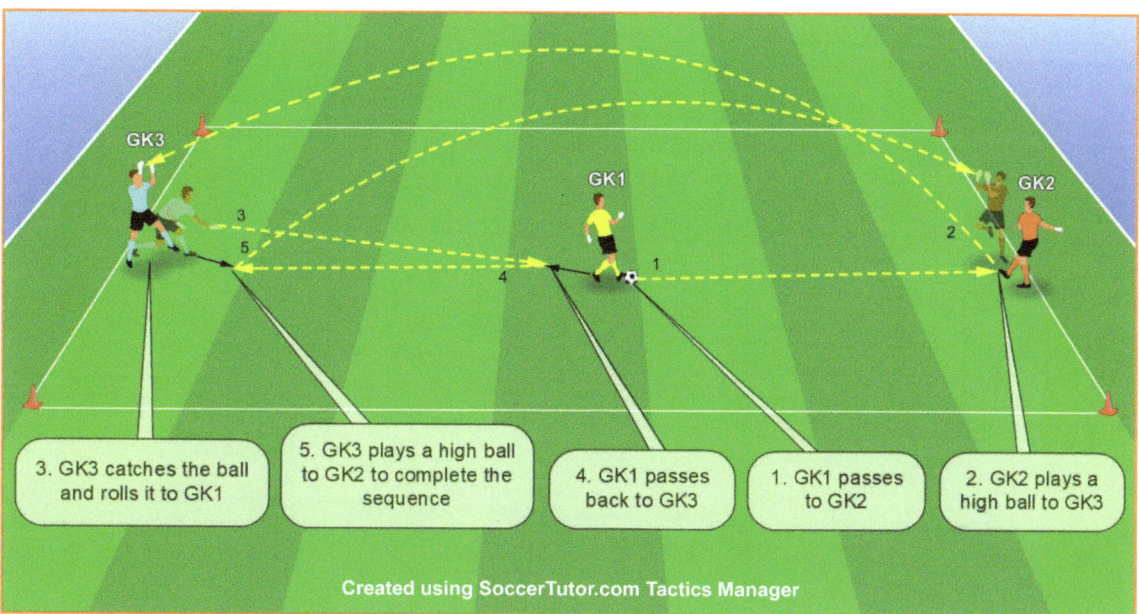

Description

1. GK1 passes along the ground to GK2.
2. GK2 plays a high ball over the head of GK1 and into the hands of GK3.
3. GK3 catches the ball and rolls it to GK1.
4. GK1 has turned and passes it back to GK3 (along the ground).
5. GK3 plays a high ball to GK2 to complete the sequence.

Variations

1. For lower ages/levels, GK2 and GK3 can stop the ball before playing the high ball.
2. You can add movement with the GKs following their passes: GK1 can move to GK2's position after passing to GK2 and GK2 can move to GK1's position after his pass to GK3 etc.

Coaching Points

1. GK2 and GK3 shout "Keeper" before the ball goes over the head of GK1.
2. The GKs should all practice using their weaker foot equally.
3. Depending on the level of the GKs, adapt the distance between GK2 and GK3.

CHAPTER 8: Technical Skills with Feet

9. One-Two Combinations with Short and Long Passing

GK2 turns around and receives the ball of GK3

GK1 passes to GK2 and asks for it back

Description

(1) GK1 passes to GK2 and asks for it back. **(2)** GK2 passes to the side of GK1. **(3)** GK1 passes to GK3. **(4)** GK2 turns around and receives the pass from GK3. **(5)** GK2 passes to the side of GK3. **(6)** GK3 completes the sequence with a pass back to the start (GK1).

Variations

1. Use chip passes.
2. Rotate positions: After GK1 plays the long pass, he moves to GK2's position etc.

Coaching Points

1. GK2 is key: If his passes are well-weighted, it's easy for GK1 and GK3 to make good passes.
2. GK1 and GK3 have to play the longer passes in a straight line.
3. The quality of the GKs determines how big the area can be.

CHAPTER 8: Technical Skills with Feet

10. "Wall Ball Game" with Passing Against Low Bench

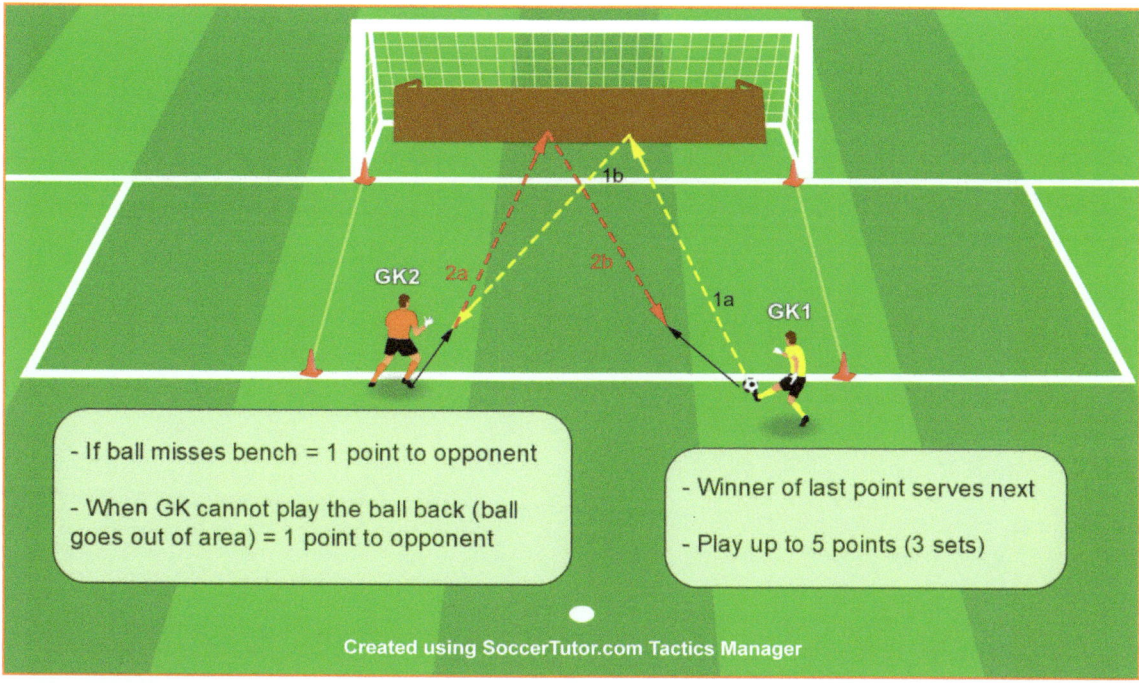

Description

- GK1 starts by passing from the edge of the 6-yard box to the bench lying on the goal line. GK2 has to return the ball against the bench with 1 touch. The game continues like this with the GKs and ball staying within the marked out area.

- If the ball misses the bench, 1 point is given to the opponent. When a GK cannot play the ball back (ball goes out of area), 1 point is given to the opponent.

- The GK who wins the point serves next. Play up to 5 points (3 sets).

Variations

1. Play with more than 2 GKs. Every GK has a number and they kick the ball in order.
2. Start with 5 points: Every mistake that is made, you lose a point (0 points and you're out).
3. Only play with the weaker foot.

Coaching Points

1. Put the bench 1 metre behind the goal line (every ball passes the goal line).
2. To score a point, the ball has to bounce within the area before it goes out.
3. This is a perfect warm-up game before training with many ball touches.

CHAPTER 9

FOOTWORK

CHAPTER 9: Footwork

1. Movement in All Directions with Ankle Resistance Band

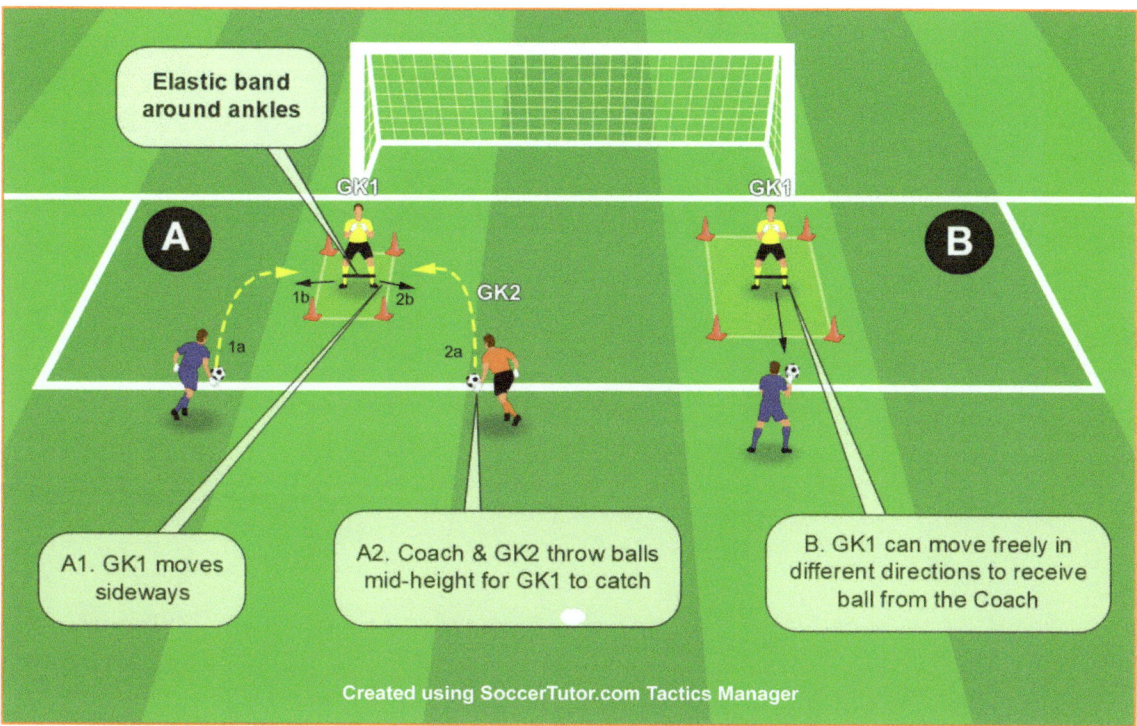

Description

A1. GK1 has an elastic band around his ankles. He can only move sideways.

A2. Firstly, the Coach throws the ball to GK1's right - GK1 catches the ball at mid-height and throws it back. Then, GK1 moves across to his left and GK2 throws the ball at mid-height to catch. The Coach and GK2 throw the ball as soon as GK1 passes the cones.

B. GK1 moves freely in different directions (with the elastic band still around his ankles) to catch balls from the Coach in front, behind, right and left. The Coach can also throw low and high balls, so GK1 can practice all types of catching techniques.

Variation: Don't use a band: The legs must not be further apart than if the band was on.

Coaching Point: Move on the balls of the feet (front part of feet).

CHAPTER 9: Footwork

2. Sideways Movement and Catch with Jump

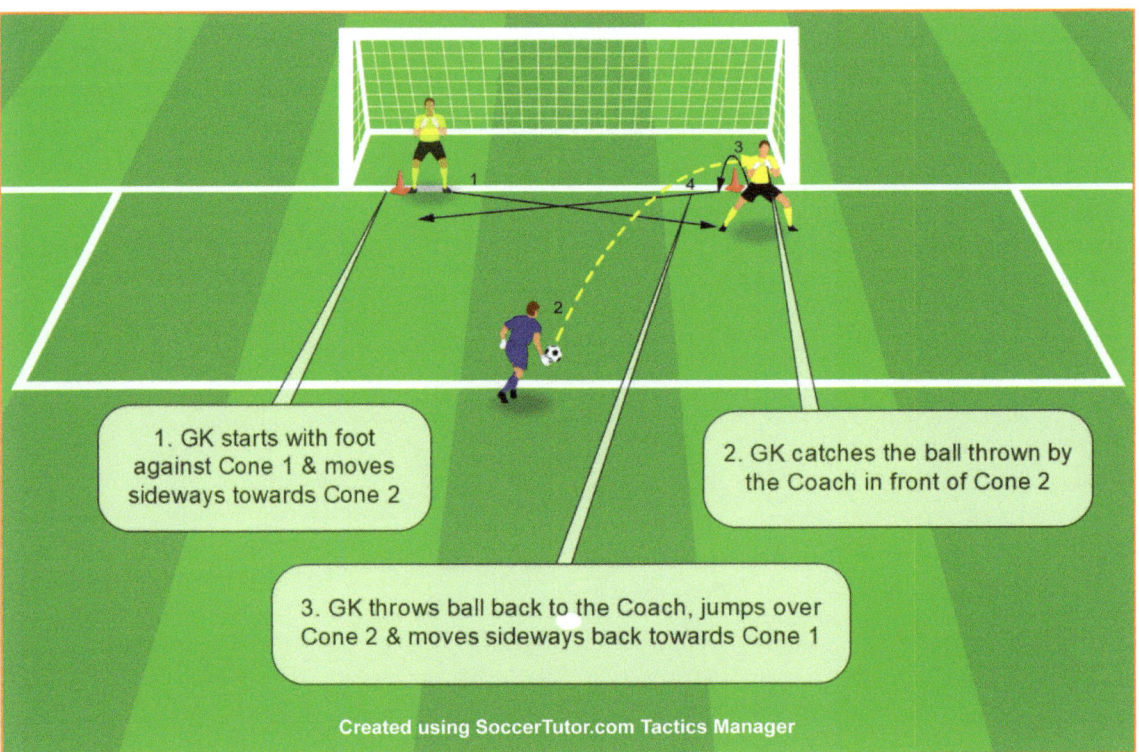

Description

1. The GK starts with his foot against Cone 1 and moves sideways towards Cone 2.
2. The GK catches the ball thrown by the Coach in front of Cone 2.
3. The GK throws the ball back to the Coach, jumps over Cone 2, lands with his feet close together and moves sideways back towards Cone 1.
4. Repeat the same sequence.

Variation: The GK starts from the other side (Cone 2).

Progression: More jumps before moving to the other cone.

Coaching Points

1. Move along the goal line.
2. As the GK moves sideways, the knees should be a little bent, he should be on the balls of his feet and the upper body should be straight.

CHAPTER 9: Footwork

3. Awareness and Quick Movements in Different Directions within a Square + Catch

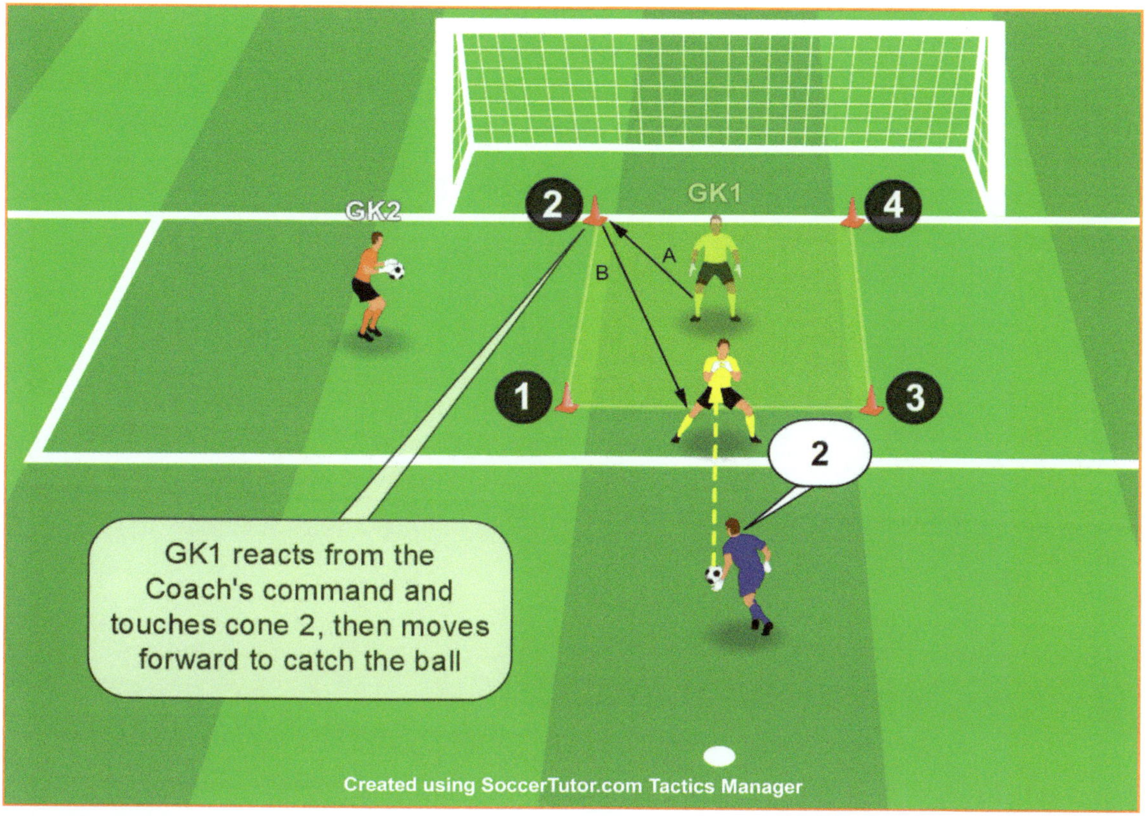

GK1 reacts from the Coach's command and touches cone 2, then moves forward to catch the ball

Description

- GK1 starts in the middle. Every cone has a number.
- The Coach calls out a number e.g. "2!"
- GK1 moves quickly to that cone, touches it and then moves forward between the cones to catch the ball out in front. GK1 throws the ball back and moves to the middle, waiting for the next command.
- Cones 1 and 2 are for the Coach to throw and cones 3 and 4 are for GK2 to throw.

Variation: Jump over cone instead of touching it and the Coach/GK2 can throw a high ball.

Progression: The Coach and GK2 kick the ball out of their hands, instead of throwing.

Coaching Points

1. Keep using small steps, even after touching the cone.
2. The cones should be close together.

©SoccerTutor.com   Goalkeeper Training Program - 120 Drills

CHAPTER 9: Footwork

4. Side-steps and Jumps in All Directions within a Square + Catch

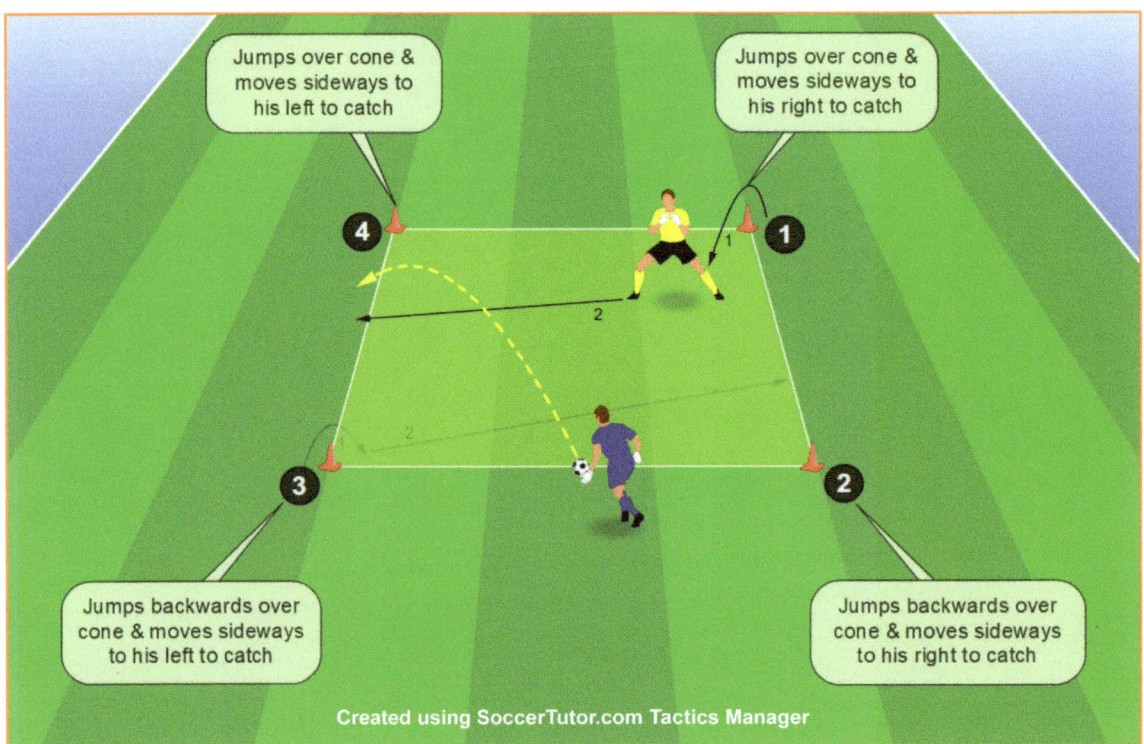

Description
- **Cone 1:** The GK jumps over Cone 1 and moves sideways to his right to catch the ball.
- **Cone 2:** The GK jumps backwards over Cone 2 and moves sideways to his right to catch.
- **Cone 3:** The GK jumps backwards over Cone 3 and moves sideways to his left to catch.
- **Cone 4:** The GK jumps over Cone 4 and moves sideways to his left to catch the ball.

Variations
1. Start in the middle and wait for the Coach to call out a number (1-4).
2. Change the numbers of the cones all the time (mental training).

Coaching Points
1. Land with the feet close together at all times.
2. After landing, don't stop: Immediately move across to the other side to catch the ball.
3. This is a high speed drill, but the quality of catching should be consistent throughout.

CHAPTER 9: Footwork

5. Speed and Coordination Training with a Ladder + Catch and Throw

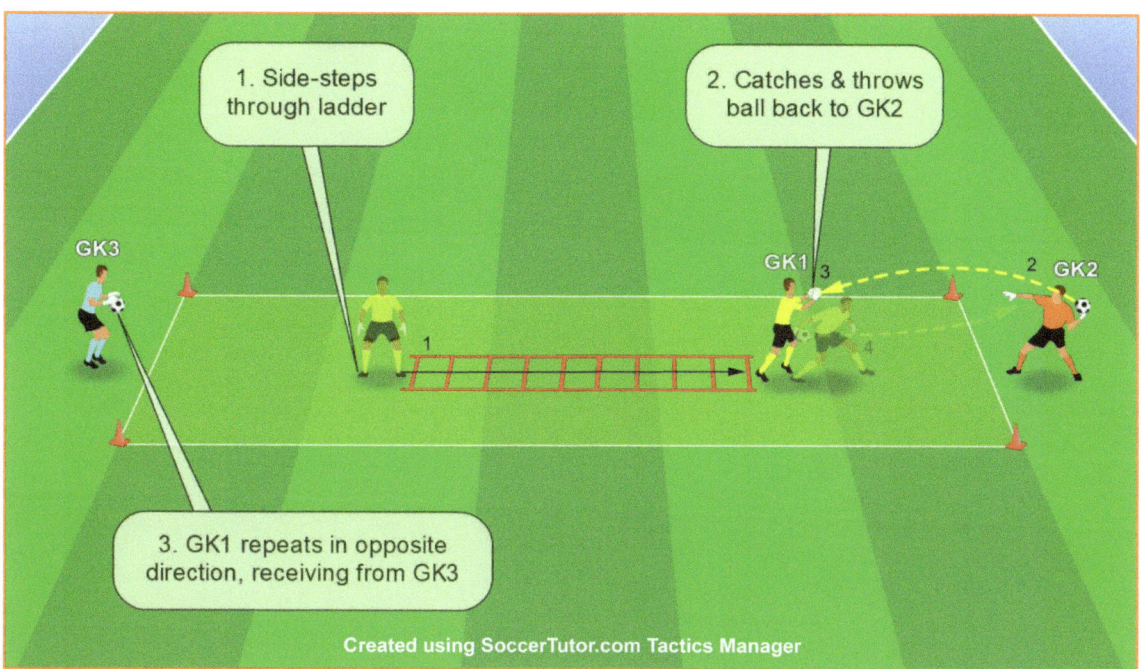

Description

1. GK1 moves with quick sideways steps through the ladder.
2. At the end, GK2 throws a ball for GK1 to catch. GK1 catches and throws the ball back.
3. GK1 repeats the same sequence in the opposite direction: Move through ladder, catch throw from GK3 and throw it back.

Variations

1. GK2 and GK3 kick the ball out of their hands, instead of throwing.
2. GK1 moves backwards through the ladder and turns at the end to catch.
3. GK1 is in the middle of the ladder and the Coach calls out whether he goes left or right.

Coaching Points

1. Only use the ladder for game-related steps of a GK.
2. When doing the steps through the ladder, always watch the ball.
3. Play at a high speed but with no more than 6 repetitions.

CHAPTER 9: Footwork

6. Turn, Big Step + Small Steps to Receive a Pass

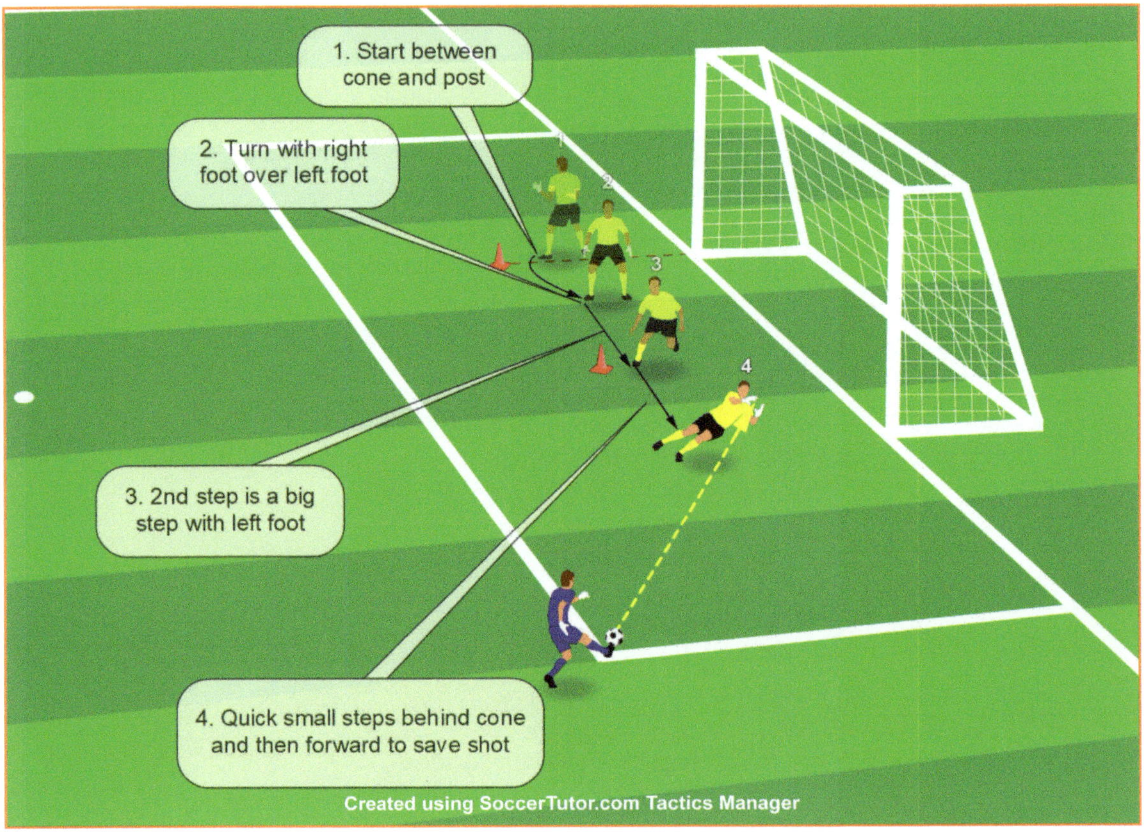

(Diagram labels: 1. Start between cone and post; 2. Turn with right foot over left foot; 3. 2nd step is a big step with left foot; 4. Quick small steps behind cone and then forward to save shot)

Description

1. The GK starts between the cone and the post, with his bodyweight planted on both feet.
2. He turns with his right foot moving over his left foot.
3. The GK's 2nd step is a big step with the left foot.
4. He takes quick small steps behind the cone and then forward to save the shot.

Variation: After turning, jump up (2 feet) and touch the crossbar in the middle of the goal.

Coaching Points

1. Starting position = When a player has the ball close to the goal line and close to the GK.
2. Get into the 2nd position as quickly as possible.
3. Be ready with 2 feet on the ground when the shot comes, even when you are not in the optimal position.

©SoccerTutor.com · Goalkeeper Training Program - 120 Drills

CHAPTER 9: Footwork

7. Quick Back-steps Towards Goal + Jump to Save

On the Coach's command, the GK takes quick backwards steps before making the save

Description

1. The GK starts in the start position just behind the cone with 1 foot in front of the other.
2. After the Coach's command (to go left or right), the GK steps back by crossing 1 foot over the other and with quick steps he moves backwards.
3. The Coach throws the ball over the head of the GK.
4. The GK's last step has to be big, in order to be able to jump with enough power to catch or tip the ball over the crossbar.

Progressions: (1) The Coach can also throw a short ball and the GK has to catch it before it touches the ground. (2) The Coach can also shoot from his hands or from the ground.

Coaching Point: This starting position should be used when the ball is far away from the goal. It enables the GK to move quickly forward, but also quickly backwards towards the goal when the ball is played over his head.

CHAPTER 9: Footwork

8. Sprinting with Different Types of Resistance

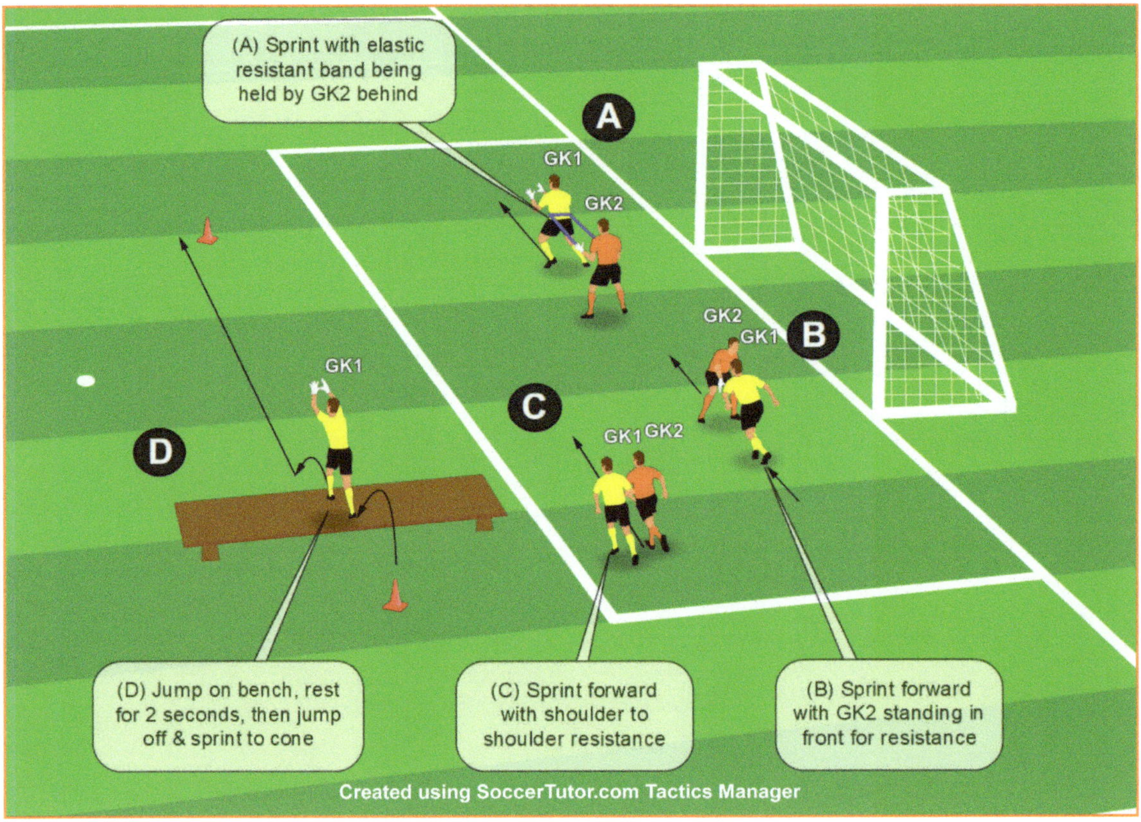

Description

A. GK1 sprints forward with an elastic resistant band around the waist, which is being held by GK2 from behind.

B. GK1 sprints forward with GK2 standing in front (moving slowly back) for resistance.

C. GK1 sprints forward with shoulder to shoulder resistance from GK2.

D. GK1 jumps onto the bench, rests for 2 seconds, then jumps off and sprints to the cone.

* After 2 repetitions, switch the role of the GKs.

Coaching Points

1. When you train sprint resistance, the GKs should already be warmed up. Also, don't train sprint resistance at the end of a session when the GK is tired and more prone to injury.

2. Both GKs should be fully focussed and concentrating, not only the one sprinting.

©SoccerTutor.com   Goalkeeper Training Program - 120 Drills

CHAPTER 9: Footwork

9. Sprint Out of the Penalty Area Towards the Ball and Accurate Chip Pass

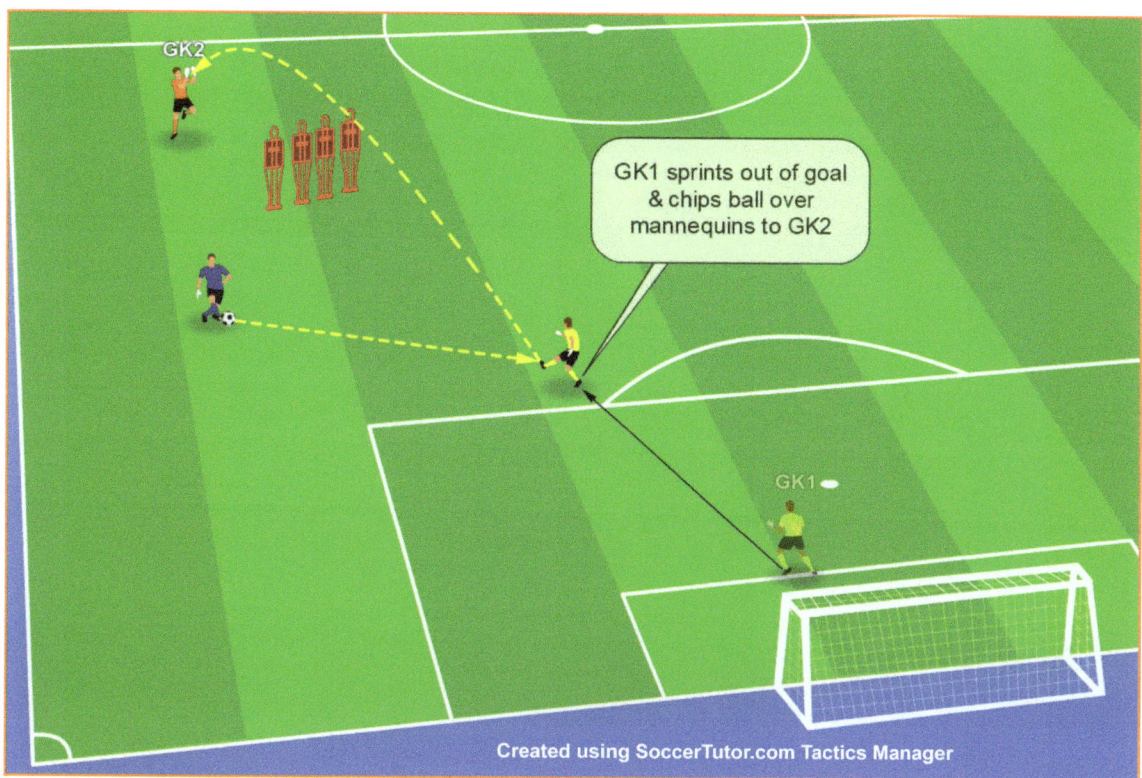

Description

1. The Coach plays a short pass to just outside the penalty area.
2. From a starting position inside the 6-yard box, GK1 sprints out of his goal and towards the ball outside the penalty area.
3. GK1 kicks the ball (with his 1st touch) over the mannequins and into the hands of GK2.

Variation: Position the mannequins closer to the penalty area, the Coach throws up a high ball and GK1 heads the ball over the mannequins and into GK2's hands.

Coaching Points

1. Placing 1 foot in front of the other allows you to immediately put the power on your leg and foot to sprint at maximum speed.
2. Ball on the left side = left foot in front / Ball on the right side = right foot in front.
3. Heading is also an important technique that GKs need to practice and use. When heading the ball outside of the penalty area, head it to the side.

CHAPTER 9: Footwork

10. Different Types of Footwork and Catching Techniques within a 6-Yard Box Circuit

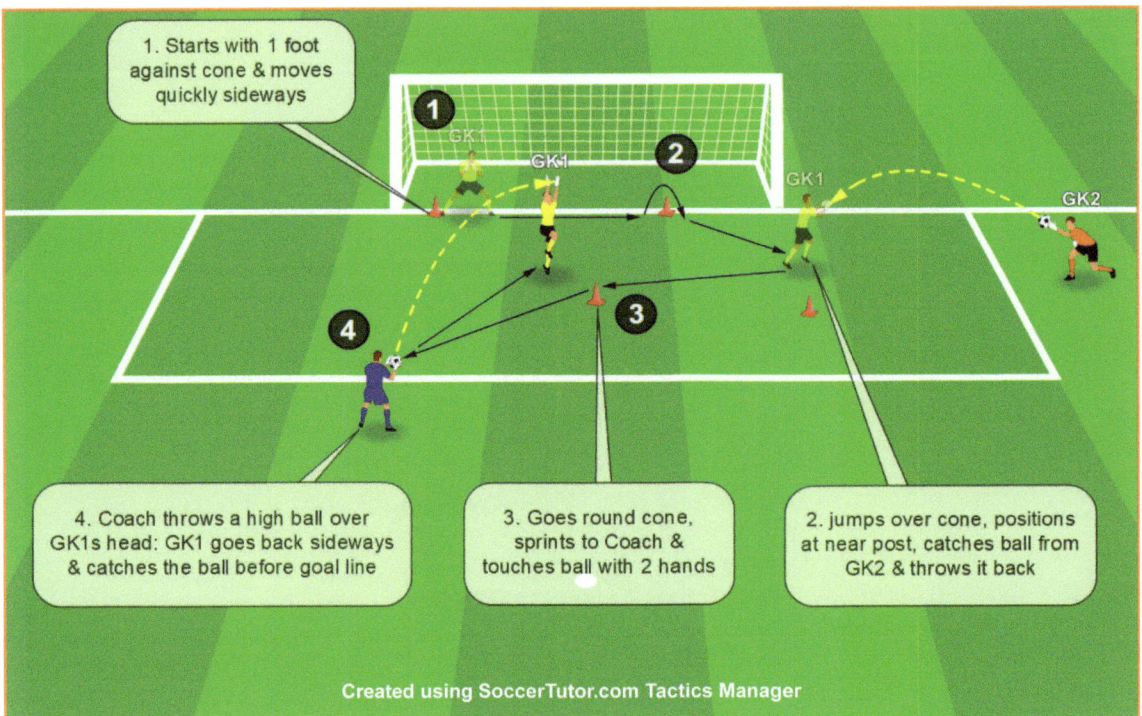

Description

1. GK1 starts with 1 foot against the cone and moves quickly sideways (side-steps).
2. GK1 jumps over the cone, moves into a position at the near post, catches the ball thrown by GK2 and throws it back to him.
3. GK1 crosses 1 leg over the other to turn, runs around the cone, sprints to the Coach and touches the ball with 2 hands.
4. The Coach throws a high ball over GK1's head. GK1 moves back quickly using side-steps, jumps and catches the ball at its highest point and before it reaches the goal line.

Coaching Points

1. Many footwork elements from the other drills in this section are integrated here.
2. Use a maximum of 4 repetitions, depending on the age/level of the GK.
3. This is a high speed drill, so make sure to allow enough rest time between the sets.

CHAPTER 10

DISTRIBUTION

CHAPTER 10: Distribution

1. Practicing Various Distribution Techniques (Long Kick, Drop Kick, Rolling Ball, Overarm Throw)

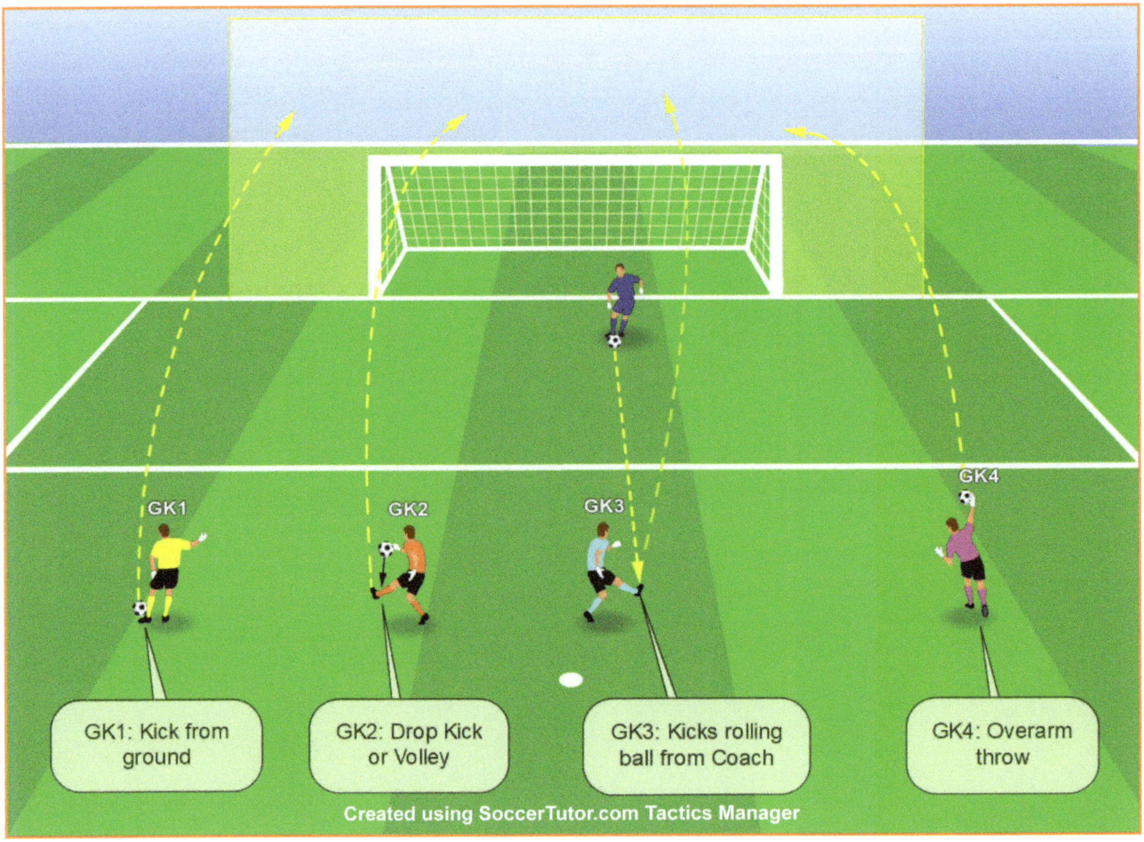

Description

The GKs practice the following techniques while targeting a fence behind the goal:

1. Kicking from the ground
2. Drop-kicks, half-volleys or volleys.
3. Kicking a rolling ball passed by the Coach.
4. Overarm throws.

Progression: The GKs try to kick/throw at the exact same position on the fence each time.

Coaching Points

1. GKs should practice this in their own time before training or after training.
2. When you increase the distance between the GK and the fence, the position the ball hits should still remain the same.

CHAPTER 10: Distribution

2. Accurate Distribution Through Channels in a Competitive 1 v 1 Game

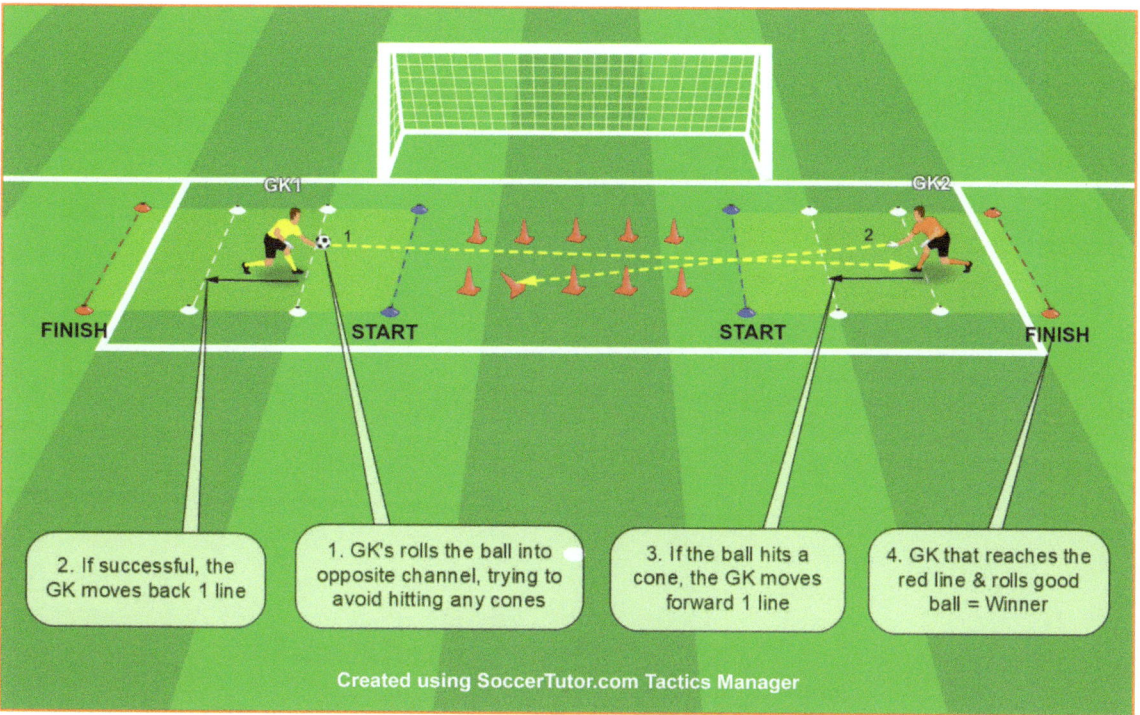

Description

1. Both GKs start at the front line (blue cones). GK1 starts with the ball and rolls it between the cones to the opposite channel.
2. If GK1 rolls it successfully and doesn't hit any cones, he can move back 1 line. GK2 also starts at the front line (blue cones) and has the exact same objective.
3. If a GK makes a mistake and hits a cone, he must move forward to the next line (like GK2 in the diagram example).
4. The GK that reaches line D first and rolls a good ball from behind this line is the winner.

Variation: Play with feet (you can make the distance between the cones wider).

Coaching Points

1. The ball has to leave the hands close to the ground = No bounce.
2. Gather the ball with 1 foot in front of the other but never put 1 knee on the ground, as this limits movement.
3. Practicing with a competitive game will automatically increase the concentration.

CHAPTER 10: Distribution

3. Hitting Targets: Rolling, Throwing and Kicking

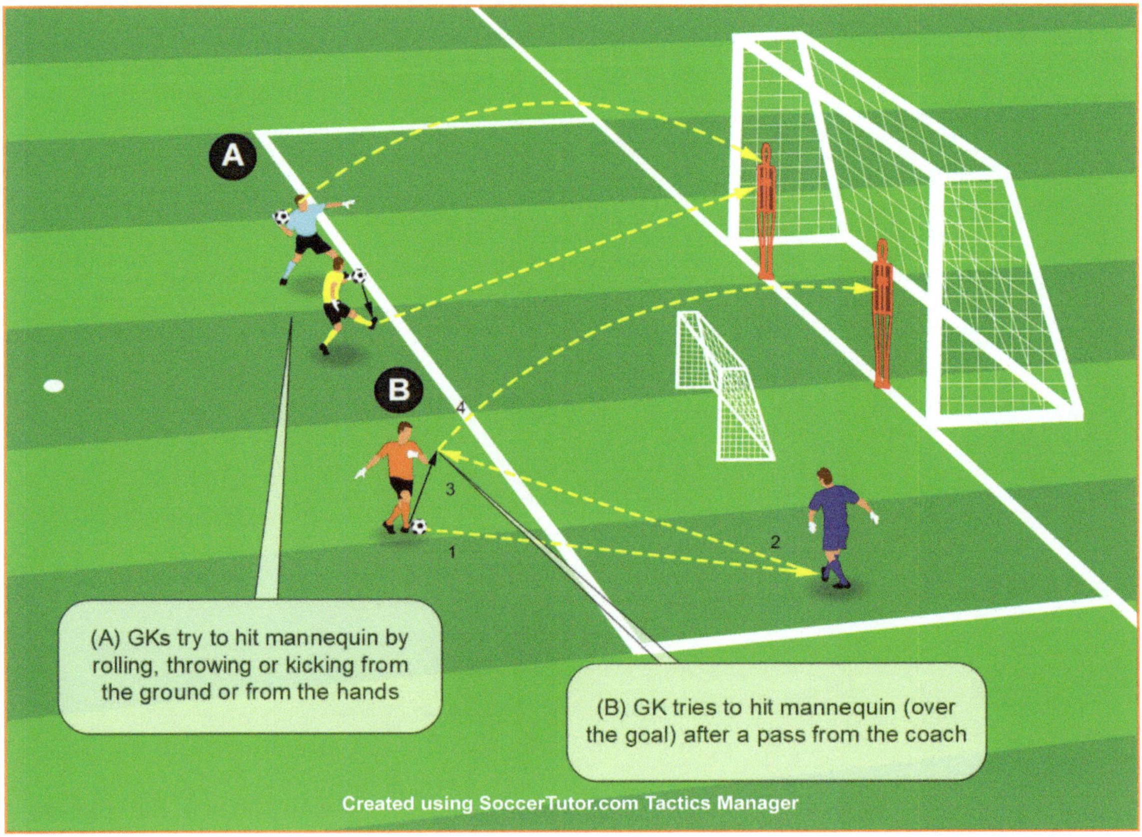

(A) GKs try to hit mannequin by rolling, throwing or kicking from the ground or from the hands

(B) GK tries to hit mannequin (over the goal) after a pass from the coach

Description

A. The GKs try to hit the mannequin in the goal. They can roll the ball, throw it, kick it from the ground or from the hands.

B. GKs try to hit the mannequin (over the mini goal) after a pass from the Coach.

Variation: Make a game between the GKs, who score 1 point each time they hit the target.

Coaching Points

1. Before throwing, bring the ball back with your arm outstretched.
2. The other arm is also outstretched in front and goes down when the ball leaves the back arm. Both arms work like a "windmill."
3. When kicking from the ground, make sure to practice using both feet.

Goalkeeper Training Program - 120 Drills

CHAPTER 10: Distribution

4. Accurate Passing into Small Goals

Description

1. GK1 passes along the ground to GK2 outside the penalty area.
2. GK2 passes first time to the Coach with his right foot.
3. The Coach passes back to GK2 to the right side and GK2 moves across.
4. GK2 passes into the bottom right mini goal with his right foot.
5. The Coach moves to the other side and we repeat the same drill, but now GK2 only uses his left foot and passes into the mini goal in the bottom left corner.

* Each goalkeeper gets 10 attempts - the GK with the most goals wins (loser does 10 push-ups).

Variation: GK2 tries to score in the space above the mini goals (between pole and post).

Coaching Points

1. This is a game that needs high concentration levels.
2. Play a strong ball with confidence.
3. GK2 has to play the ball while it is still rolling.

©SoccerTutor.com Goalkeeper Training Program - 120 Drills

CHAPTER 10: Distribution

5. Goal Kick, Drop Kick and Catch in a 3-GK Group

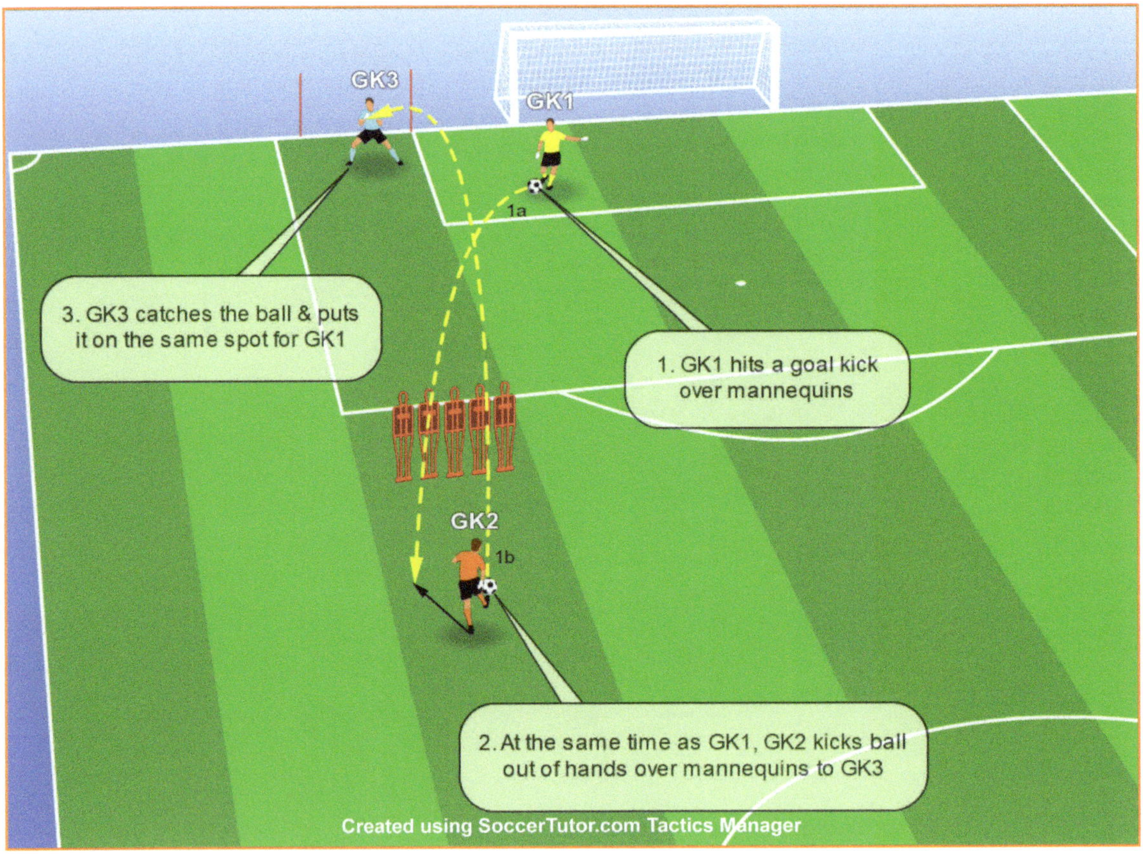

Description

1. GK1 hits a goal kick over the mannequins (1a).

2. At the same time GK1 kicks the 1st ball, GK2 kicks the 2nd ball out of his hands (drop-kick or volley) over the mannequins, to GK3 (1b).

3. After kicking the ball, GK2 must be alert to try and catch GK1's goal kick. GK3 catches the 2nd ball from GK2 and puts it on the spot for GK1 to restart.

Coaching Points

1. For lower ages/level, work with just 1 ball. GK2 catches the goal kick and kicks it to GK3.

2. When working with 2 balls, first concentrate on the kick and then react to the 2nd ball.

3. GK3 should catch the ball with the proper technique.

©SoccerTutor.com — Goalkeeper Training Program - 120 Drills

CHAPTER 10: Distribution

6. Catch, Throw Out, One-Two and Long Kick in a Dynamic Circuit

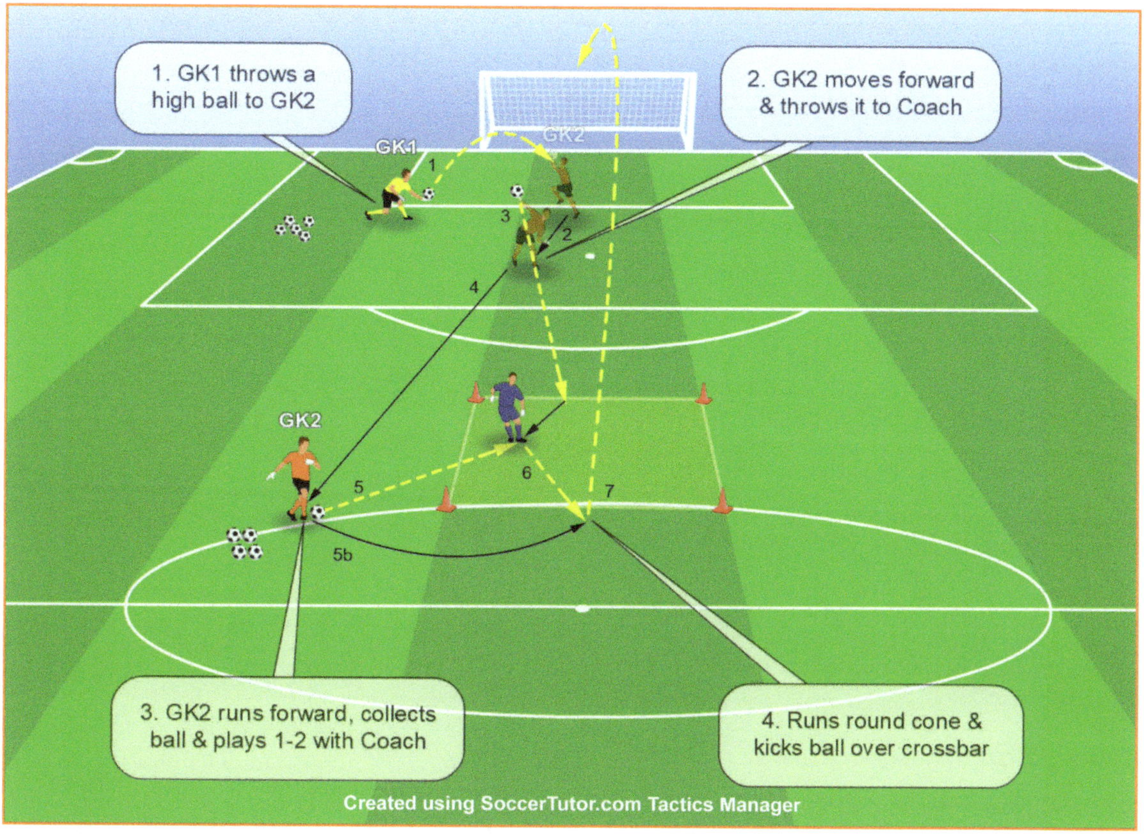

![Diagram of drill setup]

1. GK1 throws a high ball to GK2
2. GK2 moves forward & throws it to Coach
3. GK2 runs forward, collects ball & plays 1-2 with Coach
4. Runs round cone & kicks ball over crossbar

Description

1. GK1 throws a high ball for GK2 to jump and catch.
2. GK2 moves forward and throws the ball to the Coach.
3. GK2 runs forward to collect the ball and plays a 1-2 with the Coach.
4. GK2 runs outside the cones to receive the return pass and kicks the ball over the crossbar.

Variation: GK2 can use a drop-kick or volley to the Coach.

Coaching Points

1. The distance to the goal depends on the age and/or quality of the GK.
2. Make sure the GKs also practice using their weaker foot. When playing with the weaker foot, the distance to the goal should be reduced.

CHAPTER 10: Distribution

7. Accurate Overarm Throws to the Left, Right and Centre

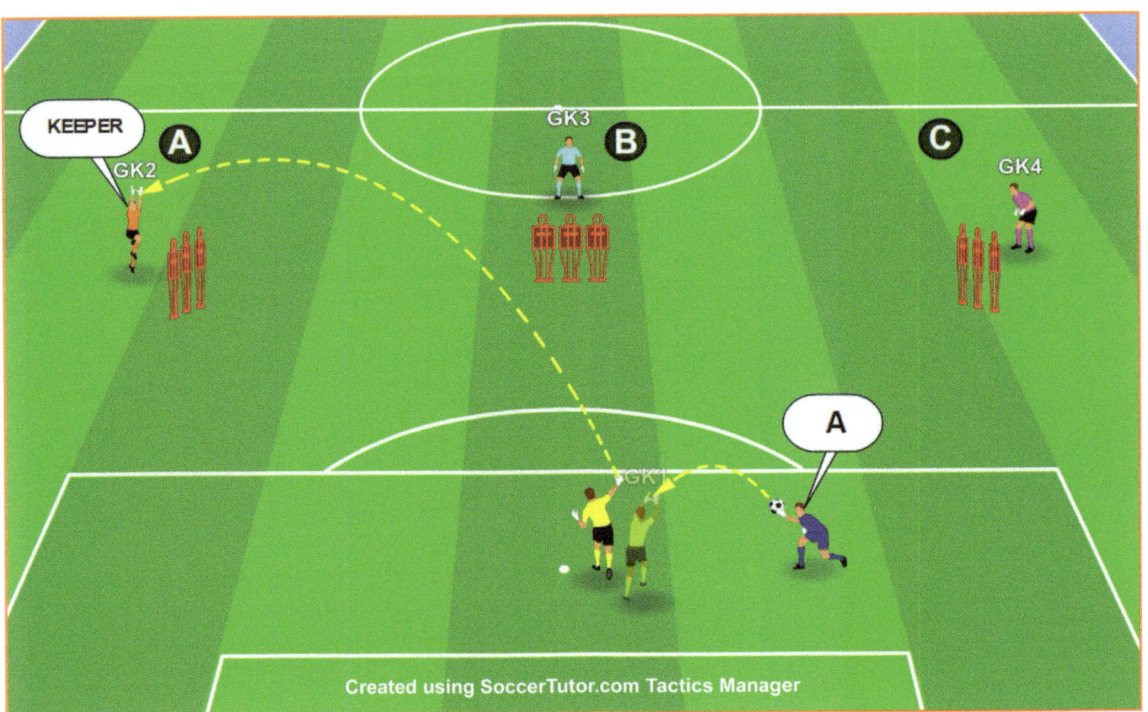

Description

1. The Coach throws a high ball for GK1 to jump up and catch.
2. The Coach then calls out a command (A, B or C) and GK1 throws the ball over the mannequins to the correct GK e.g. GK2 in the diagram example.
3. GK2 catches the ball.

Variation: The Coach can also kick the ball from the hands, instead of throwing.

Progression: GK1 gets a rolling ball from the Coach and kicks the ball off the ground.

Coaching Points

1. Balls should not only be played over the mannequins, but also into the hands of the GKs.
2. GK2, GK3 and GK4 have to shout "Keeper" before the ball goes over the mannequins.
3. For kicks from the ground, you should practice using both feet, but kicks from the hands or throws should always be with the strongest arm or foot.

©SoccerTutor.com   Goalkeeper Training Program - 120 Drills

CHAPTER 10: Distribution

8. "Piggy in the Middle" Distribution Game

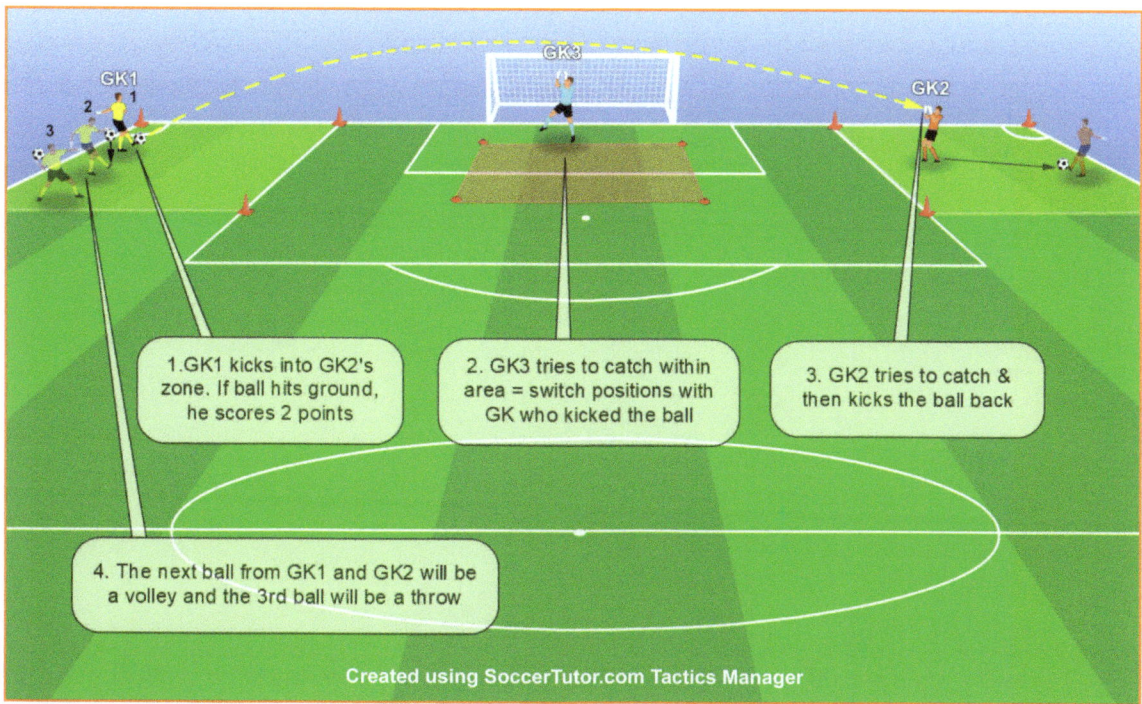

Description

1. GK1 starts round 1 with a "goal kick" from the side-line into GK2's zone on the other side. GK2 tries to catch it. If the ball hits the ground within GK2's zone, GK1 scores 2 points.

2. Every ball has to be high enough so that GK3 cannot catch it within his area. If GK3 catches the ball, he swaps positions immediately with the GK who kicked the ball.

3. GK2 tries to catch the ball and then has the same aim in the opposite direction.

4. For round 2, GK1 and GK2 both use a volley and they throw the ball for round 3.

* Every time a GK misses the other GK's zone, 1 point goes to their opponent. The first GK to score 10 points is the winner. The loser switches positions with GK3.

Coaching Points

1. The age/level of the GKs determines the size of the area you should use.
2. Lower ages/levels should simply concentrate on one technique, like throws or volleys.

©SoccerTutor.com

Goalkeeper Training Program - 120 Drills

CHAPTER 10: Distribution

9. Different Distribution Techniques in a 5-Part Points Game

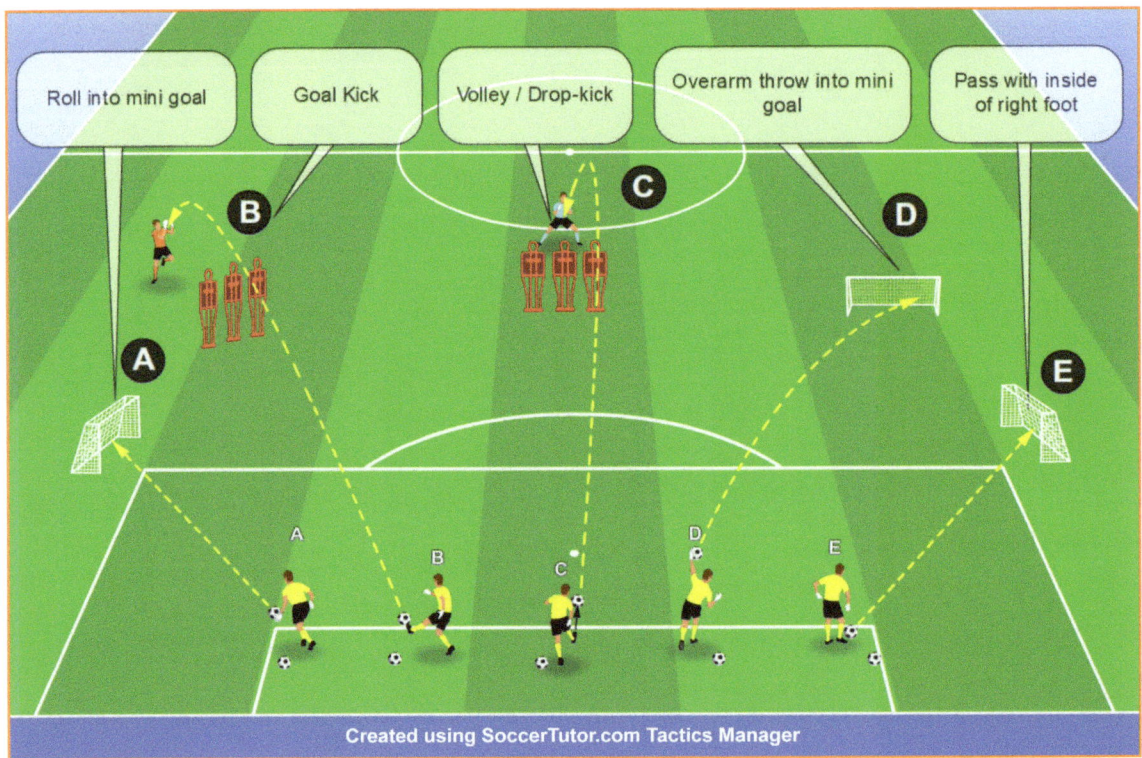

Description

The GKs have to play 5 balls as fast as they can and the fastest GK wins.

A. GK starts with the ball in his hands and rolls it into the mini goal.

B. Goal kick over the mannequins for the orange GK to catch.

C. Volley or drop-kick over the mannequins for the blue GK to catch.

D. Overarm throw into the mini goal.

E. GK uses his right foot to pass into the net (switch the techniques of A and E to practice with the left foot).

Coaching Points

1. GK starts with 1 ball in his hand and the 4 other balls are already lying in position.

2. You can complete 2 rounds in a row (9 balls are lying in position for the GK).

CHAPTER 10: Distribution

10. Short and Long Distribution in a Circuit Points Game

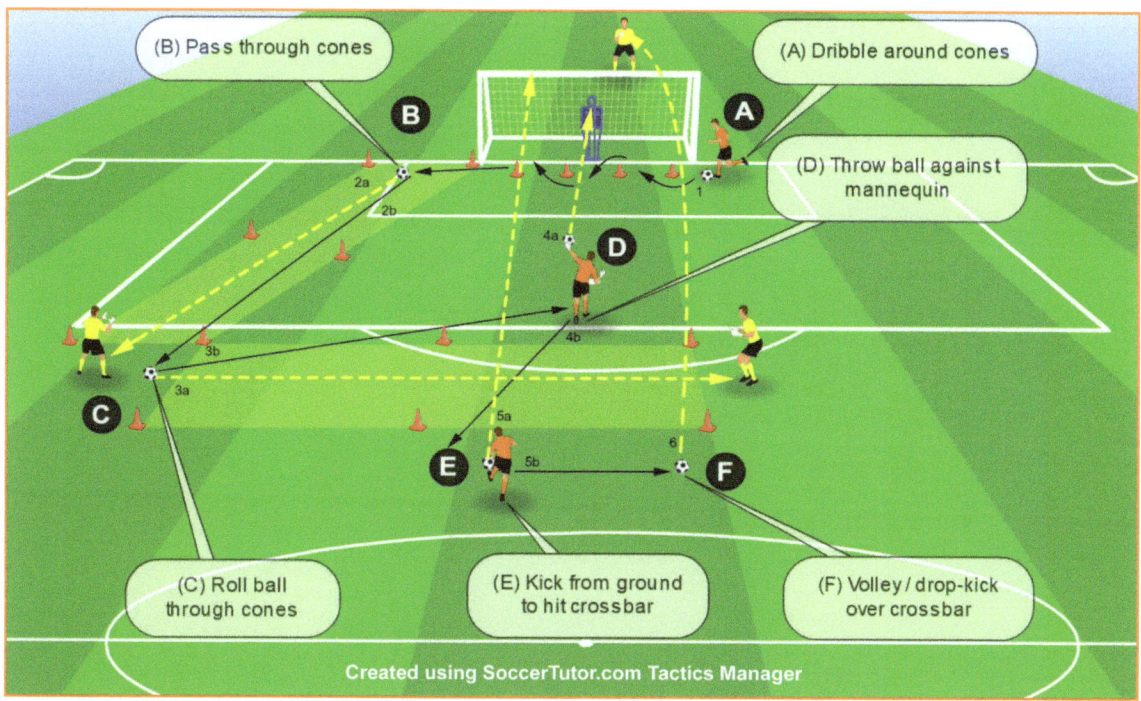

Description

This distribution circuit is time based and the fastest GK wins.

A. Dribble around the cones (Mistake = add 5 seconds to time).

B. Pass ball with inside of foot through the cones (Mistake = add 5 seconds to time).

C. Roll ball between the cones (Mistake = add 5 seconds to time).

D. Throw the ball against the mannequin (Hit = 5 seconds off time).

E. Hit the crossbar by kicking a ball from the ground (Hit = 5 seconds off time).

F. Kick the ball with a volley/drop-kick over the crossbar (Mistake = add 5 seconds to time).

G. Sprint to the mannequin and touch it to stop the time.

Coaching Points

1. Instead of a mannequin, you can use other objects.
2. The other GKs are helping in different positions (B, C and behind the goal).
3. You can set up the same circuit on the other side of the pitch.
4. The first round is a trial and then it is a competitive game. Losers do sit-ups and push-ups.

CHAPTER 11

DRILLS WITH OUTFIELD PLAYERS

CHAPTER 11: Drills with Outfield Players

1. Catching Aerial Balls in the 6-Yard Box

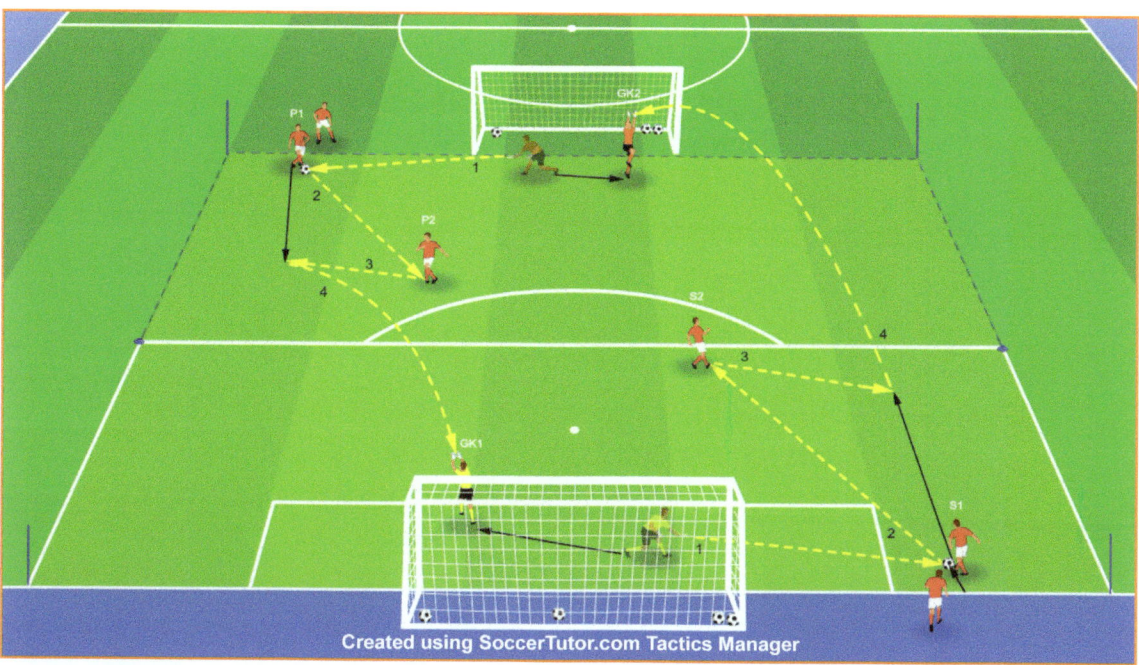

Description

1. GK2 rolls the ball out to P1.
2. P1 plays a 1-2 combination with P2.
3. P1 moves forward to receive the return pass.
4. P1 kicks the ball (in the air) into the hands of GK1.
5. The drill runs simultaneously on the other side in the direction of GK2 and starts with GK1 rolling the ball to S1.

Variation: P1 and S1 kick a low ball to the near or far corner.

Progression: P1 and S1 try to score with a shot.

Coaching Points

1. Working with outfield players is the ultimate test for the GKs, to see if they can use all the techniques under pressure.
2. This training drill is also important for the outfield players, who practice playing the ball to a specific area of the goal.

CHAPTER 11: Drills with Outfield Players

2a. Throwing the Ball Out and Catching Headers in the 6-Yard Box

P1 heads the ball up for P2 to head the ball to GK2

Description

1. GK1 throws the ball up to P1.
2. P1 heads the ball across for P2.
3. P2 moves forward from the cone and heads the ball into the hands of GK2.
4. GK2 starts, throws to P1 and P2 will head the ball into GK1's hands on the opposite side.
5. Switch P1 and P2 and repeat.

Progression: P2 tries to score with the header. The GK must react and make the appropriate type of save.

Coaching Points

1. Make sure the distance between the goals is not too big (consider the age/level).
2. Beginners can throw the ball with 2 hands.
3. If the header goes wide or over, that player has to do 5 push-ups.

©SoccerTutor.com

Goalkeeper Training Program - 120 Drills

CHAPTER 11: Drills with Outfield Players

2b. Rolling the Ball Out and Saving First Time Shots After Lay-Off

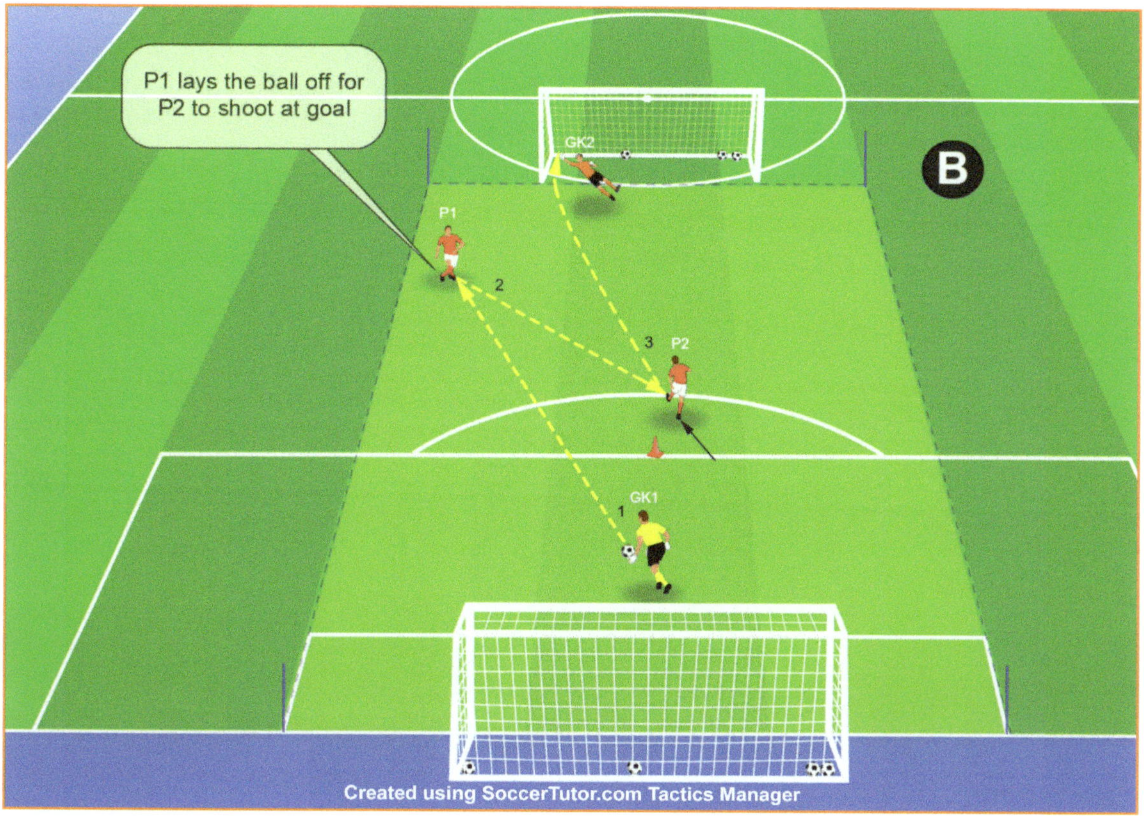

Description

1. In this variation of drill 2a, GK1 rolls the ball out to P1.
2. P1 lays the ball back to P2.
3. P2 moves forward from the cone and shoots at goal. GK2 must try to save.
4. GK2 starts and rolls the ball to P1, who will lay-off for P2 to shoot at GK1's goal on the opposite side.
5. Switch P1 and P2 and repeat.

Coaching Points

1. Position the goals further apart than in the last drill when the players were heading.
2. If the shot goes wide or over, that player has to do 5 push-ups.

CHAPTER 11: Drills with Outfield Players

3. 2 GKs (+2 Players) vs 2 Players in a Dynamic 2 Goal Possession Game

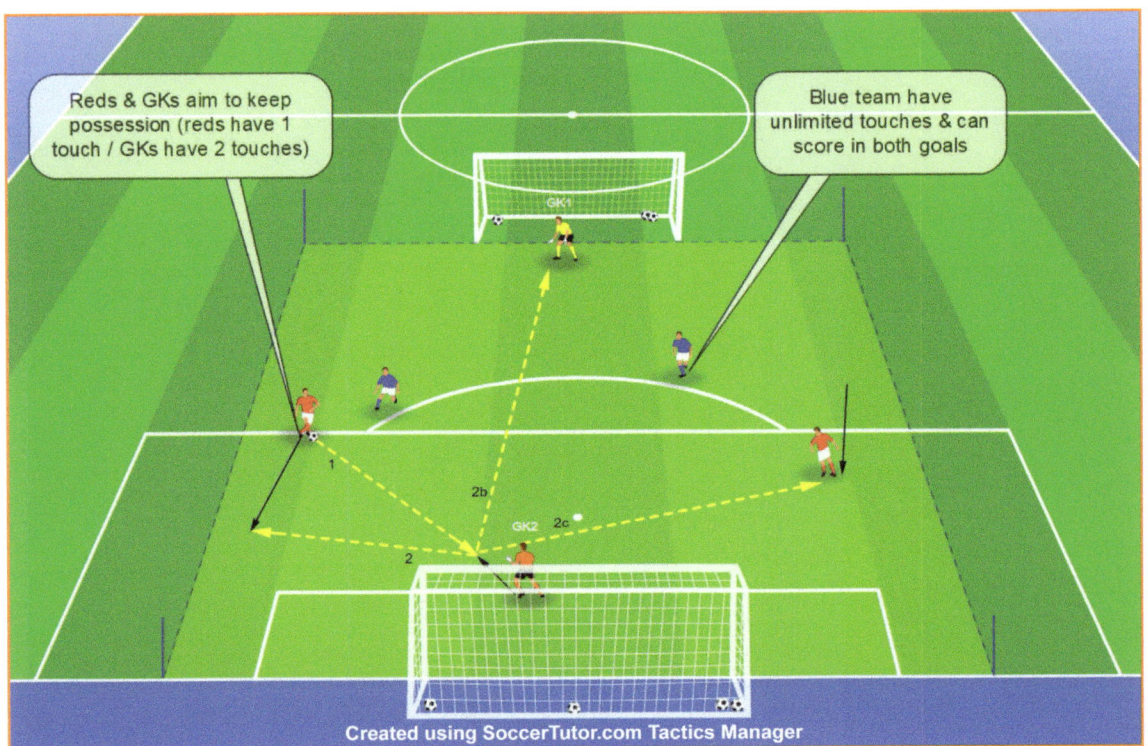

Description

- 2 GKs and 2 red outfield players play against 2 blue outfield players. The GKs and red players aim to keep possession within the area.
- The red players are limited to 1 touch and the GKs can use 2 touches.
- The blue team try to win the ball and then score in either goal. The blue players have unlimited touches.

Progression: Restrict the GKs to 1 touch, depending on their age/level.

Coaching Points

1. Both GKs need to coach the outfield players and always create a free passing line when asking for the ball.
2. GKs: Don't play the ball when there is no pressure from the blue players!
3. When losing the ball, the 2 red outfield players should move inside to defend the goal.
4. If the ball goes out, the blue team take a free ball from the middle of the pitch.

CHAPTER 11: Drills with Outfield Players

4. Dynamic Goalkeeper to Goalkeeper Rondo Possession Game

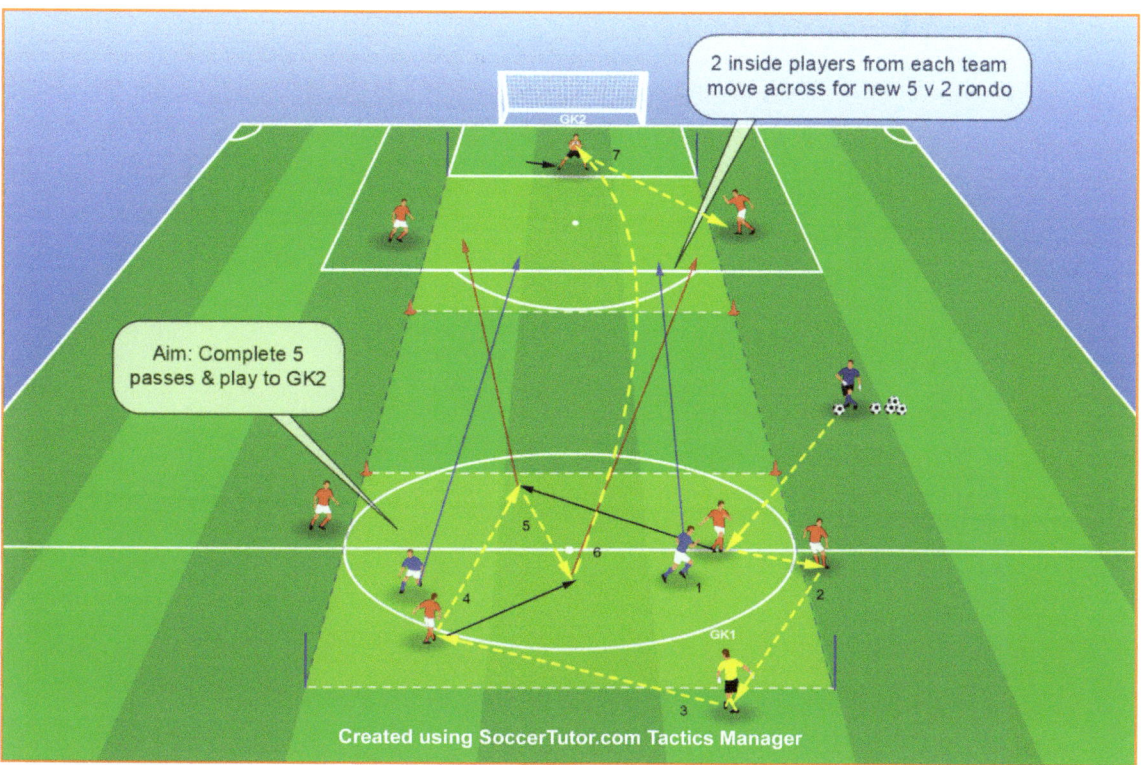

Description

- GK1 plays a 5 v 2 rondo possession game with 2 red players inside and 2 outside. The 2 blue inside players try to win the ball (1 point).

- The aim is to complete 5 passes and then play a long pass to GK2 (1 point).

- The 2 red inside players and 2 blue players move across to the other side. We play the same rondo possession game, with the aim to complete 5 passes and play back to GK1.

Variation: Only GK1 and GK2 can play the long pass to the other side.

Coaching Points

1. This is high intensity for the red and blue inside players, so change these players every 2 minutes (maximum).
2. The GKs have to create a free passing line to receive. When the ball is played to the GK, the red players then need to create a free passing line.
3. When the GK has to play the long pass, the back pass should be slow.

CHAPTER 11: Drills with Outfield Players

5. Distribution and Catching within a Passing Combination Drill

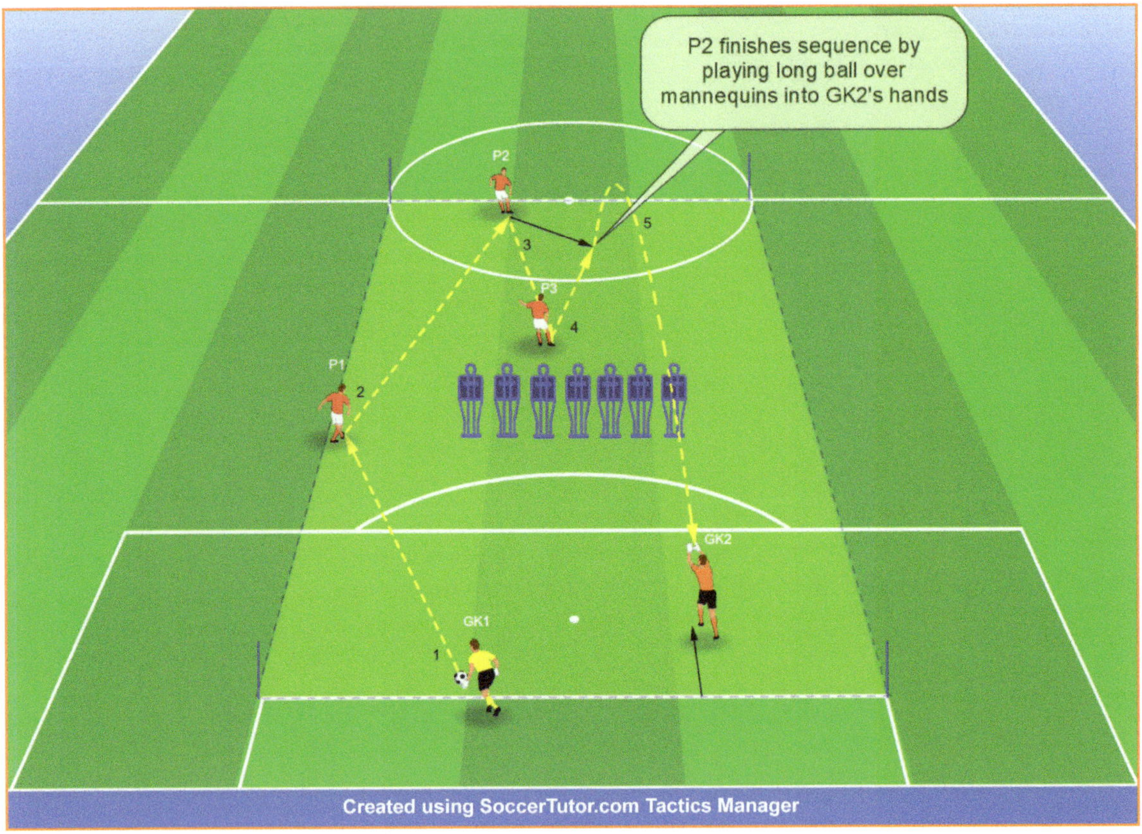

![Diagram showing drill setup with P2 finishing sequence by playing long ball over mannequins into GK2's hands]

Description
- GK1 rolls the ball to P1 and P1 passes to P2, who plays a 1-2 combination with P3.
- The sequence is completed with P2's long pass over the mannequins into GK2's hands.
- GK1 and GK2 switch positions and the sequence is repeated.

Variations
1. Play on the other side - P2's long pass is hit with the other foot.
2. Adjust the height of the mannequins (or any obstacle) depending on the age/level.

Coaching Points
1. This drill can be done with 4 or 5 goalkeepers instead of using outfield players.
2. GK2 has to call out "Keeper" before the ball crosses over the mannequins.
3. P1 has 2 touches, P2 and P3 use just 1 touch.

CHAPTER 11: Drills with Outfield Players

6a. Sprinting Out of Goal to Win the Ball in a 1 v 1 Against an Oncoming Attacker

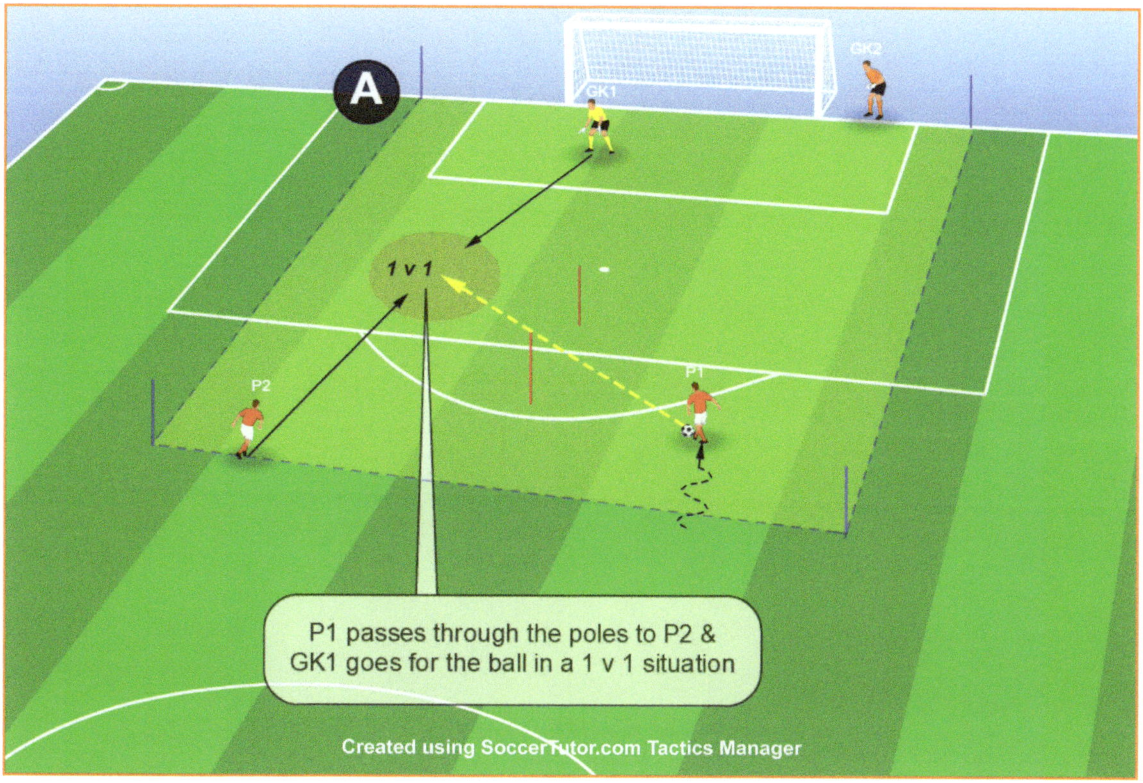

P1 passes through the poles to P2 & GK1 goes for the ball in a 1 v 1 situation

Description

1. P1 starts by dribbling the ball forward and passing through the poles for P2 to run onto.
2. P2 runs forward with the aim of getting to the ball first and scoring in a 1 v 1.
3. GK1 sprints out of goal and goes for the ball in this 1 v 1 situation. If P2 scores, he gets 1 point. If he doesn't, GK1 scores 1 point.
4. The outfield players and GKs both switch positions and we play again. This time, it will be P1 against GK2 in a 1 v 1.

Coaching Points

1. The starting point for P1 and P2 is at the edge of the marked out area.
2. Position the poles in such a way that allows the GK time to sprint out and go for the ball.
3. This drill can also be done by 2 teams of 2 GKs.

CHAPTER 11: Drills with Outfield Players

6b. Sprinting Out of Goal to Close the Angle for an Oncoming Attacker

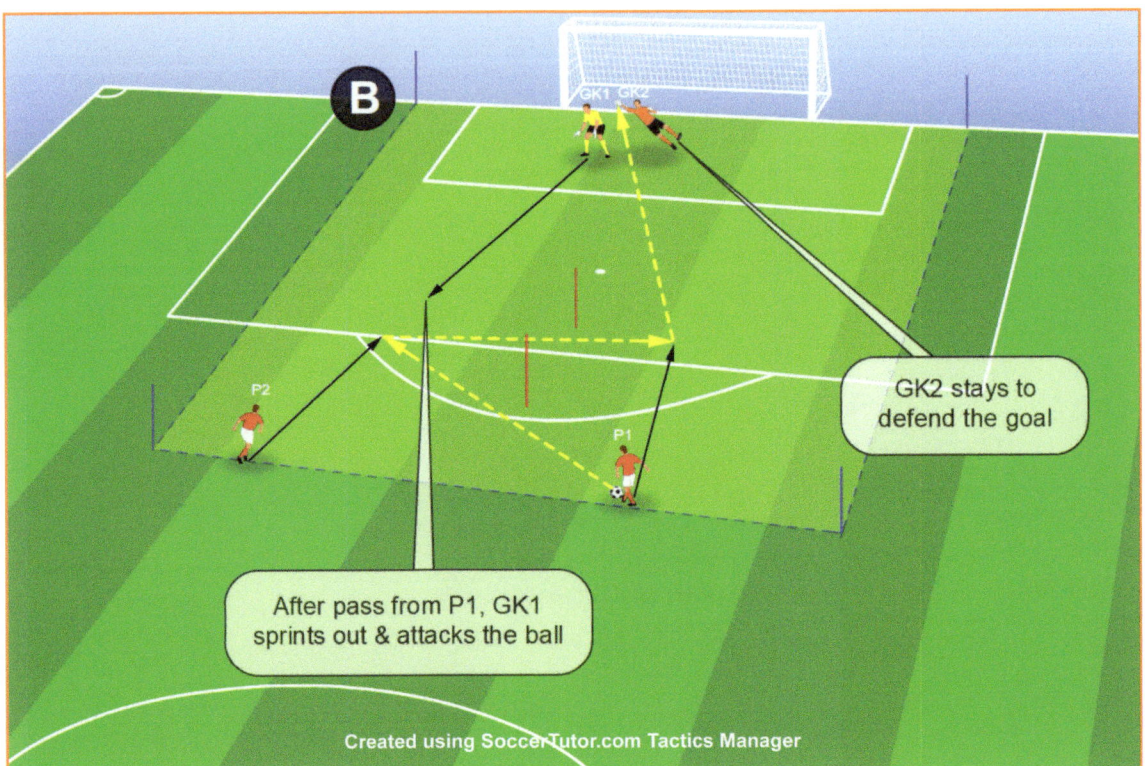

Description

- In this variation of drill 6a (previous page), both GKs are now active.
- The drill starts with P1's pass for P2 to run onto.
- From this point, P2 can either move forward for a 1 v 1 with GK1 or pass through the poles for P1 to run onto (as shown in the diagram example).
- GK1 sprints out of goal to close off the angle and prevent P2 from scoring, while GK2 stays back to defend the goal.
- If the outfield players score, they get 1 point and if they don't, the GKs score 1 point.

Coaching Points

1. The starting point for P1 and P2 is at the edge of the marked out area.
2. GK2 is behind and closer to goal, so has to coach GK1 as to what to do.
3. This drill can also be done by 2 teams of 2 GKs.

©SoccerTutor.com · Goalkeeper Training Program - 120 Drills

CHAPTER 11: Drills with Outfield Players

7a. 1 v 1 Against Attacker from Either Side

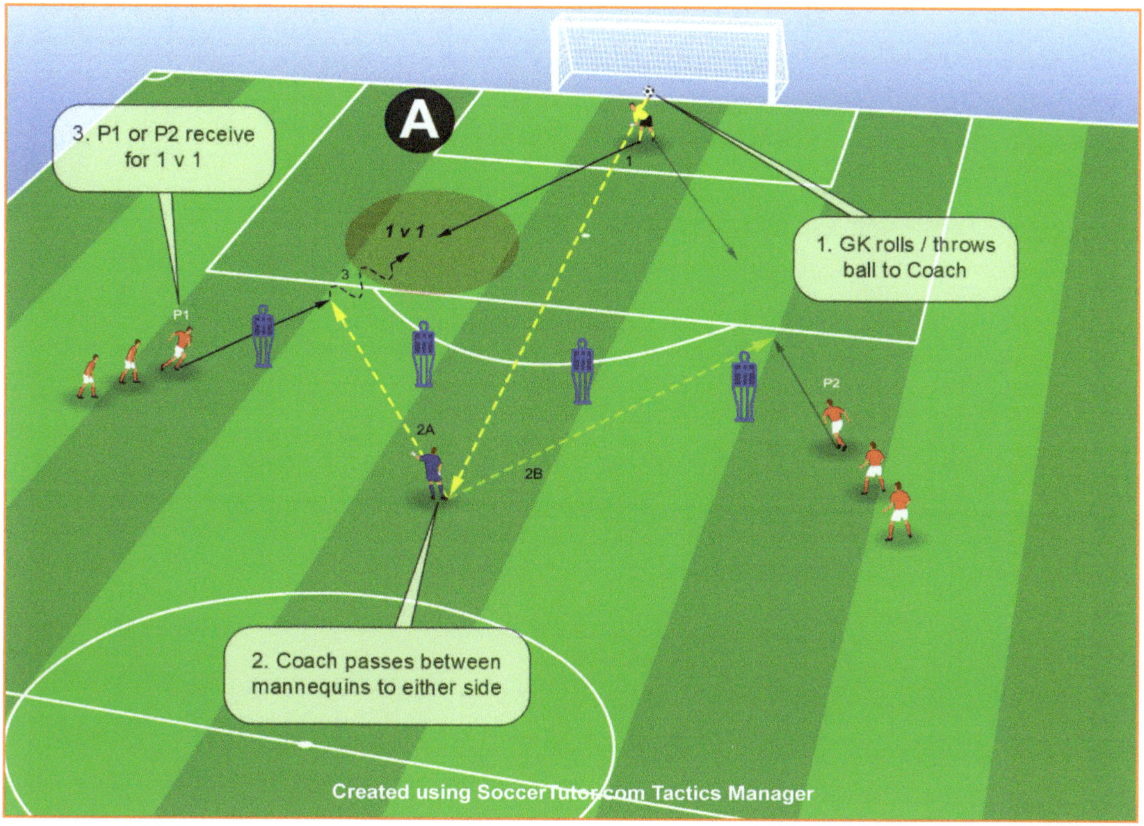

![drill diagram]

Description

1. The GK rolls or throws the ball to the Coach.
2. The Coach passes the ball through the mannequins to either side (Coach decides).
3. The player that receives (P1 in diagram example) goes into a 1 v 1 against the GK, who moves out of goal to contest the attacker.

Coaching Points

1. The GK starts with 1 foot in front of the other and away from the goal line, but still in control of the space behind him.
2. Instead of mannequins, you can use poles or cones.

CHAPTER 11: Drills with Outfield Players

7b. Protecting the Goal Against 2 Attackers with the Help of 1 Defender

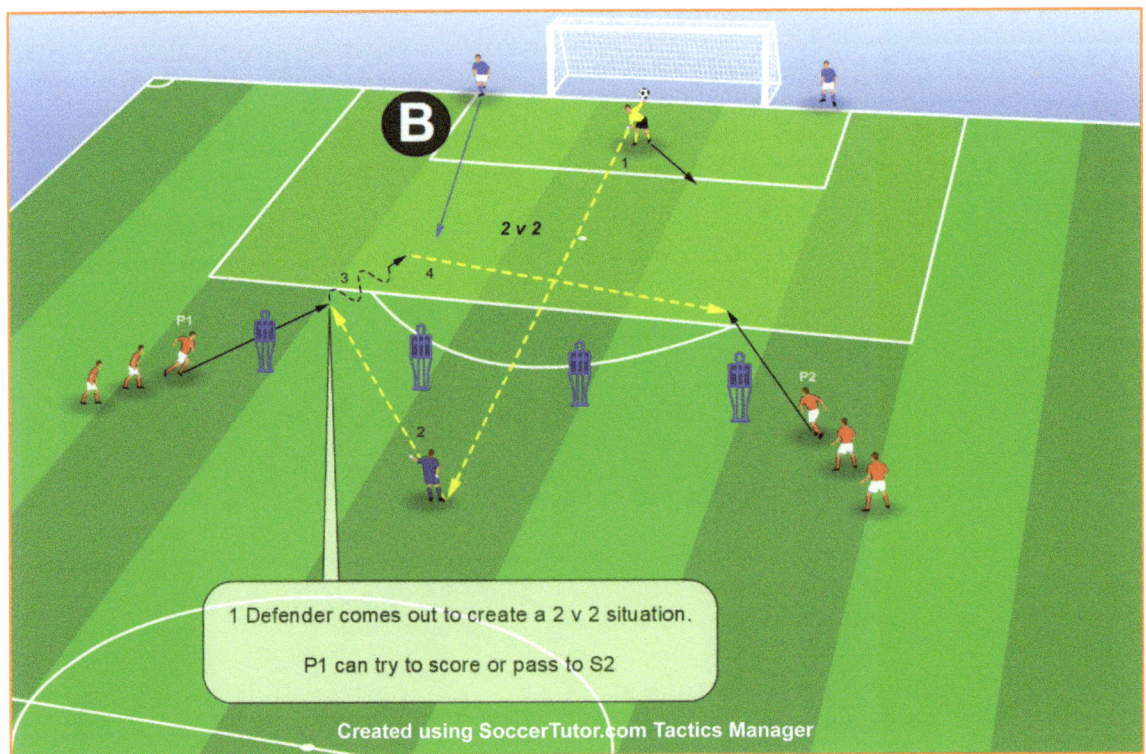

Description

In this variation of drill 7a, both P1 and P2 are active, and we also have a defender.

1. The GK rolls the ball to the Coach.
2. The Coach passes the ball through the mannequins to P1.
3. The blue defender moves out after the pass from the Coach.
4. P1 can try to score himself or pass to P2 in this 2 v 2 situation.

Coaching Points

1. The GK starts with 1 foot in front of the other and away from the goal line, but still in control of the space behind him.
2. Instead of mannequins, you can use poles or cones.
3. The GK has to coach the defender and should go to win the ball if there is an opening.

©SoccerTutor.com   Goalkeeper Training Program - 120 Drills

CHAPTER 11: Drills with Outfield Players

8. 4 v 1 / 8 v 2 Rondos with the Goalkeeper in the Middle

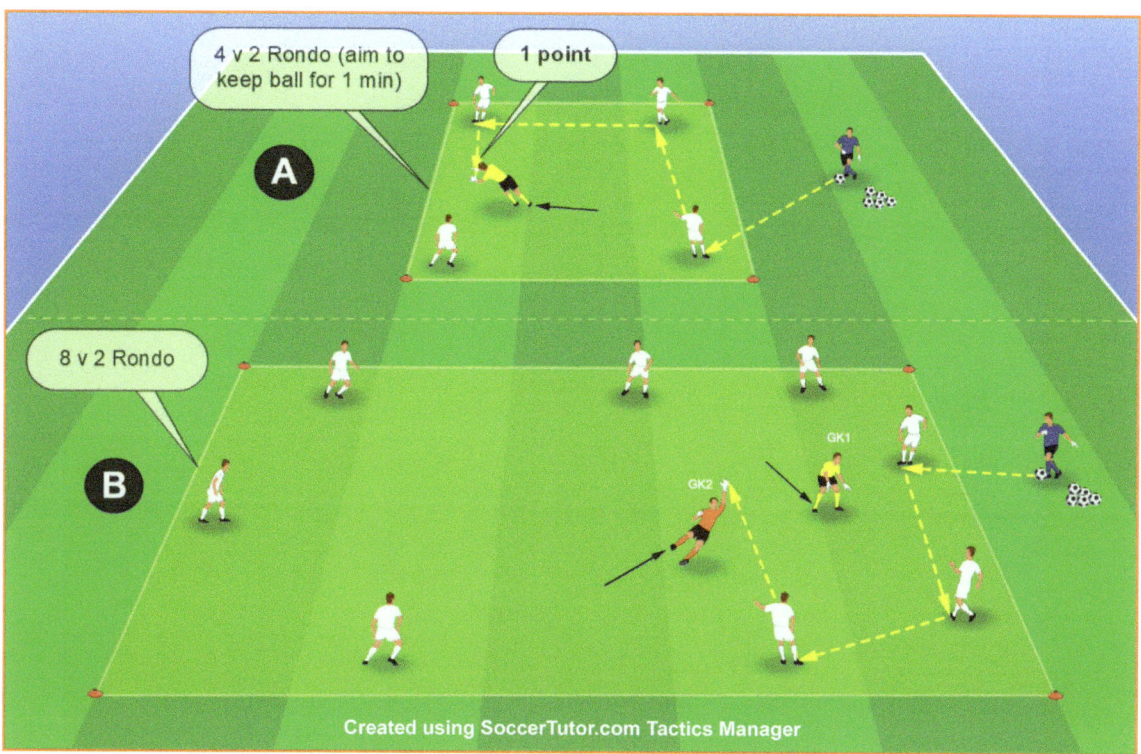

Description

A. **4 outfield players v 1 GK rondo possession game. Game = 1 minute (first pass is free).**
- Ball goes out of play = 1 point for GK.
- GK touches the ball = 1 point for GK.
- GK catches the ball = 2 points for GK.
- GK drops down to the floor but doesn't touch the ball = GK loses all his points.
- Players keep possession for 1 minute without a mistake = GK loses all his points.
- Player passes the ball between the GK's legs = GK loses all his points.

B. **8 v 2 rondo possession game in a larger area with the same rules.**

Coaching Points

1. This is a high intensity drill for the GK, so only play for 1 minute and then change.
2. The GK has to count the points out loud.
3. For the 8 v 2 rondo, both GKs have to communicate well and coach each other.

CHAPTER 11: Drills with Outfield Players

9. Saving First Time Shots from the Edge of the Penalty Area in a 2 Team Game

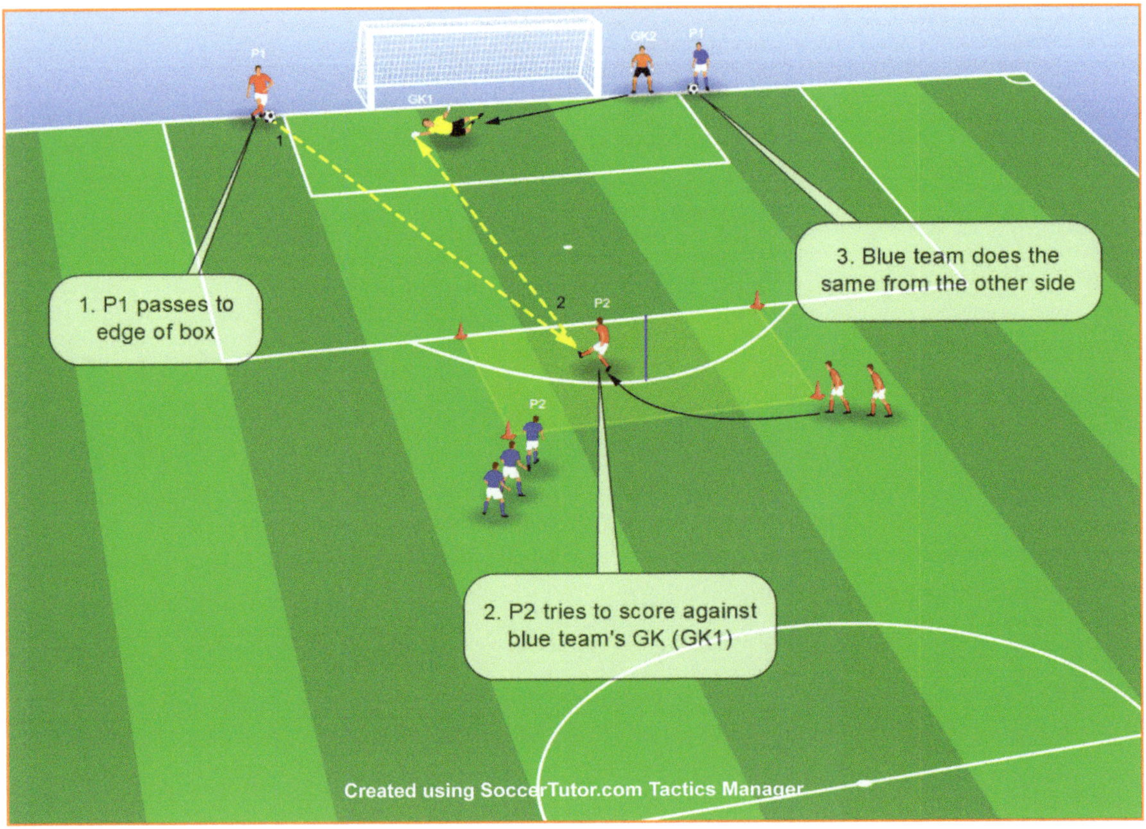

Description
1. Red P1 passes along the ground to just outside the penalty area.
2. Red P2 moves around the pole and tries to score against the blue team's GK (yellow GK1).
3. GK1 and GK2 switch positions and blue P1 passes to blue P2.
4. Blue P2 now tries to score against the red team's GK (orange GK2).

Variation: Players beside the goal throw the ball and both teams try to score with headers.

Coaching Points
1. The GKs have to be ready when the shot comes.
2. When P1 plays the ball, look at the top corner to check your positioning.
3. When the shot comes, both feet of the GK should be on the ground.
4. High level: When the GK parries the ball, P2 can try to score the rebound.

©SoccerTutor.com   Goalkeeper Training Program - 120 Drills

CHAPTER 11: Drills with Outfield Players

10. Defending Crosses in a Dynamic 2 Zone 4 (+1) v 4 (+1) Small Sided Game

Description

1. A blue player crosses over a small goal (or other obstacle like mannequins).
2. The blue team try to score directly from the cross (2 points). The red team's GK (orange) tries to catch or punch the cross.
3. If the ball stays in play, we play a normal game and both teams can score (1 point). If the GK catches the cross, he plays the ball out to a teammate as part of the normal game.
4. If the ball goes out of play or a goal is scored, the red team restart the game with a cross. The Coach gives the signal when the cross should be taken.

Variation: Add a neutral player that plays with the team in possession.

Coaching Points

1. The GKs need to coach the defenders.
2. After catching the cross, the GKs should look to launch a quick counter attack.
3. Vary the crosses: In-swing and out-swing, so the GKs have to take up different positions.

CHAPTER 12

GOALKEEPER GAMES

CHAPTER 12: Goalkeeper Games

1. Head and Catch Goalkeeper Circle Game

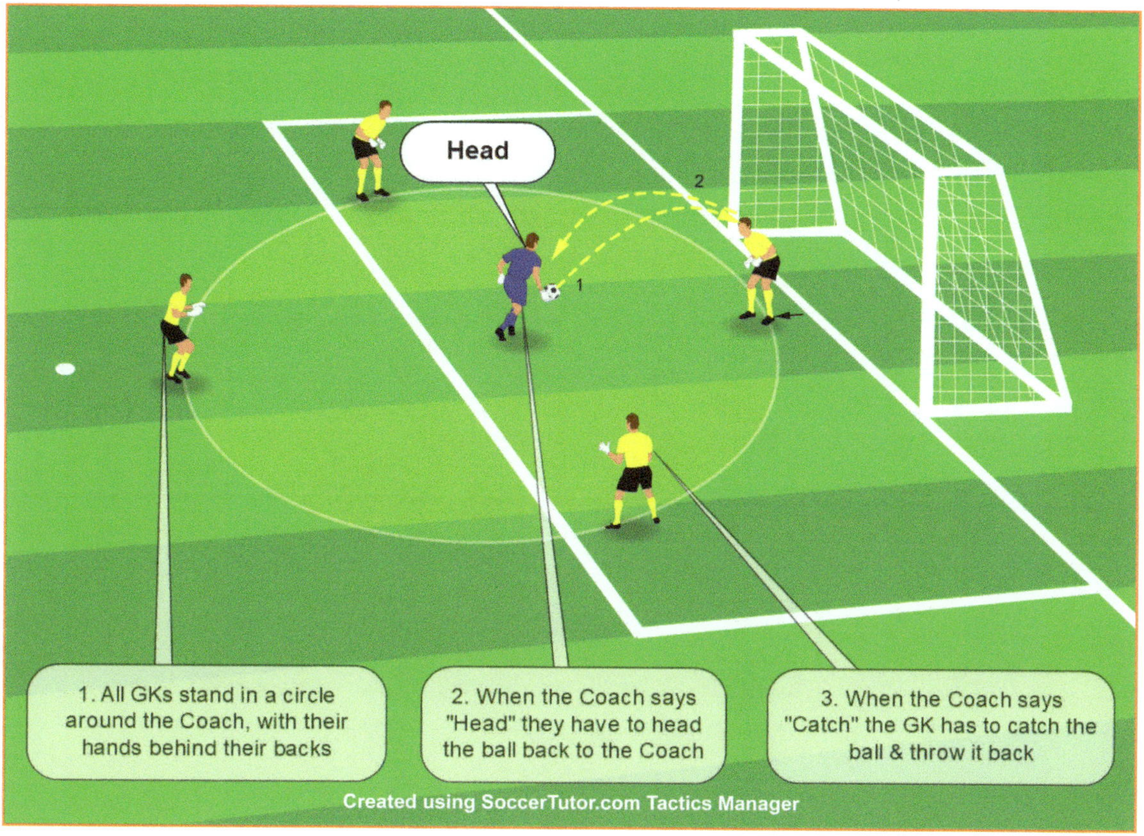

[Diagram: Goalkeepers stand in a circle around the Coach.
1. All GKs stand in a circle around the Coach, with their hands behind their backs
2. When the Coach says "Head" they have to head the ball back to the Coach
3. When the Coach says "Catch" the GK has to catch the ball & throw it back]

Description

1. All the GKs stand in a circle around the Coach, with their hands behind their back. The Coach can throw the ball to whichever GK he chooses.

2. When the Coach says "Head," the GKs have head the ball back to the Coach.

3. When the Coach says "Catch," the GK has to catch the ball and throw it back to the Coach.

Variation: When the Coach says "Head," the GK has to catch the ball and when he says "Catch," the GK has to head the ball. Every mistake is 5 push-ups and you're out of the game.

Coaching Points

1. This is a nice game to finish the training session.
2. Make the circle small.
3. Throw every ball at head height.

CHAPTER 12: Goalkeeper Games

2. "Goalie Wars" Game

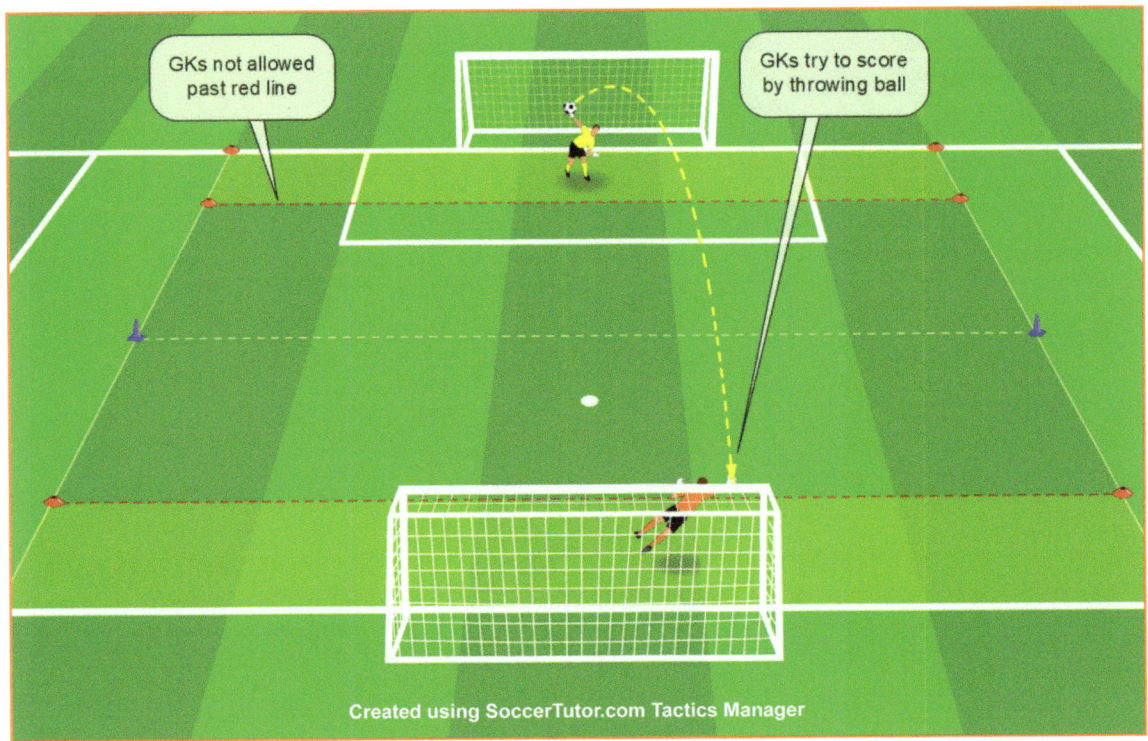

Description
- Both GKs stay within their own zones behind the red line.
- GK1 starts the game by trying to throw the ball into GK2's goal from within his zone.
- If GK2 saves it and the ball rebounds away back into GK1's half, GK1 can throw again.
- If GK2 saves it or the ball misses the goal, GK2 then tries to throw the ball into GK1's goal.
- Play for a set amount of time and the GK with the most goals wins.

Variations
1. Instead of throwing, the GKs try to score with a volley or half-volley.
2. Kick from the ground.
3. Mix all these elements: Start with a throw, then a volley and finally kick from the ground.

Coaching Point: The distance between the goals and the size of the goals depends on the age/level of the GKs.

CHAPTER 12: Goalkeeper Games

3. "Goalkeeper Squash" Game with Rebounder

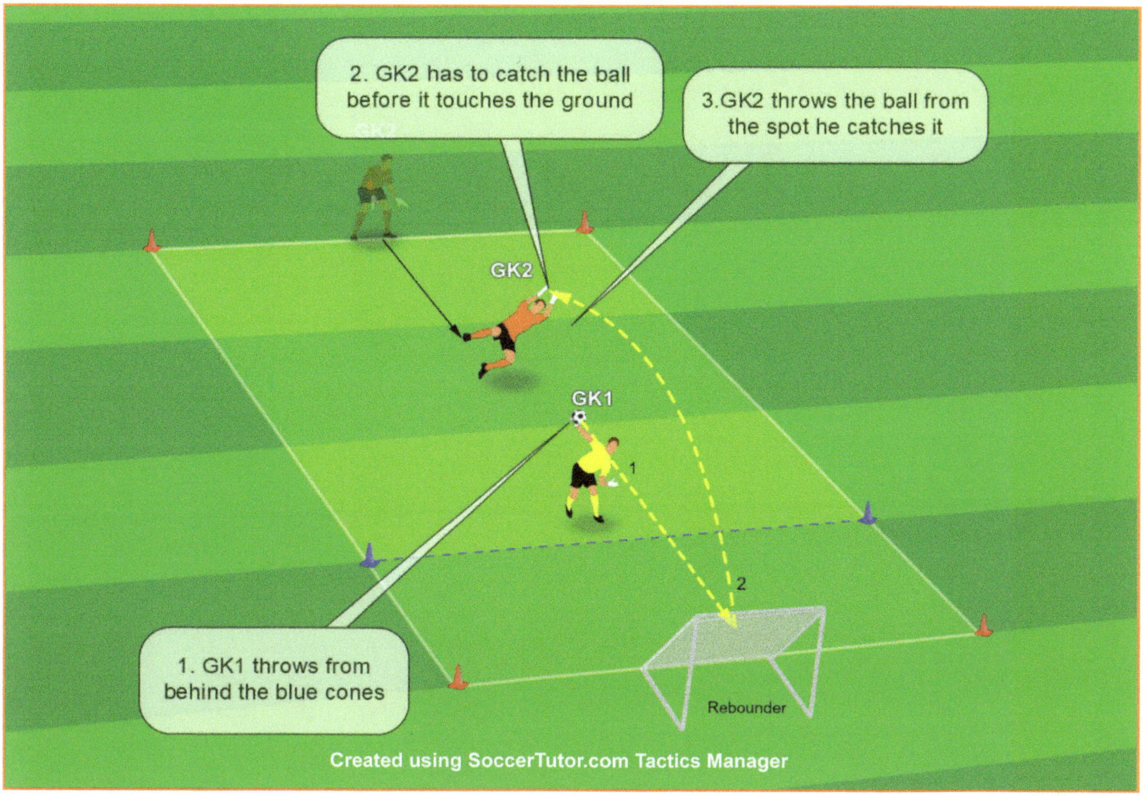

Description

1. GK1 serves (throws) the ball from behind the blue cones.

2. GK2 has to catch the ball before it touches the ground in the main area (behind the blue cones), otherwise GK1 scores 1 point. If GK1 misses the rebounder or the ball lands outside the main area, GK2 scores 1 point.

3. GK2 throws the ball from the spot he catches the ball from. The rules and point scoring remains the same. The GK who scores a point will always serve next.

Variation: Play with 4 GKs.

Coaching Points

1. Adjust the size of the area depending on the age/level of the GKs.
2. The serve (throw) must be from above the shoulder.
3. The GKs can only throw using 1 hand.

CHAPTER 12: Goalkeeper Games

4. Throw and Catch Goalkeeper Tennis Game

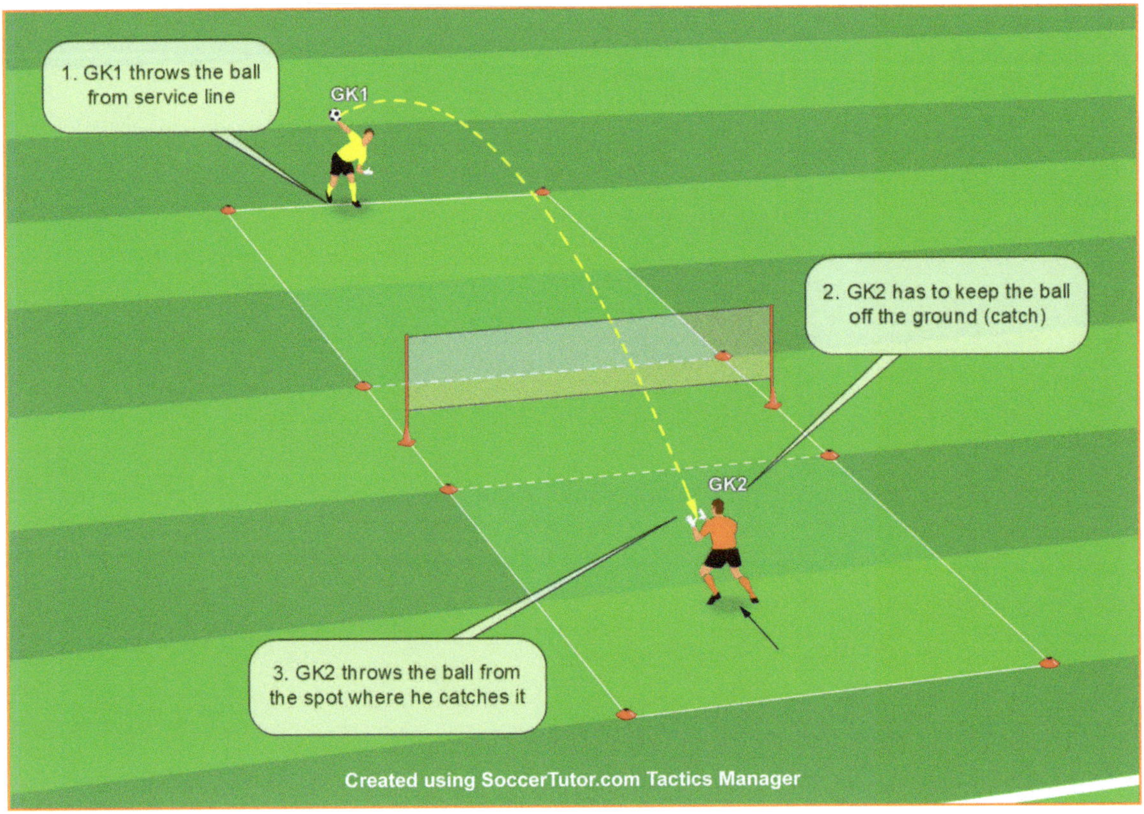

![diagram]

Description

For this tennis game, create a neutral zone in the middle as shown, where no points are allowed to be scored.

1. GK1 throws a ball from the service line over the net and onto GK2's side.
2. GK2 has to keep the ball off the ground or GK1 will score 1 point.
3. GK2 throws the ball back from the spot where he catches the ball.
4. The GK who scores the point serves next.

Coaching Points

1. Adjust the size of the area depending on the age/level of the GKs.
2. The serve is an overarm throw. During the game, all 1 handed throws are allowed.
3. The GKs that are not playing can be the line judges.

CHAPTER 12: Goalkeeper Games

5. Goalkeeper Tennis Game with Volleys

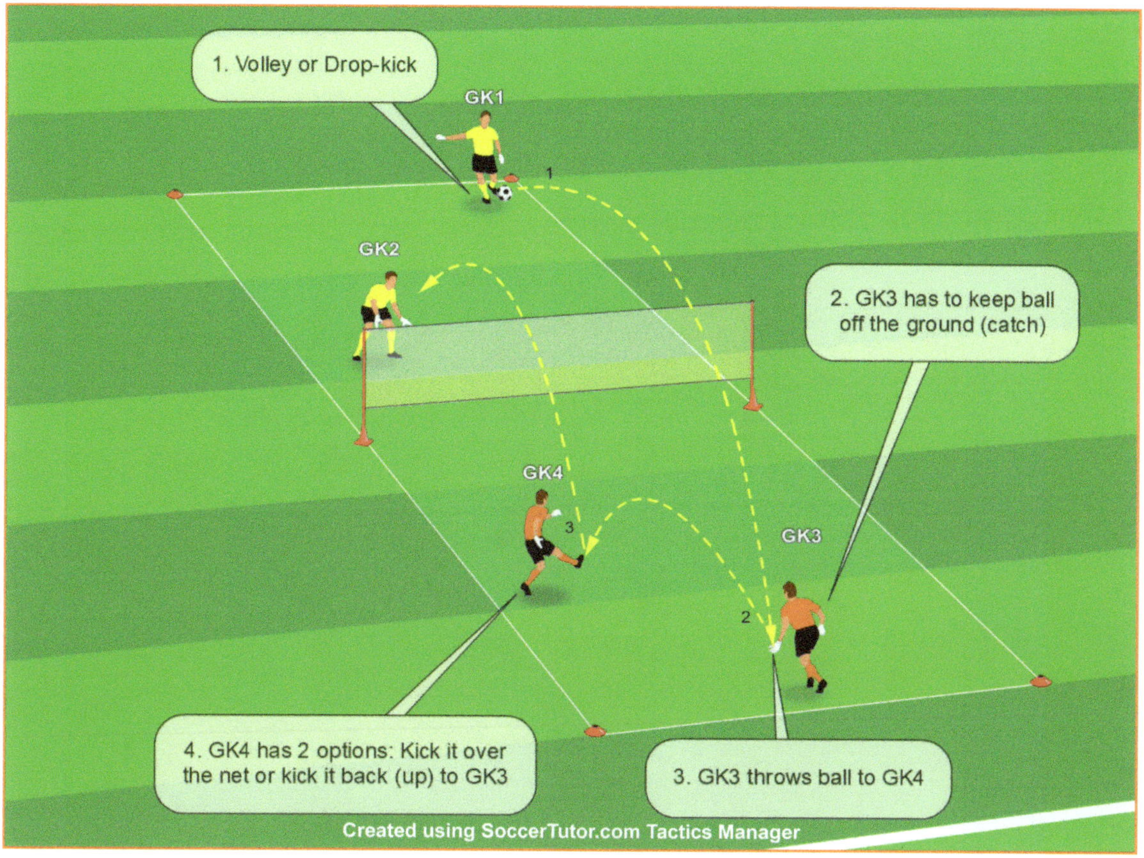

Description

This is a variation of drill 4 on the previous page and we now play with 4 GKs.

1. GK1 serves with a volley or drop-kick.
2. GK3 has to keep the ball off the ground and tries to catch it.
3. Once GK3 catches the ball, he throws it to GK4.
4. GK4 has 2 options: Kick it over the net or kick it up in the air for GK3 to kick it over the net.
5. Each team has a maximum of 4 touches. The team that scores the point serves next.

Rules

1. When a GK is touched by the ball without catching it, the other team score 1 point.
2. The GKs are not allowed to walk with the ball.

CHAPTER 12: Goalkeeper Games

6. End to End 2 Zone Rebounder Game

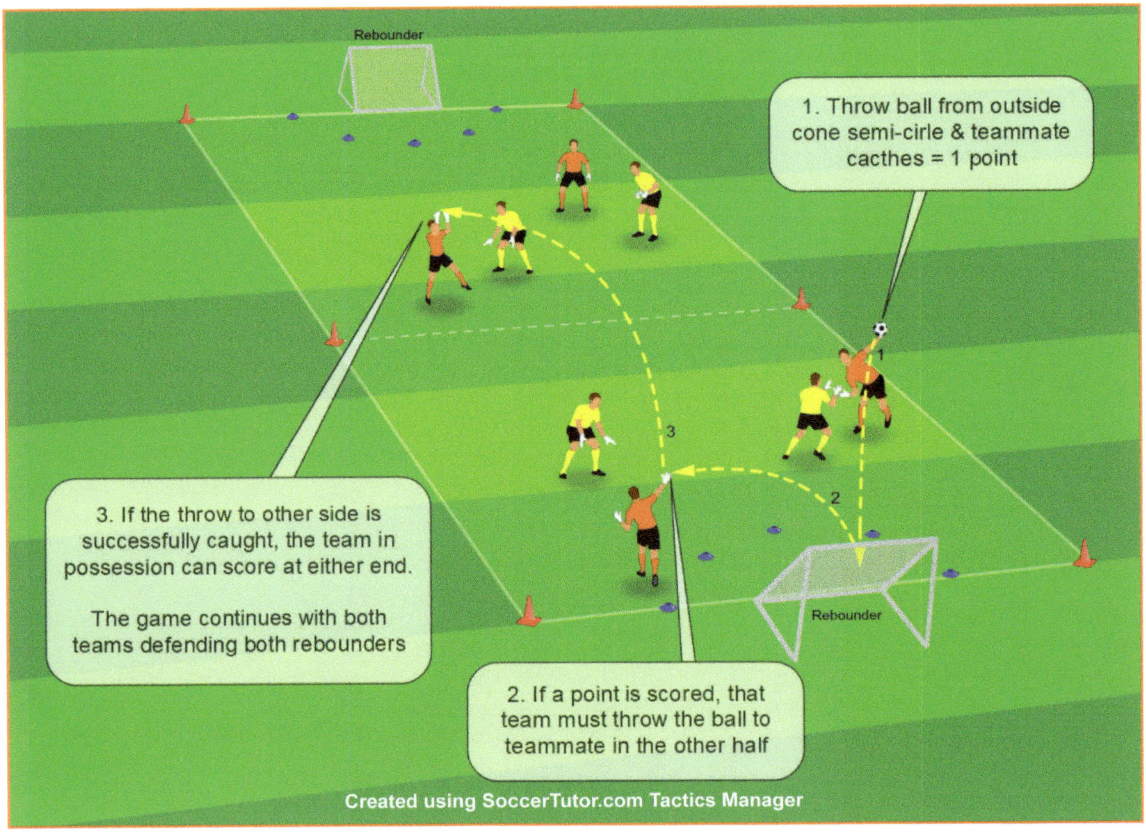

(diagram annotations):
- Rebounder
- 1. Throw ball from outside cone semi-cirle & teammate cacthes = 1 point
- 3. If the throw to other side is successfully caught, the team in possession can score at either end. The game continues with both teams defending both rebounders
- 2. If a point is scored, that team must throw the ball to teammate in the other half
- Rebounder

Description

1. Throw the ball from outside of the cone semi-circle and a teammate catches = 1 point.
2. If a point is scored, that team must throw the ball to a teammate in the other half.
3. If the throw to the other side is successfully caught, the team in possession are then free to score at either end.
4. The game continues with both teams defending both rebounders.

Coaching Points

1. Throw the ball with 1 hand.
2. GKs can jump inside the cone semi-circle circle when attacking, but they must be in the air when they release the ball.
3. The defending team is not allowed to enter the cone semi-circle at any point.

©SoccerTutor.com   Goalkeeper Training Program - 120 Drills

CHAPTER 12: Goalkeeper Games

7. Goalkeeper Penalty Competition

![Diagram]

- Score a penalty = 5 points
- Miss a penalty = 5 points to GK
- GK saves penalty = 10 points

After every shot, all GKs rotate to next position

Description

- Score a penalty = 5 points.
- Miss a penalty (fail to hit target) = 5 points to other GK.
- GK saves penalty = 10 points.
- After each penalty, all GKs move to the next position (GK1 -> GK2 -> GK3 -> GK4 -> GK1).

Variation: GK3 stays in goal and all the other GKs take a penalty before the next GK goes in goal.

Coaching Points

1. The Coach gives the signal (whistle) before shooting.
2. The GK stands with his toes on the goal line.

©SoccerTutor.com · Goalkeeper Training Program - 120 Drills

CHAPTER 12: Goalkeeper Games

8. Goalkeeper "One v One" Competition

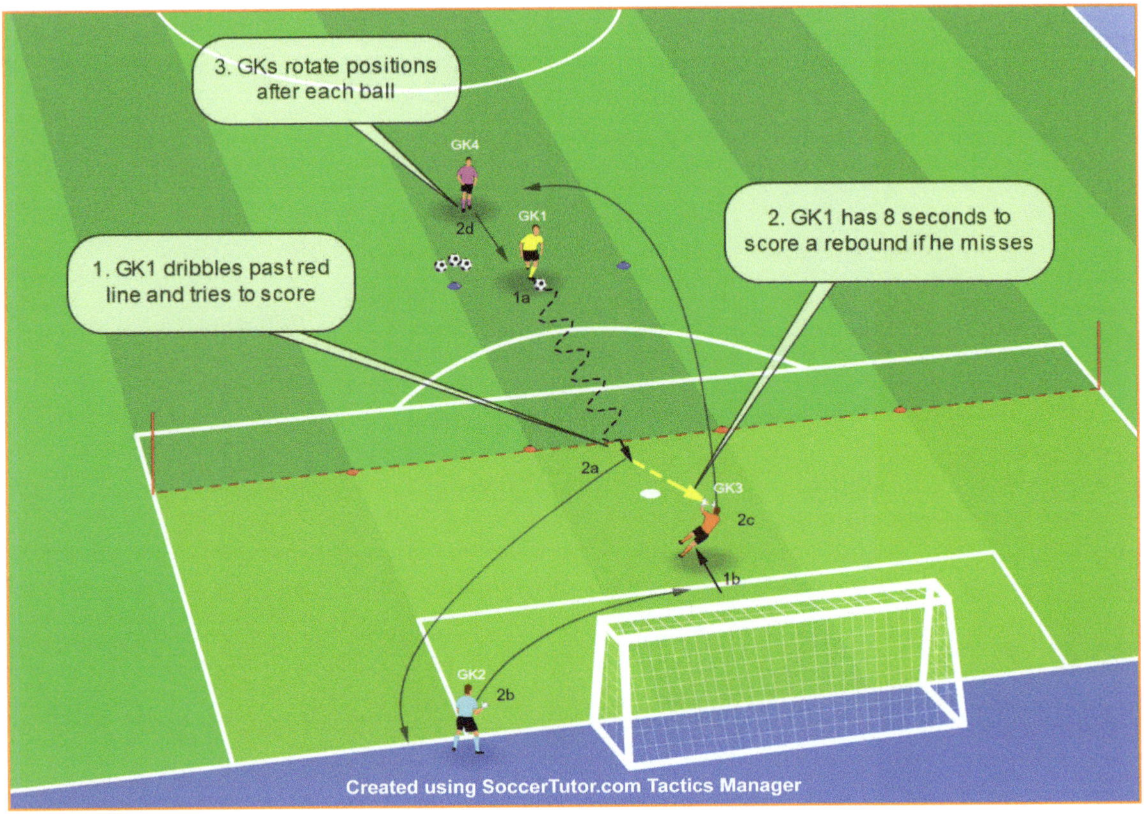

![diagram]

Description

1. GK1 dribbles past the red line and then tries to score (he cannot shoot before crossing the red line).

2. If GK2 saves the shot, GK1 has 8 seconds to try and score the rebound.

3. After each attempt, all GKs move to the next position (GK1 -> GK2 -> GK3 -> GK4 -> GK1).

Variation: GK3 stays in goal and all the others GKs attempt before the next GK goes in goal.

Coaching Points

1. GK1 can start when GK3 raises his hand to show that he is ready.

2. GK3 starts on the 6-yard line.

3. When the ball goes outside the box or outside the cones, there will be no rebounds.

©SoccerTutor.com — Goalkeeper Training Program - 120 Drills

CHAPTER 12: Goalkeeper Games

9. Goalkeeper "Head Ball" Small Sided Game

Description

- The yellow GK in goal starts with a throw to one of his teammates.
- Every ball must be headed. You can only score by heading.
- If the ball is on the ground, the GK has to throw the ball up for himself and head the ball to another player.
- After every goal, both teams change the GK in goal.

Variation: Play handball, but you can only score by heading the ball.

Coaching Points

1. GKs should be able to head the ball without fear.
2. Keep your eyes open at all times.
3. In possession, 2 GKs should go wide so the GK in goal can throw the ball to them.
4. When you lose the ball, move inside to defend.

©SoccerTutor.com

Goalkeeper Training Program - 120 Drills

CHAPTER 12: Goalkeeper Games

10. Players vs Goalkeepers Small Sided Game

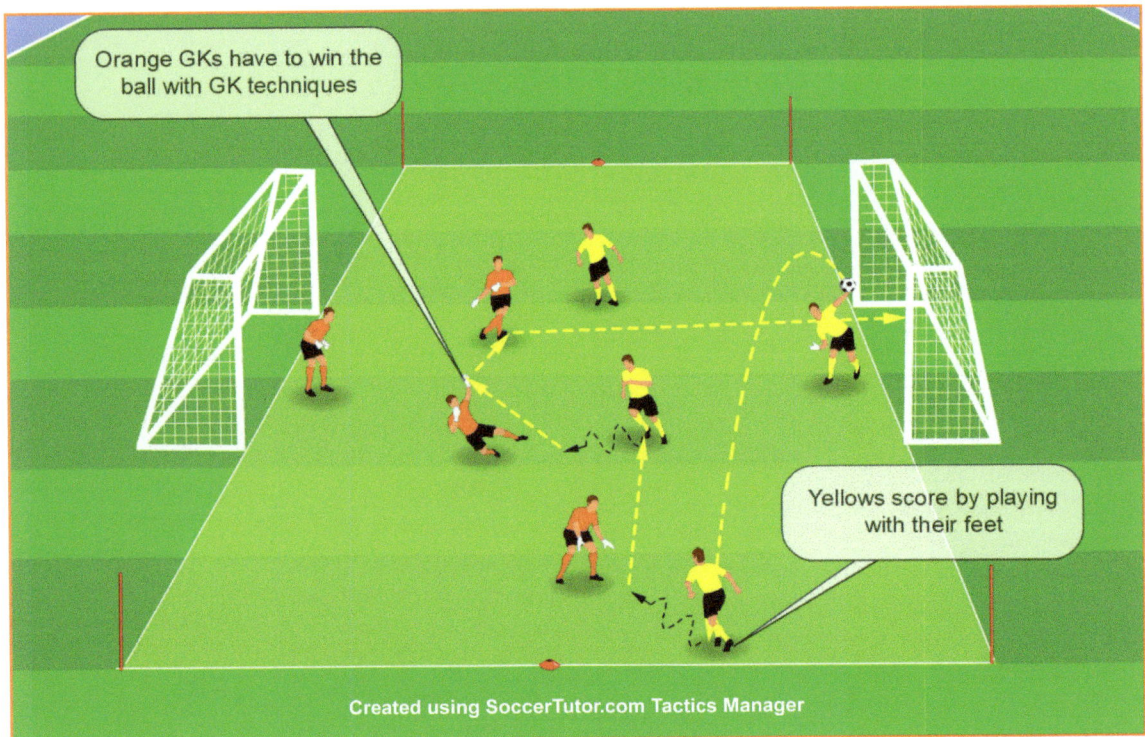

Description

- The yellow GK in goal starts with a throw to one of his teammates.
- The team in possession (yellow) play with their feet and try to score a goal.
- The defending team (orange) only use goalkeeper techniques (e.g. 1 v 1) and try to win the ball.
- If the orange defending team win the ball, they then only use their feet and try to score. The yellows will therefore use GK techniques to try and win the ball back.

Coaching Points

1. Coaching by the GK in the goal is very important.
2. After every goal, change the GKs in goal.
3. When you go down, you must win the ball. Otherwise, it is a free kick to the other team.